Steeles on Wheels

Also by the Authors

The Rules of the Game (published under the name Donia
Whiteley Mills); Viking Press, 1969.
A Long Way Home from Troy (published under the name
Donia W. Mills); Viking Press, 1971.

Steeles on Wheels

A Year on the Road in an RV

Mark and Donia Steele

CAPITAL
BOOKS, INC.

CAPITAL BOOKS, INC.
Sterling, Virginia

A Note from the Steeles:

Steeles on Wheels is a personal account of our experiences entering the world of full-time RVing. It is not meant as a how-to-manual. Everyone's vehicles and equipment, driving skills, technical knowledge, and life experiences are unique. Unless you are certain of your abilities, seek appropriate professional help in maintaining, repairing, driving, and living in your RV.

Capital Books, Inc.
P.O. Box 605
Herndon, Virginia 20172-0605

ISBN 1-892123-67-3 (alk. paper)

Library of Congress Cataloging-in-Publication Data
Steele, Mark
    Steeles on wheels : a year on the road in an RV / Mark and Donia Steele.—1st ed.
        p. cm.
    ISBN 1-892123-67-3
    1. Recreational vehicle living. 2. Recreational vehicles. I. Steele, Donia. II. Title.
    TX1110.S74 2002
    796.7′9—dc21   2001043033

Printed in the United States of America on acid-free paper that meets the American National Standards Institute Z39-48 Standard.

First Edition

10 9 8 7 6 5 4 3 2 1

Contents

Grateful Thanks to . . .

Our families, for cheerfully waving us good-bye, over and over, even though they wanted us to stay.

Our RV mentors, Ron and Barb Hofmeister, who showed us the full-timing way through their book, newsletter, and e-mails long before we ever met them.

Pete and Robin Hendricks, always there for us, east and west, with an electric hookup, evening campfires, and good grub.

Our old D.C. bridge crowd, the Dream Team, for meeting us at tournaments all around the country and showing us what true friendship is all about.

Ken Kaufman and JJ Armour, the best friends a burnt-out sheepdog could ever have.

And Dr. Ed Wilson, beloved Romantic Poets professor from Donia's Wake Forest College days, whose encouragement was the final push that set this book in motion.

WA

OR

ID

MT

WY

NV

UT

CO

CA

AZ

NM

ND

SD

NE

KS

Kalispell

Cheney Lake State Park

OK

TX

Kerrville

Pharr

- - - June through December

- · · · January to July

- · - July to October

Kerrville e-mail stop

Introduction

We Did It!

If you asked me to pick the single most exciting moment of our first year on the road, it would have to be 10:04 on that perfect morning in early June—Departure Day. Our mountain cabin was locked up tight, trailer packed, hitching checklist completed, seatbelts fastened, and Cleo in her usual perch, front paws resting on the console between the truck's front seats. The baseball cap from my farewell office party said, "I'm Retired—This Is As Dressed Up As I Get." The glee that rushed over us in that moment was like the old school's-out excitement multiplied a millionfold: This time it was like, finals are over and classes dismissed—*forever*.

When Mark put the truck in gear and slowly began driving down the narrow gravel road toward the highway, it was hard to ignore the enormous leap we were taking into the Great Unknown. We were literally leaving an entire lifetime behind us: a solid editing career that I had spent twenty years building; Mark's successful home inspection business; the house in the suburbs of Washington, D.C., where we had raised two children; my beloved flower gardens; the Virginia cabin Mark had built with his own hands; nearly all our household possessions; good neighbors; and a close circle of friends we played bridge with nearly every weekend.

In place of this stable suburban lifestyle we would be traveling around the country full-time, living in a thirty-four-foot recreational vehicle that held all the clothes and other goods we would ever need. Gone, too, were our comfy his 'n' hers compact cars; now we had only our tow vehicle, a heavy-duty Ford F-350 diesel-powered pickup truck.

Most important, we had each other—The Eight-Legged Steele

1

Family Traveling Trio. In our life on the road, we three would be closer companions than ever before, by necessity if nothing else. Cleo, a fluffy white mixed sheepdog with attitude: coal-black eyes and a button nose and a puppylike mischievous streak despite her six years and seventy pounds. Still, an excellent hug. And Mark, the Alpha male of our pack, organized and fearless and able to figure out most any challenge, given a few minutes to think about it. Another good hug. And Donia (rhymes with Sonia), who grew up as a Navy junior in the 1950s and never lost the yen to travel to new places, through all those dutiful decades of working nine-to-seven.

Our dream of becoming RV full-timers—modern-day no-mads—had begun nearly a decade earlier, when I read a newspaper article about Ron and Barb Hofmeister and their life on the road. We ordered their book, subscribed to their newsletter, e-mailed them, and got encouraging e-mails in return. When we told our friends and families we were thinking about taking early retirement and selling the house to live full-time on the road, they thought we were kidding—especially since we had never spent so much as one night in an RV. We didn't believe it ourselves at the beginning, but somewhere along the way the pipe dream turned into a serious plan. The more we read and talked and learned about it, the more feasible this wild idea became.

"You really should rent an RV and try it out before you buy," we were advised over and over—but we scoffed at this idea. To paraphrase the classic movie line, "We din' need no stinkin' rentals!" We wanted to buy a rig and jump right in. We knew we would love it.

During the final year we methodically cut loose every element of our old life, one by one—announced our retirement plans, shopped for a secondhand truck and trailer, put our house and cars up for sale, gave most of our furniture to the children. If by chance we didn't love RVing, we would still have the cabin and a few pieces of furniture as a safety net. But as we pulled away that bright June morning, we felt confident that we would never live in Virginia again. In our hearts, we were already full-timers.

Our escape route that day took us down I-81 through the scenic Shenandoah Valley of Virginia, one of the country's loveliest highways. At lunch time, when we pulled off into a rest area, we experienced the strange first-time feeling of following the "Trucks and Trailers" arrow instead of the one for "Cars." From now on we would be sharing the extra-long parking sites with huge transport trucks. Mark carefully eased our rig into a spot between two eighteen-wheelers; lucky for us rookies, there was plenty of room to maneuver that day.

Our first meal on the road was ham sandwiches, potato chips, and pickles, fixed in the trailer and carried to a tree-shaded picnic table on the hillside. Cleo was on a long leash, indulging in her favorite sport—browsing for crumbs.

With a "pinch-me-I-must-be-dreaming" feeling, Mark and I kept looking back down the hill to our new home parked against the backdrop of the Blue Ridge Mountains. On the back of the trailer we had put a stick-on map of the United States that Mark's sister had given us as a farewell gift, with stickers for all the states just waiting to be applied. Today the map had only Virginia; how many states would be added by August? December? June of next year? It didn't matter—sooner or later, we would see them all.

I remember at our first freshman convocation in college, the speaker told us to look at the student on our right and at the student on our left. Then he said, according to statistics, one of the three of us would be gone by the end of the year. That long-ago speech would come back to haunt us a year later. Little did we know, on this exciting June day, that by the end of our first year on the road one of our little family of three would have dropped out of the RV lifestyle for good, to live in a regular house again.

All we knew right then was the giddy promise of open-ended adventure, of having our life all neatly packed into a thirty-four-foot RV, of really being on the road at last. After so many years of dreaming about it, *we did it!*

1 Cherokee, North Carolina
June 6

Dear Friends and Pen Pals one and all,

Team Steele is alive and well after the first forty-eight hours on the road, and we wanted to share our departure adventures with you. Having organized our pack-up and getaway from our mountain cabin in Front Royal, Mark and I went over our final checklist on the morning of June 4 (awning secured? outside compartments locked? countertop items stowed? brake safety cable latched? etc.) and finally pulled away about 10 a.m.

We were quite an elated trio as we entered the ramp onto I-81 South, sitting up high in the cab of our huge Ford diesel pickup truck, with Cleo the dog happily viewing the scenery from her carpeted spot on the console between our seats. According to our campground directory, I-81 is one of America's Ten Most Scenic Highways, and that day the view of woods, farms, and distant mountains was indeed lush and green and heavenly all around.

Our rear view was blocked by the mountainous RV, a thirty-four-foot Dutchmen Signature model, so that our only view of traffic behind us was from the truck's extended side mirrors. It tickled us to see that the truckers, who were on the highway in droves, showed us the same courtesies they do other big rigs— like blinking their lights when it was safe for us to move back over into the right lane after passing.

Some truckers also saved us from getting bogged down in a highway shutdown up ahead, caused by a bad wreck. We were listening to their irreverent, static-filled chatter on our CB radio ("Overturned U-Haul on fire, wooo-eeee! Got any marshmallows?") when they started giving advice about which exits to use as a detour and reentry back onto the highway once the wreck was safely passed. I happened to be the one driving at this point (amazing, but true!), and I noticed that the detour exit was the very one we were approaching, so I took it.

This stroke of good luck was followed by another one a little while later, when our pickup mysteriously stalled out as I was turning to get back onto I-81. There we were, creeping to a halt sort of crosswise in the middle of the road, all forty-nine feet and nine tons of truck and trailer, with zero engine power. But fortunately, from that exact point we could coast downhill into an empty paved lot that connected to the I-81 ramp on the other side. After a minute's rest, the truck started up again and we were back on the highway with no more trouble. We began to think that our RV Angel was looking out for us, showing us Not To Worry about these little calamities that come and go.

About 3:30, we pulled into the campground near Salem, Virginia, where we had made a reservation earlier in the week. We picked this one out of the campground directory because it was about the right distance from Front Royal and could accommodate big rigs. We wondered why it was only $17 per night when many of the others advertised were $25 or more. When we got there, we saw why: It's right next to an aging tourist attraction with dilapidated outbuildings and concrete foundations scattered here and there, where buildings once stood. The roar of traffic from I-81 can be heard constantly from the fringe of trees bordering the camping area.

But it wasn't crowded, so we got our pick of grassy "pull-through" sites. That's the easy kind where you don't have to back the trailer into the space, but pull straight into the site when you arrive and drive out the other side when you leave. Mark leveled the trailer, unhitched the truck, and unfurled the awning like he'd been doing it all his life. It rained on and off the whole time we were there, but in the late afternoon we sat out and read in lawn chairs under the awning, and after dark our trailer became a cozy den where we read some more and listened to classical music on our built-in tape deck.

In the end we decided there was a certain down-home charm to this campground, which had everything from pup tents to beat-up fourteen-foot trailers with makeshift awnings to a brand new thirty-six-foot Southwind motor coach. Our favorites were the three converted school buses up on blocks that seemed to be permanent fixtures. They were distinguished mainly by their window coverings: One had shirred white curtains, another opaque blue paint, and the third a large Confederate flag.

Cleo made friends with a malamute-wolf dog down the way; his owner is a construction worker who lives in a small Winnebago with his girlfriend, a freelance nurse. She moves from town to town on assignment for several nursing contract agencies, while he picks up construction work wherever they go. We heard that another of our RV neighbors would empty your sewage holding tanks into the dump station for $10 if you didn't want to be bothered, but Mark said heck no, he wanted to do it himself.

First RVing disaster! When we pulled up to the dump station the next morning and unscrewed the sewer cap so we could fasten the drain hose onto the end, the unthinkable happened. We may be novices, but even we knew that the black water (translation: toilet sewage) wasn't supposed to come gushing out until *after* we had hooked up the hose and pulled the valve open on the black-water holding tank. Something wasn't working right, to say the least. We grabbed buckets and tried to stop the flow, but by that time the damage was done. So we let it run its course, finished dumping the gray water (shower and kitchen waste), hosed down the dump area thoroughly, washed ourselves up in the shower house, and continued on down the road.

Our second-night destination was a snazzy KOA campground in the mountains outside Cherokee, North Carolina—about as different from our first-night camping experience as could be. We arrived on a weekend in high season (major miscalculation!) and, once again, I was doing the driving. I guess I was still so traumatized by our dump disaster I didn't fully realize how narrow the streets and turns were going through downtown Cherokee (jammed with tourist traffic, of course). Or how steep and winding the mountain road was leading up to the KOA, and totally lacking in shoulders and guardrails. Or how white Mark's knuckles were. ("Better you than me," he said later.)

When we were parked and settled we tried to find a quiet place to take Cleo for a walk. Hah! Everywhere we looked, kids were running around on foot or zooming around on bikes, and families were outside cooking on the grills and eating on the picnic tables. We finally found a rocky area full of underbrush on the other side of a small stream, where Cleo could do her business in relative peace. Then we ran the kids-and-bikes gauntlet back to our campsite.

But the tradeoff at this busy KOA was dozens of camper amenities, including a swimming pool, hot tub, and snack bar. It even had a special modem hookup for us campers—a phone jack installed on the outside wall of the porch, right above the newspaper vending machines. Mark thinks he may be able to balance the laptop on a newspaper box while he plugs in to send the e-mail. If you get this letter, you'll know it worked. There's also a nifty pavilion where a country-and-western concert is due to start in just a couple of minutes.

So we'll sign off for now and catch up with you again down the road. The dealer in Richmond where we bought our RV gave us a thirty-day warranty, starting from the day we picked it up. So we're now on our three-week shakedown cruise—we'll visit Mark's family in Atlanta, then over to Myrtle Beach to visit some old friends. Then we circle back up to Richmond by the last week of June to get any little problems fixed before heading north and west for the summer.

Hope you are all enjoying summer fun in your own home-towns—and we look forward to hearing from you whenever the inspiration strikes.

Love to all,
Donia

P.S. from Cleo:

Dear Friends, four-legged and two-legged alike:
I am a dog who likes to speak for herself, and right now I would like to set the record straight about that malamute-wolf combo at the Virginia campground. When a dog comes up to you that's half wolf and double your size, you don't do anything but stand there nicely and let him sniff you, embarrassing as it may be. That's not quite the same as "making friends." And speaking of embarrassing, Mom, how would you like it if I discussed the details of YOUR bathroom business in an e-mail sent out to dozens of friends and family members all over the U.S.A.? So much for species equality in our family.

On a positive note, these campground places are filled with great smells everywhere you go—Humans cooking outside, kids spilling stuff on the ground around the trash cans, dogs marking every bush, little squirrel feet on tree trunks leaving their special fragrance that can drive you wild. . . . Yes, I think I'm going to like this new life just fine.

Love 'n' Licks,
Cleo

2 How Do You Decide on an RV?

A t our first two campgrounds Donia and I saw a colorful cross-section of the RVing world, complete with examples of every type of rig that can be bought, borrowed, or cobbled together out of salvaged parts. Still, after all our travels, we're continually impressed by the many ingenious variations of these mini-homes on wheels—much more eclectic than the range of automobile designs.

If you're into piggybacking or towing your home with a separate vehicle, there are truck campers and pop-up tent campers, regular travel trailers that attach to a bumper hitch, and split-level fifth-wheel trailers with a hitch like a miniature tractor-trailer's, which fastens into the bed of a pickup truck. You can even get tiny pop-up tent units built to tow behind a motorcycle.

In the motorhome, or motor coach, family—with living space, driver's area, and engine all in one unit—you've got your Class B van conversions, bed-over-cab Class C campers built on a truck chassis, and the popular Class A motorhomes ranging from under twenty to over forty feet in length and based on chassis built specifically for them. At the high end of this category are bus conversions, those humongous luxury pads on wheels favored by touring rock stars and other high-rollers. The newer and pricier models of both motorhomes and trailers nearly all feature slide-out rooms—telescoping wall units that roll outward at the flip of a switch—to extend the interior floor space when the rig is parked in a campground.

I have to say, shopping for a recreational vehicle is one of the most delightful forms of recreation known to man—even if you don't intend to buy one but are just indulging in Total Freedom fantasies. When Donia and I first got the full-timing bug, we visited RV shows every chance we got. Early on we narrowed the field down to two basic choices for us rookie full-timers: a medium-sized Class A motorhome or a medium-sized fifth-wheel trailer. Donia thought up a clever Flip Side research plan that went like this: We would walk up to a motorhome dealer at the RV show and say, "We're beginners and we were kind of leaning toward a fifth-wheel trailer, but. . . ?"

The sales rep would then hammer us with reasons why motorhomes were better than trailers: "So much more comfortable for traveling, you can go back and use the bathroom any time you want. And the wife can go in the kitchen and fix you a sandwich right while you're rolling down the road. They're all one piece, so they're easier to handle and back up into parking spaces . . . trailers take forever to hitch and unhitch, and watch out while you're backing up, or they'll jackknife on you! It's a snap to tow a small car behind your motorhome, something economical to run around in while you're parked." There was also the subtle suggestion that motorhomes were more attractive and upscale, definitely the choice of quality people like ourselves.

Then we would walk around to a trailer exhibit on the next aisle and do the same thing in reverse to get the other side of the picture: "Foot for foot, you get a lot more usable space in a fifth-wheel, without the driver's seat and dashboard in your living room. And you don't have all those complicated mechanical systems to break down and put your home in the shop for a week. Hitching takes five minutes, max, and backing up is easy, once you get the feel of it. When you get to a campground, you just unhitch, and then you have the truck to run around in. Bottom line, trailers are just more economical—beats me why anyone would want to tie up so much cash in one of those fancy motorhomes." (Certainly not sensible people like ourselves. . . ?)

In the end, our unanimous gut decision was to go with a fifth-wheel, which is easier-handling than a traditional travel trailer, and to look for a late-model used one rather than buying one new. I would like to state here that we know motorhomes have many advantages, and we have met many sensible, intelligent people who would never travel any other way. The same goes for other types of RVs. But for us, a fifth-wheel was the right choice. We liked the private feeling of the "master suite" they usually have, located a few steps up from the living room, behind a closed door. We liked the idea of unhitching the truck for local driving around rather than towing a car behind a motorhome, which struck us as cumbersome. We liked the idea of having only one engine to maintain. And most important, we wanted to spend as little money as possible on this first RV, figuring it would be a learning experience and not a lifelong choice.

A fifth-wheel trailer meant we would need a pickup truck to tow it, a very large and heavy-duty pickup truck. We developed a list of must-haves: We wanted a diesel, three-quarter-ton truck, for the power we would need on all those mountain roads we planned to travel. It had to have an extended cab behind the front seats, for Cleo to ride in. And we wanted an upgraded passenger interior rather than a bare-bones work truck—conveniences like automatic transmission, cruise control, and upholstered seats—for comfort on those long days of driving.

We browsed a few dealers in the D.C. suburbs, but that's not exactly monster-truck territory. Then, one weekend in March when we were out in the Virginia mountains, several locals advised us to "Go see Bubby Settles out in Flint Hill—he'll take good care of you." Settles was a small, rural, used-car dealership in a red brick building that had been there since early in the century. When we told Bubby what we were looking for, he said, "Yep, I got just what you want. Come on around back. I'll sell you my truck."

There sat our dream truck, sure enough. It was a little more than we wanted, actually—a one-ton, fire-engine-red F350 Ford Power Stroke diesel with dual rear tires (my first acquaintance with a "dually"). It was less than a year old and had six thousand miles on it, mostly put on by Bubby himself as he pulled his auto-hauling trailer to and from auctions in surrounding states. And its interior was heaven, with power windows, a good stereo, a middle seat that folded down to create a console storage compartment, push-button lumbar support, even a CB radio that Bubby said he would throw in for free. We just sat in that pickup truck and laughed. Its cab was more luxurious than the interior of any car Donia or I had ever owned.

The price was $24,800—firm. "That's what I got in it, and that's what the price is," Bubby said in a tone that meant *no bargaining*. It sounded to us like a deal, in any case, as the same truck would have run close to $35,000 new. We did the paperwork and gave him a check. Bubby gave us each baseball caps imprinted with "Settles Cars and Trucks." Then he handed over the keys and we drove his truck away.

 Other Lessons Learned

- There are vast quality differences between expensive and cheap RVs. But many costly features are subtle, and not necessary for everyone. If you're a novice, consider buying an inexpensive rig the first time around—a $20,000 instead of a $90,000 trailer, or a $60,000 instead of a $200,000 motorhome. This leaves room for learning what you really care about in an RV for a few years, before you spend the big bucks.
- What kind of weather will you be encountering? Anyone who's really going to stay away from cold winters can save a lot by passing up such features as "Arctic" insulation, an enclosed underbelly, and heated water tanks.
- Jalousie-style windows are not as weathertight as other kinds, but they have one major advantage—you can leave them open for ventilation in all but the heaviest of downpours.
- Remember that as a 100 percent full-timer, your motorhome or trailer (but not the truck) is your *home*—and interest on any loan you take out to pay for it is tax deductible as a mortgage. (Consult your accountant for details.)

Now that we had the truck, the trailer shopping began in earnest. This did not go quite so smoothly. Again we had our list of priorities: The length should be about thirty feet. We insisted on having the toilet enclosed in a separate compartment, rather than in a "pass-through" bathroom area between the living room and bedroom. We wanted a freestanding dinette table and chairs rather than a built-in booth, and plenty of large windows and ceiling vents and fans throughout for ventilation. And oh yes, it had to have a comfortable rocking chair for Donia—a hopeless rockaholic since childhood. They all came with platform rockers, it seemed, but she wanted a *good* one.

With list in hand, we began scanning the local classifieds and Internet ads for used RVs. We were such eager shoppers that we returned three times to look at the only used rig for sale in the D.C. area that remotely fit our requirements: a twenty-eight-foot Fleetwood Prowler that had seen better days. There were plenty for sale in California and Texas, but that didn't help. On a trip to visit my folks in Georgia, we briefly considered a peachy fifth-wheel that was marked down to $18,500 because of an unsightly stain on the carpet.

Then we had a really close call in North Carolina, where we fell in love with a used twenty-nine-footer in fine condition. This time we got as far as handing over a deposit before we came to our senses and asked for a couple of days to check out the specs for this trailer's model year—information the dealer did not have. After several calls to the factory and many faxed pages of specs, we discovered that the trailer's Gross Vehicle Weight Rating was only four hundred pounds higher than its Dry Weight, once all the extras were factored in. This technical distinction meant, in plain English, that we would be *way* over our legal weight limit when we were fully loaded. Sure enough, in the very next model year the company significantly upgraded the axles on that trailer. We later learned that weight-bearing inadequacy is a widespread problem in trailer manufacturing. Buyer beware.

So it was back to the Internet. A salesman for a huge dealer in Florida had a thirty-foot Carriage Cashay for $23,500 that he wanted to sell me via video. He overnighted us an eight-minute home movie he had filmed by walking around the trailer with a video camera, inside and out, narrating its features as he went. We watched it three times. A fascinating sales technique—but were we really going to buy an RV from Florida, sight unseen?

Then, that same night, I spotted an Internet ad for a thirty-foot used RV at a dealership in Richmond, Virginia, two hours from our home. Over the phone the salesman was vague about details but very enthusiastic, insisting that we come on down and see what he had.

"Is *that* the one?" Donia asked in amazement when we saw the gleaming white Dutchmen Signature parked in the service area. It was huge, both taller and longer than any fifth-wheel we had ever looked at. Of course, the thirty-footer in the ad had already been sold; this one was thirty-four. It was last year's model but looked brand new—had only been used a couple of times before its owner traded up to a larger, super-luxury rig, the salesman said. "We can't buy this, it's too big!" Donia babbled about sixteen times as we went inside. And yet, it was our dream house for sure, containing every item on our list and more, thanks to those four extra feet. It had a large living room slide-out and a smaller one in the bedroom; more kitchen counter space than we had ever seen in a fifth-wheel; a bedroom clothes closet across the full front end and a hall closet perfect for jackets, laundry basket, and vacuum cleaner; a long vanity opposite the queen-sized bed, where we could spread out all our computer stuff; *and the couch upholstery exactly matched Cleo's fur.*

Luckily the salesman had the proper specs on hand for us to review, so we knew this trailer was fine, major design-wise. The quoted price was $22,500, but we did some hard bargaining. We thought a more reasonable figure was $20,500—and we wanted a fan installed in the bedroom ceiling, and a second twelve-volt battery, and we needed free storage for two months till we were ready to move out of our house and pick up the RV. The salesman pondered a minute, scribbled some figures on a pad, and pushed it across the desk to us. It said, "OK fan, battery, storage. $21,500." We were happy. He was happy. It was a done deal.

We love our thirty-four-foot Signature, though it doesn't have the heavy-duty construction or luxury appointments of higher-end brands. We've looked at dozens of fancy new fifth-wheels during our time on the road but have never found one we like as well. And, after 100,000 hard-working miles, our faithful Ford dually is still going strong.

3 Myrtle Beach, South Carolina

June 17

This report comes to you from a high-season, beachfront campground in Myrtle Beach, South Carolina. Lakewood RV Park is total luxury. There are fine motorhomes, trailers, fifth-wheels, and even a few tents as far as the eye can see. Donia and I are set up on a sunny site of sand and sawgrass, in a large, breezy field. This campground has "only" 1,930 sites, as opposed to the one next door that has more than 3,000!

We are about fifty yards, just six campsites away, from the steps over the dunes to the ocean. Our Xanadu-on-the-Beach has fifty-amp electrical service, so we have our big cord plugged in and can run the air conditioner, microwave, TV, and everything else we own all at the same time. It also has water, sewer, cable TV . . . even a phone jack right at our site, just for us.

So here I sit. Shirtless. At the kitchen table, writing my friends. I'm on my second pot of coffee and am eating the last of the garlic mashed potatoes (Breakfast of the Stars), saved in a doggy bag from our final dinner in Atlanta. I've had my early-morning walk on the beach, my cool shower. Life is glorious. As one of our fellow campers said yesterday morning, "I'm retired, I don't do anything—and I don't start that until 9:30."

Too bad it can't always be this way. Let me tell you about two days ago.

First of all, backing up a bit . . . we had a great visit with the family in Atlanta. After years of staying in the guest room at Mom and Dad's condo, it felt strange at first to be living in our own "house" while visiting them. But we love the leafy, lakeside campground out at Stone Mountain. Mom and Dad got a kick out of visiting us out there, for a change. In fact, they brought a couple of their friends with them to show off their son's crazy new lifestyle.

On our last day in Atlanta, we went to my brother-in-law's office to be available by fax and phone at 10 a.m. for the real estate closing on our Alexandria house. First news was that the settlement was delayed an hour because the basement flooded the night before. (Why yesterday, of all days???) The problem turned out to be just a clogged drain outside the back basement door, but it caused much hooing and hahing. Finally the closing occurred, with a few hundred dollars less on our side of the settlement sheet so the buyers can clear out the drain and recarpet one room. We got on the road at 3 p.m. But it was only the beginning.

At 5:30 p.m. (mistake #1, rush hour) in Augusta (mistake #2, a city) we pulled off the interstate to get fuel. Turning into the service station, me driving, Donia starts pointing at the diesel pumps and telling me, "Go over *there*" (mistake #3, don't point and gesture with a white-knuckle driver at the wheel; use words like, "Go beyond the *far left* pump").

Well, in my high anxiety, something like a fear-biter dog, I start yelling at my trusty helper (mistakes #4–36: don't yell at your wife, don't yell at somebody who's trying to help you, don't yell at somebody who is going to be making your dinner that night . . . and so on to #36).

And while yelling, don't stop watching where you're going (mistake #37)!

Hey, friends, do you know what those very rigid concrete and steel posts at the end of gas-pump islands are for? They are so people trying to turn too sharp with ridiculously big RVs in tow don't smash into gas pumps.

They work. I impaled the camper, scraping up the right side pretty well in the process. Yep. I stuck it tight. Despite the Ford Power Stroke diesel most-powerful-production-truck-made-in-America, I couldn't move. Forward or back.

I was ready to call the wrecker when a knight in coveralls suggested, "Maybe if we let the air out of the tires on the far side, it'll tilt enough t' git free." So we let those two tires down almost to the rims, and lo, we got free. (Then we had to pay for air—two quarters, because it took so long to reinflate the two tires. Insult to injury, if you ask me.)

We circled around and bought our fuel across the street in a roomier service station and, thoroughly depressed, hit the road again. Donia wanted to stop and call ahead for campground reservations. But oh, no—I thought I'd feel better just leaving the state. So off we drove into South Carolina with no idea where we would stop for the night (mistake #38). The first campground we tried was full. The second had a vacancy, but I couldn't maneuver the rig into it. The manager was gone, but one of the tenants at the campground said she was just off feeding her horse and she'd be back soon. We waited, wondering if she'd simply let us park for the night in her wide-open office parking area.

After a half hour or so, and she wasn't back, the friendly tenant wandered by again. "You can't get into that site?" he asked skeptically. "Let's us take a look." We walked down to the site and he suggested, "Why don't you drive all the way around the horseshoe and pull in from the other side? Looks like enough room to me."

Well, of course there was enough room from *that* side. So, saved again by a good ol' boy with some smarts. I'm going to have to work on "thinking outside the box" as they say in the corporate world.

This morning, from our private-phone luxury pad here in Myrtle Beach, I called our dealer in Richmond. Apparently I'm not the first one to impale his new RV on a stanchion. The dealer says a scraped and dented entry door and a couple of cargo doors, and this and that, can be taken care of in "only" about two days (once parts are ordered) whenever we come back through Richmond. Or, to avoid the hassle of waiting on ordered parts, we can wait until we're going through Indiana and take it directly to the factory for repairs.

By now, the sun is high. The ocean beckons. I'm off for a swim.

Love,

Mark (and, of course, Donia, who through it all never did stop speaking to me)

P.S. from Cleo:

Thanks to all of my friends who e-mailed us back to say they liked hearing the dog's point of view. Your support is truly appreciated.

Once again, I must speak up and tell the Myrtle Beach story like it REALLY happened. In his excitement over the ritzy campground, Dad forgot to tell about our arrival. It seems all 1,930 campsites in this place are the "back-in" type, instead of the pull-through type we had in all our other parks up till now.

So Dad turns on the CB radio in the truck and gives Mom the little hand-held CB radio he bought in a truck stop. She's supposed to go behind the trailer and tell him which way to turn and everything, so he can back straight in. It's a pretty geeky scene to begin with, Mom running around talking into her CB, plus something is wrong with this thing. Dad and I can hear what she's saying, but when Dad says something back to her, she can't understand him. So she has to keep running back up to the truck window to ask him what he said.

Things are getting a little tense, because the backing up is not going the way Dad was hoping. Like, he was hoping the rear end would go right, and it goes too far right and then starts going left. Plus, all these people are standing around watching us back into the space, like they've got nothing else to do on their vacation. Grandfathers, little kids with ice cream cones, teenagers on bikes stopping to catch the action, etc.

Finally, after a lot of backing and forthing, we hear Mom's voice squawking, "Great job with the trailer, Sweetie, except oops! Now you just knocked over the signpost with the rear end of the truck." Dad turns off the engine and gets out, cool as can be, paying no attention to all these other campers. He walks around and picks up the little wooden signpost with our campsite number on it and sticks it back in the ground like nothing happened.

Later we went for a walk on this soft stuff called "sand" that goes right down to the "Atlantic Ocean." Definitely a weird type of water. It kept rushing up at you and then running away. And the TASTE. Yuk! Take my advice, if you ever go to this Atlantic Ocean, be sure to get a drink of water before you go.

Love 'n' Licks,
Cleo

4 What Do You Do With All Your Stuff?

The June real estate closing on our Alexandria house was the final act in a drama that had been going on for six months. Starting the previous December—in a gung-ho spirit—Mark and I had begun taking steps to dispense with the house and nearly everything in it. This is probably the point at which many wanna-bees decide full-timing is not for them, after all. We've met lots of part-timers who tell us they just can't bring themselves to give up their home, lawn, garden, furniture, quilting frame, garage hobby shop, miniature lighthouse collection, or some other homey thing that normal people get attached to.

Mark and I also had treasures we couldn't part with. Things like the mounted head of a buck my father had bagged as a young man back in Texas in the 1930s. Two trunks full of my old diaries, letters, short stories, photos, and childhood mementos—some over fifty years old. Mark's sixth-grade baseball mitt. And his rare set of original, signed editions of Charles Dana Gibson drawings. Luckily, we had the luxury of the Front Royal cabin, where we could leave our keeper items until we decided whether the RV lifestyle was really going to stick.

As for the rest of our gear, I told the kids to come and get it, now or never. At New Year's, my daughter, Curry, and her husband, George, drove down from Cape Cod in a rented truck. The same day, my son, Travis, flew home from the University of Texas in Austin, bringing his amiable girlfriend, Amy, along to meet us for the first time. The two of them looked so domestic, browsing through our up-for-grabs furniture, linens, Christmas decorations, framed portraits, china, and cookware. Did this mean Amy was the One? I wondered, all atwitter. Might they have plans I didn't yet know about? At the moment, no one was saying.

In a two-day blitz, the kids packed up childhood keepsakes and household items they thought they could use some day. Mark and I hung tough on this issue; leaving things at the cabin was not an option. We'd stored their treasures long enough. Anything they didn't take now, they would probably never see again. I bought several inexpensive trunks and plastic tubs at a discount store, to make it easier for them to transport their stuff. I even prefilled a primary plastic tub for each of them, putting in such vital items as birth certificates, medical records, school report cards, photographs, and carefully preserved arts and crafts gifts they had made me for Mother's Day over the years.

Curry and George agreed to store Trav's things until he had a place of his own, so they loaded everything into the rental truck. When the kids finally drove away with their booty on January third, a heavy weight seemed to float up off our shoulders and disappear among the clouds. All that was left were the few things we would store in the mountain cabin, the clothes and supplies we would take in the RV, and the poor rejects that nobody wanted.

Nearly all the full-timers we read about had held a big garage sale before they took off, but we decided our leftovers were not worth the time and effort. So we took boxes and boxes of give-aways to the local thrift shop. Also, we lived in a rather eclectic neighborhood where getting rid of unwanted stuff was no problem. You could just put it out by the curb with a "free to a good home" sign on it, and twenty minutes later it would be gone. In fact, half the time when we set large items out front for trash collection, they disappeared long before the trucks arrived. We were always happy to think that our junk was somebody else's treasure.

With the house emptied out, it looked a lot bigger—and was much easier to spruce up for sale. We had the entire place painted inside and out, the windows deep-cleaned, the worn living room carpeting ripped out, and the original oak flooring refinished to a beautiful shine. Outside, we pressure-cleaned the wooden fences and walkways that Mark had built, trimmed the gardens bordering the house and yard, and tidied everything up with a fresh covering of mulch. When the For Sale sign went up in late February, the humble fixer-upper we had bought ten years before had become a sparkling showplace.

During this period of major divestiture, we did purchase one new item—an NEC Versa 2735MT laptop computer—and started transferring over files from our beloved (but outdated) desktop PC. At the time we didn't realize how much critical activity would be concentrated in this one little electronic companion once we embarked on our new streamlined lifestyle. Everything from communicating with friends and practicing bridge hands to banking, shopping, record keeping, doing our taxes—and writing a book.

In April we decided to start trying to sell my ten-year-old Subaru wagon. We expected this to take a while, since the brakes squealed and the air conditioning was broken and it had over 150,000 miles on it. Silly us! One Saturday I left it down at the local shopping center with a For Sale sign on the window, and by the time I got home again, the phone was ringing. Within forty-five minutes the enthusiastic buyer had test-driven the car, made the rounds of several automated teller machines, and handed me $1,650 in cash. I promptly wrapped up the money in aluminum foil and hid it away in case of emergency—like maybe, a total nationwide ATM meltdown.

I must say, it all happened so fast I wasn't emotionally prepared to part with that little Subaru that had seen me through so many years. The man who bought it lived in a townhouse nearby, and early one Sunday morning I took my exercise walk past his house so I could see my old car once more, parked at the curb, with different license plates. That seemed to satisfy me; it was his car now, and it looked perfectly happy there.

Mark still needed his station wagon and all the gear in it for house inspections, which meant that I had to drive the monster diesel truck to work every day and park it in our low-ceilinged underground parking garage. Just picture a midget in a business suit driving a Sherman tank into a cave. This scene amused my

Could *You* Be a Full-Timer?

There are many definitions of full-timing, but for Mark and me it means "living and traveling full-time in an RV." To join the true hard-core nomads, you must take the plunge and dispose of your stationary residence, so that your only home is the one on wheels.

But selling the homestead is just one of the emotion-laden issues involved in the decision to hit the road. Here are a dozen more questions to ask yourself:

- Can I afford a life of full-time travel, either as a retiree or as a traveling worker?
- Will I be happy living for an extended period without a familiar home base?
- Am I curious, adventurous, and daring in the face of the unknown?
- Can I be flexible in coping with change and the unexpected?
- Am I comfortable living among strangers?
- Can I live with a minimum amount of clothing and household gear?
- If I can't part with certain belongings, do I have a secure way to store them?
- Can my parents and children manage without having me nearby?
- Am I healthy and fit enough to withstand the physical requirements of RVing?
- Can I tackle the challenge of driving an oversized vehicle—safely?
- Will my health insurance cover medical expenses as I travel?
- Can I read a map?

If the answer to all these questions is yes, then what are you waiting for???

coworkers no end, and convinced them once and for all that I was really moving on to a completely new life in a few weeks.

The only anxiety we suffered during this time was the total absence of sales activity on our house. We had both set May 15 as our last day of work, and the following week we would fly to Austin for Travis's college graduation. After that, we planned to do a final house cleanup, pick up the trailer in Richmond, move ourselves and everything we still owned out to the cabin, and then take off. It would throw a serious monkey wrench into the plans if we hadn't sold the house by then. Mark came up with Plan B, the "cloverleaf" plan, in case our house didn't sell. We would route our travel in clover-shaped loops around the D.C. area for a few months, so we'd never be more than a day's drive away if we were needed in Alexandria to conduct house-related business.

Our local area had been in a real estate slump for some time, and there were horror stories of houses in our neighborhood that had languished on the market for over a year. We lowered the original asking price, then a few weeks later lopped off still more. The house was now a steal, yet as the end of the ninety-day listing period approached, we still hadn't had one serious nibble. We tactfully told our agent we were thinking about switching the listing to a different realty company that was bigger and more active in our area.

Two days later, out of the blue, a delightful young couple with a new baby and very little cash came along and made us an offer. We did some juggling with closing costs and came up with a price figure that was the equivalent of $187,500—only $58,000 more than we had paid for the house in the first place. Not a lot of appreciation over ten years' time in the close-in Washington suburbs. But we were thrilled, nevertheless. The last major hurdle was passed. Our new life was cleared for takeoff.

5 Richmond, Virginia
June 30

Dear Friends and Fans,

You'll be happy to hear that, based on your overwhelming praise and support, and after some cold-nosed negotiation with my Human editors, I now have my own canine column. They think my style is too long-winded, so I'm supposed to limit my column to "three thousand bites." Sounds good to me!

By the way, for all of you out there who didn't write me a fan letter, and who may be secretly wondering how a dog can write e-mail notes—GET OVER IT. I've watched Mom and Dad do it thousands of times, and when they leave me alone while they go to Wal-Mart or something, there's my chance to write. I mean, it's not exactly rocket science.

But to tell you the truth, Mom and Dad don't leave me alone all that much. Mostly the three of us hang out together. The way both of them worked all day long back home, it's a lot to get used to now, having them around all the time. This Human retirement thing sounds pretty fishy—you work for a company for only twenty years (that's about three People Years, right?) and then you "retire" and this company keeps paying you money for doing nothing, for the rest of your life. What a deal. Meanwhile, I'm still working my butt off. It's "Cleo, watch the trailer!" or "Cleo, watch the truck!" And then I also have to take my people on at least four or five walks a day in all these strange new places with no sidewalks.

But hey, I'm not complaining. Back home in Alexandria we never had all these picnic tables and trash cans with all the crumbs and great smells all around. And now I see many more fellow dogs than I ever got to meet back home. Granted, a lot of traveling dogs are these yappy little mutts no bigger than a cat— your toy poodles and terriers and miniature dachsunds and such—

26

which I pretty much ignore. But occasionally we will see a really beautiful golden retriever or black Lab, which I consider to be in my Big Dog Quality League. Sometimes there's an opportunity for some mutual sniffing while their people are talking with my people. These moments are brief but intense. And then both families move on—us going one way, them going another, never to meet again.

So here we are in Richmond, getting the RV's little bugs fixed. There was a leaky window in the living room that poured water all down the wall one time when it rained real hard in Atlanta. They fixed that. We had a lot of noise with the water pump, and they worked on that a little bit, but if you ask me, it's still noisy. Plus they fixed something on the water heater and a tire with a "slow leak." But the top item on the list was that wacko sewer valve. The guy was on his back under the trailer with all the pipes, huffing and cussing, and Mom and Dad were so fascinated by this mystery valve that they crawled under the trailer too, so they could watch.

"Hah," the guy finally says, and he crawls out holding up this sopping wet twig. "Here's the problem." The valve wasn't closing all the way because this little stick was stuck in the pipe! Like, maybe the people who used to own the trailer were pushing something down the potty with the stick, and they accidentally flushed it down. Or maybe they flushed it on purpose because it was so icky? And then maybe they hated the mysterious broken toilet valve so much they traded the trailer in on a new one? Could it be, the whole reason we got such a great deal on our new home was this humble little twig? Anyway, the guy put the valve back together, minus the stick, and then it worked perfectly.

One thing these Richmond guys didn't fix was the mess Dad made when he scraped the trailer against the diesel pump in Georgia. He and Mom thought it would be fun to see the factory in Indiana, so they'll take it there someday. They decided they're not in any hurry. (If you ask me, I think Dad enjoys telling people how it happened.)

For now, we're only in a hurry to get up to Cape Cod for

Fourth of July. After being around nothing but strangers for so long, it will be great to visit some of my favorite Human family members—my big sister Curry lives there, and my brother Travis will be there too. Best of all, there's going to be a cookout!

A Happy and Delicious Independence Day to all my four-legged friends around the country—Spike and Sophie, Brett and Euchere, Bingo, Company C, and Alpha and Harley. And especially Daisy, who will be happy to hear that I don't bark at cats any more (unless they deserve it). I hope you all have a chance to hit the road with your people someday, too.

Love 'n' Licks,

Cleo

6 How Can You Afford Full-Timing?

Cleo's e-mail just answered a question that many people probably wonder about but are too polite to ask: How can we live this freewheeling lifestyle with no working income? First of all, it helped a lot that Mark and I both had a lifelong habit of spending less than we made, and had no debts except for our mortgage. But the real key to full-timing was my comfortable pension—"money for doing nothing," as Cleo so bluntly put it.

I had the good fortune to start my career as a small editor for a big media corporation and then work my way slowly up to a middle management job over the years. My company offered generous benefits, including early retirement with continued health coverage at age fifty-five and twenty years of service. By adding on accrued vacation days and a sabbatical I was eligible for, I could actually retire three months before my fifty-fifth birthday—and once we got the full-timing bug, every extra day counted.

One of my corporate colleagues was a witty, no-nonsense fellow editor named Mark Steele. We met in the early 1980s, shortly before he left the company to strike out on his own. He was eager to break out of working on home repair books and get his hands on a hammer and nails for real. At the time, he was in the final phase of work on his beloved cabin overlooking the Shenandoah River Valley and Blue Ridge Mountains. Fond of the old Spanish proverb "Living well is the best revenge," Mark had named his cabin the Best Revenge.

I met him just in time to spend weekends finishing up the fun stuff at the Best Revenge—the final trim, painting, and furnishing. I think I passed the critical wife test the day I agreed to stand on the top step of a very tall ladder and hold the molding in place while he nailed it around the cathedral ceiling. A year later, we were married on the deck looking out over that beautiful valley, my two children from a previous marriage flanking us as we said, "I do."

Our house in the suburbs was an inexpensive and unexciting brick rambler. But it was convenient to our work and the kids' schools, and was made much more livable over the years by Mark's handiwork. He had his own small contracting business for a while,

 Other Lessons Learned

- Plastic is the full-timer's best friend: It's so easy these days to use debit or credit cards for nearly everything. On credit accounts, know your monthly billing date and the company's 800 number. Don't wait for mailed bills to catch up with you each month—call for your balance and pay it in full before the deadline. Late fees are usurious.
- Since you're using your credit card so much now, get one that gives you cash back, or at least airline bonus miles.
- Have backup ATM and credit cards. It's surprising how often a card will fail to swipe properly because of damaged magnetic strips. Backup cards will save your life while you wait for mail-forwarded replacements.
- A backup checking account at a second bank, accessible with plastic, can also be a lifesaver if your regular bank's computer network goes down while you're standing at the only ATM within a hundred miles.
- Consider putting your assets in stable investments. Phones and Internet access are often not immediately available on the road, and having investments you must track closely or sell at a moment's notice can add a major hassle factor to your life.
- Forget about shopping at warehouse clubs to save money. You just don't have room now to store those giant bargain packages.

then specialized further, training as a home inspector. So, with two solid incomes and a frugal lifestyle, we could steadily put money away during our final career years.

Our goal as full-timers was to live on my pension alone, leaving our IRAs, 401(k)s, and other investments to build into a healthy nest egg for our "old age." We really had no idea how much money we would need for our traveling life, so we took the lazy way out. We didn't even try to establish a budget beforehand. We didn't think it would be a problem, as the pension came to just about $3,000 a month, after taxes. We would be debt-free, since we had bought the truck and trailer with cash and also wouldn't have a home mortgage to pay any more. And all the RVing books we read assured us that it was really cheaper to live on the road than in a regular house.

Instead of starting out with a fixed budget, we decided to keep track of every penny we spent and check how we were doing after a few months. I carried a small monthly calendar in my purse and, in teensy handwriting, recorded each expenditure in the block for that day, rounded off to the nearest dollar.

Our categories were alphabet-coded:

- C was for daily campground fees.
- D encompassed diesel fuel, bridge and highway tolls, routine vehicle maintenance, and minor repairs and improvements on the truck and trailer. Included in here were our annual insurance premiums for truck ($912) and trailer ($424).
- E was entertainment—entry fees at tourist attractions, video rentals, movie tickets, golf greens fees, casino gambling, and so forth.
- G was for groceries, anything we bought at a store or roadside stand to bring home and eat in the RV.
- H stood for health care, including our monthly insurance premiums of $209, all noncovered medical treatments, and various copay amounts for doctors, dentists, and prescription drugs. (Plus there was that $4 copper bracelet Mark bought in a souvenir shop, hoping to cure his achy knee.)

- R meant restaurants, including not only full meals but also snacks, cocktails, sodas, and coffee consumed away from home.
- S stood for sundries, the most elusive and dangerous category of all. Typical sundries were all the miscellaneous toiletries and household items, from toothpaste to padded mailers to electric space heaters for the trailer. Also counted here were clothes, laundromats, postage stamps, Mark's cigars, occasional air travel, haircuts, RV-club membership fees, magazine subscriptions, and the armloads of books we couldn't resist.
- U was utilities, encompassing propane refills for our twin on-board tanks, mail-forwarding fees, and monthly charges for our telephone calling card, voicemail service, and Internet provider. (Electricity and water are generally included in daily campground fees.)
- X started out as our catchall category for big one-time items like Christmas gifts and major vehicle repairs. However, these definitions soon broke down, and Cleo's vet, kennel, and grooming expenses somehow ended up here as well.

We did okay for a couple of months, but things started slipping in the fall. When we tallied it all up we were appalled to find that our spending had averaged over $3,900 a month for the first year. The bad news looked something like this:

Average Monthly Expenses

Item	Amount
Campground fees	$466
Diesel and vehicle expenses	622
Entertainment and recreation	212
Groceries	404
Health care	736
Restaurants	477
Sundries	658
Utilities	167
Extras	163
Total	$3,905

Numerous times, we had to dip into our savings to cover expenses. For example, Mark decided to take the plunge and get laser surgery on his eyes to correct lifelong nearsightedness. That was a cool $4,800—none of it covered by insurance—which alone inflated the H category by $400 a month. (Alas, Mark's plunge took place a year or two before the advent of $700 laser surgery.) Then there was some unexpected dental work for each of us, plus those unplanned RV repairs—not to mention a totally extravagant week we spent at Disney World in November with some close friends from home.

At first I argued that these were unusual expenses, and we shouldn't have to count them in with our monthly totals. "Life is full of unusual expenses," Mark said. "You always have to count them in."

The hard truth was, we went way overboard in a couple of everyday categories that seasoned full-timers spend much less on. Our diesel fuel and vehicle maintenance expenses were exceptionally high because we did so much driving our first year. RV travel is not exactly fuel-efficient: We averaged under ten miles per gallon while on the road in the rig.

Our campground fees were also a lot higher than necessary because most of the year we zipped from place to place too often to take advantage of cheap weekly rates. For peace of mind, we usually chose higher-end campgrounds with full hookups, roomy sites, and "modem friendly" offices, which often cost us over $20 per night. In time we discovered that you can find perfectly fine campgrounds for $10 or $12 if you can live without the luxurious extras at least for some days out of every week—and if you stay away from big cities and the East Coast.

Mark and I also shamefully overdid it in the Restaurants department—our biggest weakness. We just couldn't bring ourselves to pass up those famous eateries in towns we passed through. Added to our grocery tab, the overall monthly food bill came to a staggering $881. "How did two short people ever eat that much?" is a totally reasonable question. We wonder, too.

And finally, we overspent wildly in the Sundries category.

Don't even ask me how all those odds and ends added up to $658 a month. Where did we ever find room for them in our tiny house on wheels? Come to think of it, many of those sundries were for the house, expensive little gizmos to make life easier or more comfortable: area rugs, a new mattress, towel hangers, racks and bins to organize cabinets, tool boxes, plumbing pipe to create a sewer hose caddy, and so forth. These were things we might have gotten cheaper if we'd been more patient. But as newbies, whenever we thought of something we wanted, we wanted it *now*.

We settled down a lot in our second year and not only stayed within our means but actually were able to put some of my pension back into savings most months. Money spending is a very individual thing, of course, and what seems frugal to one RVer might be extravagant to another. We've met experienced full-timers who claim they can live well on less than $2,000 a month, while others are obviously spending even more than we did in our first year. "You can't count other people's," as the saying goes.

Just a short mention of banking on the road, since many people raise this question. Before we left Virginia I opened an account at NationsBank, which soon afterward merged with Bank of America. However, we generally stay away from bank buildings altogether except for dropping by ATMs to get cash wherever we are. We also deposit checks by mail, and get my pension check direct-deposited on the first of each month.

Mark enjoys doing his banking business via our laptop computer. He has free service from Citibank. I started out with a similar "electronic banking" arrangement, but my finances became so simplified after retirement I suddenly realized I was paying NationsBank a $6 monthly fee just so I could pay one measly credit card bill. So I canceled the bill-paying feature and went back to the old-fashioned method of writing a check once a month.

We've been asked if we worry about delays in the mail, the security and reliability of computers, direct-deposit glitches, refusal of out-of-state checks, and other financial screw-ups caused by our nomadic lifestyle. The short answer is no. Although managing our spending has presented some challenges, the mechanics of banking and other financial business have never been a problem. (Knock on wood!)

Note from Mark:
Oops, you caught us cheating. Yes, we paid cash for our RV, and no, we haven't formally planned for vehicle replacement. But it looms in the back of our minds. When the time comes (hopefully far in the future) we have no idea what the expense will be. Will we spend $50,000 for a used truck and trailer again? Or go for a top-of-the-line motorhome and tow-car combo costing $150,000 or more? In any event, full-timers like us who don't have vehicle loan payments in their budget *should* be factoring in a replacement amount.

7 Finger Lakes, New York
July 15

No great *sturm und drang* to report this time. The drama of our first days on the road has faded and we are settling into a routine. It's hard to believe Donia and I have been living this mobile lifestyle for more than six weeks already. When we worked, we never had a vacation that long. We've been retired now for two whole months, and neither of us (unless Donia is holding back on me) has looked back once. I keep wondering if it will hit me some day that I'm leading a totally useless, self-indulgent life . . . Naaaaah.

Since leaving Richmond with our minor repairs taken care of, we visited relatives in suburban New York, highlighted by a nice reunion with my first cousins and aunts and uncles whom I haven't visited with in, well, years. Then we stayed for a whole week in Cape Cod visiting with Curry and George, who have been married almost a year now and have bought a wonderful Cape Cod house. Travis and his S.O., Amy, drove up with us in the truck and trailer from New York, visited for a couple of days, then hopped a bus back to the Big Apple, where they are taking on Real Life, post-college phase.

Upon leaving Cape Cod we headed up, up, up. Into the Berkshire Mountains of western Massachusetts. We had a great campsite in the middle of a huge lawnlike field. We had to wear wool sweaters at night (Yummmmm), and the days were cool and sunny. (Highlights: the Norman Rockwell Museum at Stockbridge, and a walking tour of Williams College in Williamstown.)

Adams, Massachusetts, has a big statue of William McKinley. He had no connection to the town but was instrumental in passing a tariff that kept cheap foreign cotton out of the United States, thus protecting the textile mills of the state. That rates him Big Bronze. There's a statue of Susan B. Anthony at the other end of the street; the brochure says she was the offspring of Shakers, which I don't understand, as I've read that Shakers were celibate. Unfortunately, we'd made commitments and had to break camp and head west before I unraveled the mystery.

We then stopped two days in Central New York to visit George's parents (aka Curry's in-laws). The Mohawk Valley is simply breathtaking to look at, but it's definitely part of the "rust belt." Utica, the central city, is depressed from so much industry fleeing to the nonunionized South, and there are many vacant, boarded-up buildings. But having Dot and Ron Hoskey to act as tour guides brought the region alive in a way we would have missed on our own. We saw between the vacant buildings to what was charming and lively in the area. They showed us a Russian Orthodox monastery, a Revolutionary War-era church, and several parklike marinas springing up along the Erie Canal. We gambled at Turning Stone, the new Oneida Indian casino, played golf in uncrowded bliss at the local links, and ate the world's best hot dogs at Voss's on Route 5, which Ron has been enjoying for over a half century, since his grade school days.

All the family members we've visited so far have invited us to stay at their houses, like their visitors usually do. This time around, we thanked them for the hospitality, but told them we really prefer staying at a campground in our *own* house. We can get up at our leisure, get dressed and brush our teeth without having to rummage through a suitcase, and everyone has privacy and a chance to take a break from each other. What a concept!

Now we're in the Finger Lakes region of New York. We failed to connect with our mail in Cape Cod. It took eight days (seven if you forgive the Post Office July Fourth) to get from Dallas, Texas, to Cape Cod. Graciously, Curry volunteered to pick it up when it arrived and overnight it to us at our next stop. Meanwhile, our latest batch of mail has reached us in only two days, from Dallas to western New York. Go figure. Anyway, we just spent the afternoon going though new mail and some very old mail, and catching up on business.

We also found a nice vet to treat Cleo's flea bite dermatitis, an itchy skin condition she seems to get whenever the weather is warm or she's been in tall grass or woods. We find that living on the road has exacerbated the problem. Every other day we're in a brand new dog-walking environment filled with unknown flora and fauna. Anyway, Cleo now has a fancy set of flea repellents, antibiotics, and antihistamines to take. She also got a big shot of cortisone, so she's walking around licking the rug, drinking water, and peeing like a tank truck with a hole in the hull. But for the first time in two weeks, she's not scratching herself and licking, licking, licking her skin.

It's hot, hot, hot here in the Finger Lakes, so we're not sticking around. I voted for a U-turn and return to the cool Berkshires. But the COO vetoed that idea. Instead we're going to dash west to Toledo, Ohio, then turn north into Michigan and not stop until the daytime temperature is back in the seventies. Or until we reach the Straits of Mackinac, whichever comes first.

Donia sends her love, but can't come write anything right now, as she is at the coin-op laundry room staking out a dryer to pounce on as soon as the washer is finished with our clothes. Timing is all, in this competitive arena of campground clothes washing. She promises to write next time (and let *me* do the laundry).

Cheers to all,

Mark

8 How Do You Get Your Mail?

Of all the questions people ask about our nomadic lifestyle, the most frequent one is, "How do you get your mail?" Good question!

Receiving postal delivery on a regular basis is something you take for granted in America, until you hit the road full-time. Then it becomes a strategic operation. You're a moving target, and the mail is a moving target, so it takes organization and forethought to make sure you both reach the same place at the same time. When we missed our mail delivery while visiting my daughter, Curry, in Cape Cod, it was a simple goof on our part: We forgot to specify priority mail-forwarding service, and we had to leave the Cape before it got there by regular delivery. (No wonder they call it snail mail these days.)

Some RVers have a trusted family member handle their mail all the time, but we didn't want to impose on Curry or anybody else for the length of time we planned to follow this lifestyle. So, like most other full-timers, Mark and I selected a professional mail-forwarding service before we embarked. The way it works is, the service assigns you an address with a box number at their office, and that becomes your new address. You have all your business and personal mail routed there. The service receives your mail and holds it until you call and tell them an address to send it to—private home, campground, or in care of general delivery at the post office in a town you plan to visit.

Since the mail-forwarding address becomes the official "residence" address for many full-timers, it's important to pick a company located in a state you'll be happy "living" in. Legal residency is a complex matter, full of gray areas and ambiguity (see Chapter 40), but we've noticed that mail-forwarding services do tend to be clustered in places that have no state income taxes, such as Nevada and Texas.

We knew the mail service run by the Escapees RV Club in Livingston, Texas, was the biggest and most established. But in our rookie mind-frame, we didn't like the idea of having the same address as thousands of other full-timers. So, at the outset, we looked elsewhere. We first signed up with a company in Florida but immediately canceled when we found out that our address did not include a street name, as their brochure had stated, but consisted only of a long box number. That looked tacky to us.

Next we changed to a service near Dallas, Texas, which charged a small annual fee plus 50 percent of the postage costs to send your mail each time you called. They offered the glorious option of discarding all junk mail as it arrived and forwarding only first-class mail and magazines. We got a nice street address and were told that we could use "Apt." instead of "Box" in front of our number if we liked.

In April we sent out address change notices to our banks, credit card and investment companies, utilities, and other business contacts. We also sent a more personal letter to all our friends and family members explaining our full-timing plans and the various ways they could contact us. A couple of weeks before we left Virginia, we stopped our home delivery—filing a change of address at the local post office specifying the Texas mail service as our new address.

A week later, we called the service and asked them to send us our collected mail so far, in care of general delivery at a local Virginia post office branch. We kept our fingers crossed, hoping this whole deal worked as advertised. Sure enough, two days later there was our mail waiting to be picked up, all packed in a white Tyvek envelope. It was like Christmas in May, opening that package and pawing through the letters to see which companies had already made the address change in their files, and which mail was still getting forwarded from our Virginia home address.

In all the time we've been on the road, the fun of picking up our mail package has never worn off. Our favorite routine is to have the mail sent to the post office in a small town where we'll be staying or passing through in about four days—or five, if a Sunday or holiday is involved. Priority mail usually gets there in two days, but we give it some leeway just in case. Once we pick up the package, we find a visitors' center bench, a park picnic table, or just a grassy place somewhere in town, and open our mail at leisure.

In our first few months of travel, mail forwarding worked smoothly about 80 percent of the time. We have fond memories of tiny towns where the postal clerks greeted us with a jolly, "So you're the Steeles. We wondered when you'd be coming by." They gave us advice about things to see in their area, where the closest Wal-Mart was located, or who was the best veterinary doctor in town.

Of course, there were a few bummers. In at least three towns, the clerk returned from looking in the back and said there was no package for us. Yet when we returned the next day—or the next—we discovered it had been there all the time, left sitting in an unsorted pile or simply overlooked. We were later told, while sharing a table with two friendly postal workers at a barbecue festival, that mail clerks sometimes resent general delivery customers, assuming that they're locals just too cheap to rent a box.

But we soon realized the majority of the problems were with our own mail-forwarding service. A couple of times we waited extra days in a town for mail that never came, because the service slipped up and didn't send it as requested. Something about the telephone clerk forgetting to push the "save" button on her computer. They also had a customer with a name similar to mine, whose mail we kept getting by mistake—and vice versa, we could only assume. Each time, we sent back Dana Steele's mail with a note to the service, and hoped Dana was doing the same with ours. We had distinctly different box numbers, so what was the problem? The fourth time this mix-up happened, we said that's it, and eventually switched our business over to Escapees.

Then we had the annoying chore of changing our mailing address with friends and businesses again, and of paying for both services during the months it took for all our contacts to change their records. Moreover, we had no sooner sent out our second set of address-change notices than the United States Postal Service decreed that all mail-forwarding customers must use PMB, for Private Mail Box, in front of their number. Mail marked Suite, Apartment, or with the # sign would not be delivered, the USPS

 Other Lessons Learned

- Many mail-forwarding services advertise in the classified sections of RV specialty magazines: e.g., *Highways* (the Good Sam club magazine), *Trailer Life*, and *MotorHome*. Check out their services and fees carefully before deciding.
- A mail service that will throw away junk mail is a great boon. Even better is one that lets you specify particular junk mail you *do* want to receive. That way you avoid most of the bulk but still get your J.R. Cigars catalog and airline mileage statements.
- Once or twice a year even priority mail takes a week to arrive. Hopefully you'll be getting your mail sent to places where it wouldn't be so awful to have to stay a few extra days, in case it's delayed.
- Express mail, the post office's overnight service, is not all that expensive for rare occasions when you need to get your mail fast, or simply cannot commit to being in some particular place in five days. Our typical mail-forwarding package, costing $4 to $6 to send priority, runs $15 to $20 via express mail—and we have it in a day or two.
- Use the # sign instead of PMB with your mail-service box address in any situation where you want to avoid complicated discussions about residency. Examples: vehicle registration and insurance, state tax payments, cell phone "one-rate" plans, and credit applications. Oddly, it doesn't matter what address you use for your federal taxes. The IRS only cares that you pay up.

warned. So, for the third time in a year, we sent out a round of address-change notices.

The PMB thing was allegedly a measure to cut down on mail-order fraud. But RV full-timers and other legitimate mailbox customers raised such a storm of protest that the USPS softened the rule eventually, allowing PMBers to use the # sign as an alternative box prefix if they wished. We were not about to change our address again at this point, however, so PMB-stained we remain.

Mark and I have been extremely happy with the Escapees service and have not experienced a single glitch in mail delivery to date. When first starting out, we called for our mail to be sent once a week, but now that we've been traveling a while we've relaxed a lot. Sometimes we let it pile up for two weeks or even a month, if we want to keep our schedule flexible, and not be locked in to driving to some specific town two hundred miles away just to pick up mail.

From experience we've learned that we rarely get any urgent snail mail anyway—except credit card bills that have a payment deadline. We solve this possible problem, when our mail pickup is going to be delayed, by calling the credit companies to find out our balance, then prepaying by check before we actually have the bill in hand. Everybody else who has timely business just sends us e-mail. But that's a whole 'nother story.

9 Cheboygan, Michigan
July 28

 There is a geographic/culinary phenomenon Donia and I have noticed. I call it The Line.

Someplace there is a specific border above which there are no more biscuits with breakfast. There is another line, maybe coincident, where grits disappear. (Disappears?) And sausage gravy.

The Line isn't restricted to southern food. It's not a Mason-Dixon sort of thing. There's a line where "soda" becomes "pop." If you order a soda here in Michigan, no one asks you, "What kind?" You get fizzy water. Club soda.

In western New York we saw salt potatoes advertised on the roadside. They are little white potatoes that the vegetable stand guy said are for boiling in salt water. "Put a tablespoon and a half of salt in the water," he told me. I asked him how much water. "At least enough to cover the potatoes," he replied.

We're now in northern Michigan. Above some line up here, barbecue ceased to exist as a noun. There is smoke up here, however. The locals use it on all manner of fish, as well as some meats. There's smoked pork loin, whitefish, lake trout, salmon, kielbasa, and whitefish kielbasa. Plath's Meats, on Third Street in Rogers City, Michigan, is famous for its smoked pork loin. We bought two pounds just to try. While we were at it, we got a pound each of their smoked salmon, kielbasa, and teawurst.

Plath's deserves its fame. Why did I have to come all the way to this pretty little Lake Huron town to eat such a heavenly substance? It comes sliced from the whole loin in perfectly slablike pieces, slightly pink from the smoke, about half an inch thick. At the counter they wrap it in real old-timey butcher paper, tied with string yet. The butcherette told me the loin was cooked. Just grill it enough to heat through and put the grill lines on it, she advised.

The meat was buttery smooth without tasting fatty. The smoke was subtle. The result was something between a pork chop and a slice of ham, with the best qualities of each. The kielbasa was wonderful too. Again, Plath's is into subtlety. The texture of this sausage was fine-grained. More like a bratwurst than a kielbasa, but with just enough garlic punch to let you know that its family tree was rooted farther east than you will find the Autobahn.

I told our campground neighbors, Ronny and Linda, about our good fortune in finding Plath's. Turns out Linda's aunt is from Rogers City—and while Linda allowed that Plath's pork loin is okay, apparently we went way wrong on the kielbasa. Said Linda, "Nowicki's is better. We had a taste test. We bought a pound of Plath's and ten pounds of Nowicki's. Now we buy ten pounds of Nowicki's for the freezer every time we visit Aunt Pat." Nowicki's is also on Third Street, just a couple blocks down from Plath's.

Our campground this week is in Cheboygan, Michigan, on the Cheboygan River some four miles south of the Straits of Mackinac. There is, by the way, a Sheboygan, Wisconsin—larger and more widely known. Michigan also has a Zilwaukee. We were informed that these near-imitation names were chosen purposely, to fool immigrants in the nineteenth century when cities vied hard with each other for labor for their lumber camps, limestone quarries, and iron and copper mines. Agents at the docks were not above pulling the old switcheroo on the new arrivals from Scandinavia, Wales, Ireland, and eastern Europe.

Saturday was a quiet night at the campground. Jan and Ron, the owners (who also are dairy farmers and school psychologists) credited the campers' early bedtime to the nice weather. "It's always quieter when it's warm and the boaters can be out on the water all day, doing whatever it is they do," said Jan. These are campground owners who put flowers in their ladies room, provide a lawn chair next to the pay phone, and slip the phone book into a rain-proof bag, with note paper and a pen. Nice touches. We like Jan and Ron.

I found out that if you have an "amplified antenna" for your

TV, you don't have to replace it if it doesn't work. You first should try finding a switch someplace and turning it on. I never heard of turning on the TV antenna before. But sure enough, there's that little black switch on the side of the small TV cubbyhole in our bedroom (which is filled with odds and ends, not a TV). Now I've got to return a hundred-dollar replacement antenna we bought at Radio Shack. Turns out, however, that there are real Radio Shacks and franchise Radio Shacks. Real ones will take back Radio Shack merchandise no matter where you bought it, if you have a receipt. Franchise ones are not "required" to, we were informed. We were also informed that there was a real (read: company-owned) one in Sault Ste. Marie, next to the Wal-Mart.

So off we head to "the Soo."

Donia says Hi. She would add a note but she's off in the kitchen developing a close personal relationship with the famous Mackinac fudge we bought yesterday on Mackinac Island.

Cheers,

Mark

10 How Can You Live without a Phone?

It may seem strange for us to get excited over a campground pay phone equipped with a lawn chair and note paper, but little things mean a lot to telephone-deprived full-timers. Many RVers now travel with cell phones, but when we first started checking them out, cellular service was extremely expensive and not reliable enough to be worth it. Then one leading company began cracking down on full-time travelers who subscribed to its no-roaming-charges plan, leaving RVers madly scrambling to find other providers. So we decided to do without a cell phone and just use pay phones instead—often an adventure in itself.

For long distance calls, we have a service that we access by calling an 800 number. We can make calls any time, anywhere in the country, for a flat rate of 14¢ a minute. We also signed up for a voicemail 800 number with our own individual extension (called an "account code") where family and friends can leave us a message any time, toll-free. This service runs an average of $12 per month.

When Donia and I announced these arrangements, several family members suddenly developed severe phone separation anxiety, realizing they would have no way to call us directly on the road. We assured them we would stop at a pay phone and check our voicemail around 5 o'clock each evening, wherever we might be, so we'd never be more than twenty-four hours away from an emergency message. This has worked fine so far. Still, emergencies aside, the idea of having no immediate telephone access to loved ones is a stressful concept for most people, and it has remained one of the biggest frustrations for our families to deal with.

From our point of view, having no phone is mainly inconvenient when we're trying to conduct business via a pay phone, and a receptionist tells us she will take our number and have Mr. Busy call us back. There's always that moment of silence on the other end when we patiently explain that we don't really live anywhere, we don't have a phone, so we *can't* be called back. On a good day, we are put on hold and Mr. Busy himself comes on the line after a short while. Otherwise, we just have to keep trying, hoping to find him at his desk and un-busy at some moment we call.

Whenever we do leave our voicemail 800 number for business contacts, we have to make sure they take down the required four-digit account code. Some telephone clerks don't quite get it that our "home phone" has an "extension." Or perhaps the computer form they're typing the information into just doesn't have a phone extension field. In any event, anyone who tries calling the main number of our voicemail service without using our account code is just out of luck.

Our pay phone experiences in campgrounds have ranged from sublime to ridiculous, and everything in between. The typical setup is a single pay phone attached to an outside wall of the campground office, which can be a very noisy place when those big diesel pickups come roaring up the driveway. Still, this is better than a campground with an out-of-order pay phone or no public phone at all, a situation we encounter every now and then.

Once or twice, we've run across off-brand campground pay phones that block you from calling 800 numbers, or restrict the number of digits you can enter on any given call. Local phone companies also vary widely in their attitudes toward pay-phone traffic. In a couple of campgrounds, we've seen the spot where a pay phone used to be, but it had been removed because the company that installed it decided it wasn't being used enough. All you can do in these cases is: Go find a different pay phone. Or wait till tomorrow to make your calls.

The Sublime Pay Phone prize goes to an Escapees park in Alabama, where the management installed four phones in individual booths—tiny rooms with small desktops, chairs, doors for privacy, and even small windows for ventilation. As icing on the cake, each one also had a phone jack to hook up our computer and connect to the Internet.

It's always nice to have more than one phone in a park, so you don't have to line up and wait at "rush hour," the 4 to 6 p.m. period when travelers are arriving and phoning home, or wherever it is they're calling. We also appreciate it when a pay phone has a local directory attached, a shelf to write on, and an adjacent lawn chair or bench so you don't have to stand up for the duration of your call. If it's located in a quiet corner away from the surprisingly noisy soft drink machine, and sheltered from the direct blazing sun, so much the better.

Our worst-ever telephone experience was at a grungy in-town RV park in Austin, Texas, where the absentee owner had installed a Brand-X pay phone that required 35¢ to make a toll-free 800-number call. And—here's what really sent us over the edge—it wouldn't take dimes! Of course, we had already signed up and paid for a week's stay before we discovered this. Donia and I nearly went berserk, trying to make a number of important business calls. We finally just gave up and went to the airport, where we could do our pay phoning in the comfort of a sit-down booth.

Lobbies of expensive hotels are another place we've found high-quality pay phones, the more modern ones featuring data-ports to plug in a laptop computer. For conducting serious phone business, quiet public places such as libraries, hospitals, or restaurants at nonmealtimes are other options. And many times we've found that business establishments we're visiting—auto service or RV shops, tire stores, banks, real estate offices, and so forth—have a courtesy phone or at least an empty desk where we can sit down and make calls in comfort.

In three RV parks during our first year, we were spoiled by having an instant-phone hookup right at our site, next to the electrical post. We bought an inexpensive telephone and a long cord to connect the site's phone box with a jack on the side of the RV. Our rig came wired with a kitchen jack, and I installed a second jack in the bedroom, so we can chat all we want with friends and family from the comfort of our own computer desk.

We can also indulge in a frenzy of e-mailing, and unlimited Net surfing down a list of "dot.com" addresses we keep for those rare occasions when we have our own phone just like normal people. More and more, businesses are directing customers and potential customers to the Internet for information, just assuming that everyone in the world has a land-line.

As I write this, we have reopened our investigation into cell phones. Truly nationwide plans seem to be available again, thanks to increased competition among providers. But there are still many "dead spots" in the country that are outside any carrier's service area. These are mostly found in remote reaches of the western states—exactly the kinds of places Donia and I like to hang out. And it seems that e-mailing and surfing the Net by cell phone is still impractical, despite the introduction of cell-phone modems. We hear that they are expensive, their transmission rates are excruciatingly slow, and they are prone to annoying disconnects.

The rapid growth of cell phones seems to have produced a generation of brand-new, constantly changing service reps and systems and rate plans that can best be described as "shifting sands." You never know if the salesperson you're speaking to is giving you today's or last week's information. You have to be a skilled interrogator to get all the fine print about "nationwide" coverage, roaming charges, voicemail and other add-on services, and billing practices. Many full-timers have especially been burned by roaming charges not billed in the same cycle in which the calls were made, making it impossible for them to manage their monthly time limits.

Still, all these negatives aside, Donia and I will likely have our own cell phone by the time you are reading this. We are starting to feel like the last of the dinosaurs without one. In the meantime, we're savoring this last bit of freedom from telemarketers, from mad dashes to answer a ringing phone, and from long-winded callers interrupting us in the middle of *West Wing*, Scrabble, or dinner.

11 Copper Harbor, Michigan
August 8

Dear Friends and Fans,
Thanks once again for all the great e-mail feedback. As you may notice, I'm trying something new with this edition, something even Mom and Dad have never done. It's called "headlines." Let me know what you think.

Water, Water Everywhere

My theme today is The Quality of Life on the Road, which is EXCELLENT in this place called Michigan—a state that comes in two parts, as you probably know. The best thing of all about Michigan is, everywhere you look there are lakes. The really big ones, called the Great Lakes, have waves lapping on the shore just like that Atlantic Ocean—except here the water isn't all icky like at Myrtle Beach, so you can drink the water while you're wading in it!

In this one place a while back called "The Soo," we saw these humongous ships full of all kinds of cargo from around the world, passing down the channel between one Great Lake and another one, right behind our campsite. The campground was full when we got here, but they let us park on the grass right at the edge of the water. There were no hookups over there, which seems to be some kind of big-deal roughing-it experience called "boondocking." But it was a great spot for watching those ships. They were going to "the Locks," which I gather is sort of an elevator for raising ships when one lake is higher than the other lake. Boy, Humans sure do invent some fancy stuff, don't they?

Sometimes at night by these Great Lakes Mom and Dad take their lawn chairs down on the beach to watch the sunset. It doesn't get dark here till nearly 10 o'clock, because we're so far north and also so far west in the time zone, whatever that means.

Anyway, if I get bored with this sunset watching, I dig big holes in the sand with my two front paws, both paws together at the same time, throwing the sand way out behind me. This is fine except when I start throwing sand in the direction of Mom and her latest embroidery project, which she gets really crabby about. Meanwhile, Dad just keeps smoking his latest cigar, or wanders slowly up and down the beach. He says he's looking for agates, whatever those are. But Mom says they look like plain old rocks to her, and besides, where are we going to keep all these rocks in the RV?

Take This Job and Love It

Also in Michigan there are many friendly people that come around talking to us and scratching me behind the ears. Most of them are still working folks, like me, and a lot of them have more than one job. But they're not complaining. They just want to tell you about all their jobs. Like, one girl at a mini-mart gave Dad advice about how to find the best pasties (rhymes with "nasties"), because she said her second job was working at this pasty shop in Escanaba where they make the best ones. In case you don't know about pasties, they are another cool Michigan thing: little folded-over pies that have meat and potatoes and other stuff inside. More about this later.

And then there was a campground manager who also worked midnight to dawn at an Indian casino, counting the money on a computer. He was really glad he didn't have to touch the money itself, which he said was so "filthy" that if he actually had to touch it, he wouldn't do that job. And a guy we met at the Alger County Fair had THREE jobs. On weekends he goes around to fairs with a display selling big metal wood-burning furnaces. Besides that, he raises cattle, and he also has a CPA business, whatever that means. So anyway, all you people out there who are still working your butts off like I am—not just sitting around with your embroidery and cigars watching sunsets and getting paid for doing nothing—don't feel bad. Lots of people out here

in America do lots of different kinds of work, and they're proud of it.

My Best Day Ever

Now I want to tell you about the day we went to that pasty shop in Escanaba. We were out back at their picnic tables eating lunch, and Mom kept slipping pieces of pasty to me under the table, because she's still doing that weight-watching thing, you know. Then some people came and sat at the table next to us, and I couldn't help noticing that the ice cream bar one of the ladies was eating was slowly melting all the while she was talking, till pretty soon the whole thing just fell on the ground! Guess who got to clean it up?

Then we went walking on the dock looking at all the sailboats in the harbor, and I saw this green, grassy-looking place below. So when Mom and Dad weren't looking I leaped off the dock . . . except it wasn't grass, it was deep WATER covered with this green slimy seaweedy stuff! The next thing I knew I was climbing up onto the rocks at the edge covered with green slime. I heard this man walking by say, "Boy, he's going to smell great tonight!" so I waited till that guy was right next to me and then I shook real hard.

That was fun, but the best thing of all was when Mom and Dad ate dinner at a steakhouse and brought a doggy bag back to the truck. Driving back to the campground I dozed off, and when I woke up they had stopped to buy diesel fuel. They had hidden the leftover steak under Dad's backpack, but I could smell it like crazy. I started thinking how they call it a "doggy bag," but the people never have any intention of giving that steak to the dog. What a sham! Dogs don't have to take that! Who's the only working member of this family, anyway? So I waited until they both went into the service station to go to the bathroom and made my move. It was gone in two bites. When they came back I braced myself for the "Bad-dog! blah, blah, blah" routine—but they were so dazzled by my cleverness, they just laughed! Do I have great folks, or what?

Outfoxed Again

So now I want to tell you about the weird stuff Humans get into
when they don't have jobs any more to keep them busy. Like,
one day Mom insisted we go on this big expedition. She wanted
to find "The Big Two-Hearted River," which some guy named
Hemingway apparently wrote a story about a long time ago. We
had to drive through thirty miles of woods on unmarked roads.
These roads went from dirt, to sand, to gravel, to potholes,
before we finally found this dinky creek way up in Michigan.
Just about the time we got there, Dad read in a little booklet
where it said this guy Hemingway didn't really fish on the Two-
Hearted River after all, he just named the story after it. He really
fished on the Fox River, twenty miles west of there. Mom looked
at Dad. Then Dad looked at Mom and said, "Don't even think
about it!"

Water, Water Everywhere, Part Two

Things have been going pretty well in the trailer, no more crashing
into things. However, we did have a small flood in the kitchen
yesterday when we arrived at this campground up in Copper
Harbor. It happened when Dad turned on the inside pump switch
and kitchen faucet to get me a drink from our water storage tank
before he hooked up the outside hose. The thing is, he turned
off the pump switch but forgot to turn off the faucet, so when
he hooked up to the campground water supply, which doesn't
need the pump, water gushed out all over the countertop and
down through the cabinets.

Mom and Dad were outside doing all the hookups when they
noticed water pouring out. Lucky for them, we had a handy
supply of dog towels to mop up the mess. Dad was totally like,
had his tail between his legs, and even took the yucky towels
over to the laundry room himself to wash them without being
asked. Meanwhile, Mom was being really nice and cheerful, taking
the soaked stuff out and saying things like, "This is a good excuse
to clean out the bottom of these cabinets and throw away these
things we didn't have room for anyway!" Then Dad said, "It's

too late to cook now, why don't I take you out for dinner?" So see what I mean about the quality of life in Michigan? Everything always turns out good in the end.

Love 'n' Licks,
Cleo

12 How Do You Fit Everything In?

Mark's brief stint as a Great Lakes beach rock hunter calls to mind the 1954 Lucille Ball-Desi Arnaz comedy *The Long, Long Trailer*. Long-suffering hubby Desi goes bonkers when he finds out Lucy has been collecting bowling-ball-sized rocks from every state and hiding them away in various corners of their travel trailer. Now he understands why he's been having so much trouble hauling the trailer up those mountain roads.

When it came to packing up our trailer out at the cabin, Mark and I were ready. We knew about making the most of storage space and understood that every pound counts toward the critical weight limit that every RV has. Both of us are enthusiastic organizers, so the challenge of fitting all of our new life into thirty-four linear feet was actually fun, like playing house. The only tricky part was deciding what we could and couldn't live without for a year, or five, or maybe forever. But we had already gotten rid of at least 75 percent of our stuff by then, so this was just the final paring down.

In the outside storage compartments Mark stowed two boxes of carefully selected hand tools and hardware, a small tackle box that held my sewing gear, suitcases and duffel bags, a door mat, a small charcoal grill, two fold-up lawn chairs, golf clubs, a small stepladder, a drywall bucket and some rags, various lengths of lumber for leveling the RV, and a twenty-pound sack of chow for Cleo. This was in addition to the water hoses and fittings, sewer drain hoses and attachments, and electric cords and adapters needed for the campground utility hookups.

We picked out the clothes we were taking and carried them from the cabin to the trailer one armload at a time, to arrange in the drawers and closets. Talk about examining your life! There is no better way to do that than having to fit all the clothes you own into five feet of hanging closet space plus five feet of shelf. Most of my good work clothes had long since gone to the thrift shop, where I hoped they would help some other five-foot-two woman dress for success. I sat down and stared at what remained, trying to envision all the things we'd be doing in our casual new lifestyle and what I would need to wear.

In the end, I crammed in: A few long-sleeved shirts, one flannel. A dozen tee shirts and several pairs of bermuda shorts, jeans, and slacks. A denim jumper, and two skirts with tops and mix-and-match jackets. Two sweaters, one wool and one cotton. Windbreaker, sweatshirt, medium-weight jacket, raincoat. A tailored suit and another semi-dressy outfit in case of unexpected interviews, weddings, or (God forbid) funerals. Swimsuit and long-sleeved cover-up. Good shoes, flats, sandals, sneakers. Nighties and bathrobe, socks and underwear. This all turned out to be way more than I would need, but at the time I couldn't imagine taking any less. After all, the life I was envisioning was one I hadn't lived yet.

In addition to the bedroom's long clothes closet and two small "shirt closets," there were five tiny drawers next to the vanity countertop. By moving fast I was able to grab one of the shirt closets for my short hanging items, plus two drawers for my knickknacks. Mark loaded computer and office stuff into every other drawer and cabinet in the room. We were now a complete office on wheels, with a nifty computer/printer setup on the vanity and supplies ranging from paper clips to boxes full of printer labels to a postal scale. But we had no place to put our underwear.

Mark had all this figured out, too. Borrowing a tip from the how-to books, he bought half a dozen plastic baskets from Wal-Mart that fit perfectly on the top shelf of the closet to hold our socks, undies, folded tee shirts, and other small items. The rest of his clothes fit easily into half of the hanging closet. In his former life as a house inspector, casual clothes and work clothes were one and the same.

On the wall separating the living room from the bedroom area, there was a built-in entertainment center with small cubbyholes and cabinets. Here we could store books, magazines, videos, games, bridge cards, backpacks and tote bags, campground guides, zip code directories, maps, and other odds and ends. Extra linens, blankets, and dog towels we stored on the top of the upper cabinet, conveniently situated about fourteen inches from the trailer's high living room ceiling.

We pushed the platform rocker closer to the door so we could squeeze a two-drawer filing cabinet in between the chair and refrigerator. This would have to hold all our financial and insurance records, banking and real estate stuff, health care paperwork, and Cleo's veterinarian records. Prior-year tax returns, receipts, and other irreplacable papers went into a fireproof security chest in the "basement" next to the bag of Cleo chow.

Before leaving we sat down with our boxes and boxes of file folders and ruthlessly threw away anything not really vital. The rest of what we had to keep, like Mark's business files and our past-year tax records, we left stored at the Best Revenge, with our fingers crossed that we wouldn't end up needing them.

My coolest personal invention was Office in a Briefcase. I dusted off an old hard-sided briefcase that I hadn't used for years and filled it with stamps, envelopes, note cards, assorted all-purpose birthday cards, pens, address change materials, a small stapler, and a folder for correspondence. The briefcase was just the right size to tuck neatly out of the way between the couch and living room wall.

Mark and I really locked horns over kitchen gear during the packing-up phase. Our kitchen was spacious as RVs go, covering the whole rear wall. It had a small oven, three-burner propane stovetop, microwave oven, and small dual-fuel refrigerator with a two-shelf top freezer compartment. Best of all, just over the double sink there was a wide rear window, from which I imagined looking out over bucolic scenes of lakes, woods, and mountains as I did the dishes.

But we both love to cook, and it was tough cutting our kitchenware down by 70 percent. By the time the fur quit flying, we had packed in two frying pans, a dutch oven for soups and stews, three saucepans of varying sizes, a small grill pan with rack for oven or broiler, an 8×8-inch metal baking pan, a 9×13-inch glass baking dish with a cover (for those famous campground potlucks), two measuring cups, a set of stainless steel nesting bowls, a colander, and a few airtight storage containers. Our only electric appliances were a small rice cooker and a four-cup coffeemaker. We used a manual can opener for the first time since either of us could remember. A small whisk was our only mixer. It was a bare-bones collection, for us. But I have to say, we have never gone hungry for lack of a certain cooking pan.

Each of us picked out one favorite coffee mug to take, and we bought some plastic dime-store glasses to avoid breakage problems. Our one new kitchen purchase was a set of break-resistant Corelle dishes from a CorningWare outlet store—a twenty-five-piece service for four, augmented with some extra salad plates and serving bowls. This was plenty. We had only four chairs, so we couldn't very well throw big dinner parties.

We bought rolls of thin rubber padding material and carefully cut squares to separate each dish from its neighbors. All kitchen items were padded and nested inside each other in the cabinets, to maximize space. We kept this padding routine up for a year before we realized that it was not really necessary, except for cushioning glass pot lids and nonstick pans.

Our biggest kitchen bummer was lack of space inside a cabinet for a decent-sized trash can (and with you-know-who on board, we couldn't exactly leave garbage sitting out in the open). We ended up wedging a small plastic bucket into a lower cabinet near the sink. The tight fit made it hard to get larger items into the can, and it was so small we had to empty the contents into the campground dumpster at least once a day. Other annoyances were having to stand on a chair to reach dishtowels and canned goods on upper shelves, and having to remove everything from the front row of a deep cabinet to reach an item in back. (Wait— is that sad little violins I hear playing in the distance?)

We knew that before hitching up and taking off, we needed to secure everything inside and batten down heavier objects that might shift around as we drove. Some of our travel preparations and precautions were advised by the dealer; others we picked up from how-to books. And a few we learned about the hard way. For example, Mark had to install a "seatbelt" for the TV set after it shifted and got banged up our first day on the road. It still wears a scratch right in the middle of the screen. We also wedged a spring-type curtain rod vertically in front of the shirt-closet shelves in our bedroom, after the closet door flew open and office supplies came tumbling out onto the floor as the trailer jolted over a rough road.

For the first month, we were highly checklist-dependent. We had our pretravel Hitching Checklist (see box), our Unhitching Checklist (basically, the Hitching Checklist in reverse), and our

---

 Mark and Donia's Hitching Checklist

This is the long, spell-it-all-out version we used when first starting out. After a couple of weeks we knew the drill so well we were able to condense the list, then dispense with it altogether. The procedures may look time-consuming, but soon Mark and I together could knock them out from start to finish in fifteen minutes, and be ready to roll.

Inside:

1. Stow countertop and table items in sinks.
2. Put spring rods across refrigerator shelves.
3. Fasten kitchen blinds and check cookware padding.
4. Lock file drawers.
5. Fasten TV seatbelt, turn off antenna switch, crank down antenna.
6. Velcro shut closet doors and latch shower door.
7. Put spring rod in front of office shelves.
8. Close all top hatches.

continued

9. Turn off stereo, lights, heat/air conditioning, water pump, propane tank valves.
10. Clear items from slide-out paths and retract slides.
11. Spray for bugs.
12. Close hall door.

Outside:

13. Fold in steps and lock trailer door.
14. Stow doormat and dog chain in side compartment.
15. Lower and latch rear window shield.
16. Raise rear jacks and stow jack support boards.
17. Unhook and stow water hoses and electric cord.
18. Unhook, rinse, and stow sewer hose and fittings.
19. Extend side mirrors on truck.
20. LOWER TAILGATE!
21. Adjust front jacks.
22. Back truck into hitch pin and lock hitch in place.
23. Finish raising front jacks and lock in place.
24. Raise tailgate, secure electric and brake cables, check running lights.
25. RECHECK TAILGATE!
26. Pull wheel chocks, drive off leveling boards, stow chocks and boards.
27. Lock all compartments.
28. Walk around trailer to double-check all items.
29. Take off!

Awning Up/Awning Down Checklist. We literally walked around clutching lists and calling out items aloud to each other every time we left one place and arrived at another. But we traveled so much at first, hitching and unhitching about every other day, that it didn't take us long to know the routines by heart.

As we got underway, we were curious to know how much our fully packed rig actually weighed, in relation to our published truck and RV weight limits. During our second week on the road, we found a truck stop with Black Cat Scales and drove right up onto the platform, just like the big eighteen-wheelers. Let me say here that the issue of weight ratings can get pretty complicated. There's axle weight and hitch weight, dry weight and Gross Vehicle Weight Rating (GVWR), and I don't know what all. It's the Bermuda Triangle of RVing. Suffice it to say that our truck, trailer, and gear weighed in at 18,600 pounds total—safely below our Gross Combined Vehicle Weight (GCVW) limit of 20,000 pounds.

We've stayed pretty much at this weight level by keeping in mind that our space is a finite quantity, and throwing out or giving away old items as we bring home new ones. If Mark buys two new shirts, he has to toss two old ones. When we get new books on one of our bookstore splurges, we donate an equal quantity of old ones to a campground swap library. And we never keep rocks from any state, no matter how pretty they are.

13 Lake Tomahawk, Wisconsin

August 13

Here's one that maybe you had to be here for. I'll just report it "straight," and you can decide for yourself. Donia and I were enormously entertained Monday night when we went to a game of *Snowshoe Baseball.*

Except it was softball, the Midwestern sixteen-inch variety, rather than actual baseball. Same game you can see any summer night in Grant Park, Chicago. Twenty after-work guys in tees and jeans, drinking beer and playing softball. Except here they had big snowshoes on their feet. The ones that look like tennis racquets. The infield was covered with pine bark mulch, there being no snow here in August. The evening was delightful, seventy-two degrees and dry, no bugs. The concession stand run by the local Lionesses had brats, beer, and homemade cheesecake. The diamond was behind the town garage. Upwards of two hundred and fifty people turned out.

Home team Lake Tomahawk beat the visitors, Tower Tap, 17 to 9. No one broke any legs or, amazingly, any of the $140-a-pair snowshoes. The game was not much different from a game of normal baseball-shoe baseball. The fielders were much slower getting to the ball, but then the base runners were much slowed down as well. There was more falling down and tumbling head over snowshoes, though. And there was the thundering, scraping sound of running elephants as each play unfolded.

There were high-jinks aplenty, this being the last game of the season:

- The pitcher substituted a cantaloupe for the ball (twice), and big funny messes were made both times when the batters

63

swung. (Near as I could tell, the second cantaloupe was lobbed because not enough of the first one gooed up the much-beloved plate umpire.)

- Base runners were "tagged" in unmentionable places—and I don't mean between third and home.
- Fielders moved the bases farther apart when the umps "weren't looking."
- The batter "attacked" the pitcher following a "bean ball" attempt. (Pitches in sixteen-inch softball are high, loopy affairs that couldn't hurt a flea, and couldn't hit a snail if the snail tried to get out of the way.)
- The infielders fell down in unison, as if "blown over," when the visitors' big-Kahuna batter swung and missed.
- The manager kicked dirt on the umpire's shoe. Well, mulch, actually.

Lake Tomahawk is known, at least in Lake Tomahawk, as the Snowshoe Baseball Capital of the World. Whether this was *why* they play Snowshoe Baseball, or *because* they play Snowshoe Baseball, was not clear. In any event, Lake Tomahawk is said to be the only place in the world that Snowshoe Baseball is played in the summer—at 7:30 every Monday night from late June till early August. In winter, apparently, it's played all over northern Wisconsin on frozen lakes. Winter rules allow batters only two strikes; three balls constitutes a walk, and the games are only seven innings instead of nine. These measures are necessary to shorten the game so no one freezes to death.

In other news . . . Donia and I have crossed a retirement Rubicon: Yesterday we both bought Teva sandals. There's no going back now.

Today is Donia's birthday. We celebrated with beer and brats for lunch (hey, this is Wisconsin). And we were going to go play nine holes of golf, except Donia's birthday nap lasted too long, so we missed our window of opportunity. Oh, well. There's always tomorrow.

We have an appointment in late August at the factory that

built our trailer in Elkhart, Indiana, to get the dent hammered out of the side. Turns out trailer body work is lots less expensive than car body work. So I don't want to hear any more about it. Okay?

We had our truck oil changed on Tuesday. Oil changes for diesel trucks are lots more expensive than car oil changes. For one thing, we use fourteen quarts of oil. That's what you get when you own the most powerful production pickup truck made in the United States. Arrrgh, arrrgh, arrrgh.

We're at a lovely lakeside campground now that mostly has "seasonal" occupants, which means they park their trailers all season here and commute up on weekends in their cars. So it's very thinly occupied here during the week. Quiet. Peaceful. And no one is bothered if we play with Cleo off the leash from time to time.

A bit of housekeeping: If any of you are getting our periodic travel reports at work and wish you weren't, please let us know and we can remove your name from our mailing list. We won't take offense, either. We understand about snoopy bosses and clogged e-mailboxes.

Thanks to those of you who reply to our missives. Especially thank you to those who do not forward our entire letter back to us with your reply. (You think they're long when *you* download them once!) We love hearing what's happening back in what still seems to us to be the "real world." You know, the world without Snowshoe Baseball.

Cheers,
Mark

P.S. Cleo sends thanks for all the fan mail, which, she has pointed out to us, is twice as much as Donia and I combined have ever received. However, we are *not* going to let her write all the rest of the e-travelogues from now on, as she has suggested. Her head is already swelled quite enough, thank you.

14 What Do You Do All Day?

Like many other busy retirees, Mark and I wonder how on earth we ever managed to get everything done, back when we spent ten hours a day working. But as retirees who are also full-time travelers, we have a special kind of busy-ness all our own—and actual travel time is the least of it. We probably spend only six or seven hours a week, on average, hauling the rig from one place to another. The rest of our waking hours are devoted to exploring and having fun. Going to that antic snowshoe baseball game in Lake Tomahawk, Wisconsin, was just one of maybe six hundred different things we saw and did in just our first year on the road.

Of course, we do a lot of regular sightseeing. Over time, we have hit all the normal tourist spots like Graceland, Mount Rushmore, Dollywood, Disney World, Mammoth Cave. We laughed our heads off at the music and comedy shows in Branson, Missouri. Rode the historic steam railroad up the canyon from Durango to Silverton, Colorado. Enjoyed free samples at the Blue Bell Ice Cream Factory in Brenham, Texas, and the Tillamook Cheese Factory in Tillamook, Oregon. Drove the seventeen-mile loop through the red rock spires of Monument Valley straddling the Utah-Arizona state line. And of course, stopped by world-famous tourist mecca Wall Drug just outside Badlands National Park in South Dakota.

We also poke around wacky places you've probably never heard of. Would you believe, the Wisconsin Concrete Museum in Phillips, Wisconsin, featuring statues of lumberjacks and Indians and Mary Todd Lincoln, molded in concrete and decorated with shards of bottle glass? Or the James Dean Museum in Fairmount, Indiana, housing an amazing collection of memorabilia including Jimmy's discarded motorcycle parts and childhood gym suits? Or how about Windmill Park in Electric City, Washington, where a now-deceased hobbyist named Emil Gehrke built dozens of colorful whirligigs out of things like pie pans, cups and saucers, hard hats, kitchen funnels, and prison food trays? At many such places, we're the only ones there.

What we do in our travels often depends on where we are—like tourist chameleons turning local colors. In Lexington, Kentucky, we hung on the fences as teenage girls ran sleek horses through the Jump Start Horse Trials. In places like Lava Hot Springs and Hagerman, Idaho, we soaked in steaming mineral water from natural hot springs. In Bandera, Texas, self-proclaimed Cowboy Capital of the World, we joined a crowd of ranchers and geezers and bikers at a rustic dance hall where country music legend Kitty Wells, still spunky at eighty, was performing on her farewell tour. And on the Olympic Peninsula, we went on a lumber company's mini-van tour of logging operations.

Eventually, though, museum fatigue sets in and we get the Tourist Heebie Jeebies. *We can't see everything! It's got to stop somewhere! Forget about the Confederate Air Museum—we'll catch it next time!* As an antidote to heavy sightseeing, we take whole days off to do what normal people do: We watch TV, read books, play computer games, shop for groceries, make a big pot of soup that leaves the kitchen a mess, clean house. We go on picnics, float in the campground pool, take naps in the shade. Or do truck repairs, make business calls, catch up on mail, rent videos. We can spend half a day just doing laundry in a downtown laundromat.

We strike up conversations with RV park neighbors, swapping tips on rig maintenance or good campgrounds down the road. Sometimes we join these fleeting friends in whatever they're doing. In Seaside, Oregon, we enjoyed nightly jam sessions with a group of bluegrass buffs who had rendezvoused at the campground from three states. We went line-dancing with fellow Escapees in Knoxville, Tennessee, and have played golf and cards with countless fellow campers around the country.

But then we hitch up and we're off. For us, each new town is like opening up a nifty new picture book. On the map, all

Mark and Donia's Top 25

Where should we go today? What should we see? The best answers come from personal recommendations offered by fellow full-timers we meet on the road. Here are our recommendations to you—Mark and Donia's Top 25 attractions. There is no common quality that ties them together, except that each one far exceeded our expectations in one way or another. Listed in no particular order, they are:

1. National Storytellers Festival, Jonesboro, Tennessee (early October)
2. Oregon Trail National Interpretive Center, Baker City, Oregon
3. The Willow City Loop scenic drive, Willow City, Texas (April)
4. National Oldtime Fiddlers Championship, Weiser, Idaho (mid-June)
5. Buckstaff Bathhouse and Fordyce Bathhouse Museum, Hot Springs, Arkansas
6. The Norman Rockwell Museum, Stockbridge, Massachusetts
7. Ozark Folk Center (and town square jam sessions), Mountain View, Arkansas (summer)
8. Atomic bomb historical sites in Oak Ridge, Tennessee, and Los Alamos, Albuquerque and Alamogordo (twice yearly tour to Ground Zero), New Mexico
9. The Soo Locks, Sault Ste. Marie, Michigan
10. Oregon's Pacific Coast beaches
11. Big Bend National Park, Texas, and Boquillas, Mexico (early spring)
12. Agecroft Manor House, Richmond, Virginia
13. Pink Palace Museum, Memphis, Tennessee

continued

14. LBJ Library and Museum, Austin, Texas
15. Jekyll Island, Georgia
16. Cades Cove, Smoky Mountain National Park, Tennessee
17. The Biltmore Mansion, Asheville, North Carolina
18. Mud Island, Memphis, Tennessee
19. Smokejumpers Base Aerial Fire Depot, Missoula, Montana
20. Independence Rock, between Alcova and Muddy Gap, Wyoming
21. Badlands National Park, South Dakota
22. Chaco Culture National Historic Park, New Mexico
23. National Lewis and Clark Interpretive Center, Great Falls, Montana
24. Kentucky Horse Park Museum, Lexington, Kentucky
25. National Historic Site and Prisoner of War Museum, Andersonville, Georgia

dots look alike—but when you actually get there, every town in America is different. And we want to see them all. We drive past the store fronts on Main Street, or take the historic district walking tour, reading plaques on handsome buildings from past centuries. We check out the local hardware store (Mark's perennial favorite) and quilt shop (Donia's latest passion). We drive around the grungy warehouse district of town, which, in places like St. Louis and Oklahoma City and Little Rock, is being spruced up into a happenin' entertainment scene.

We find the town library and check out its computer stations and architecture and books and magazines. Sometimes we spend a couple of hours just browsing the shelves, reading, and enjoying the interior spaciousness and quiet of a big solid building. Later, we'll drive around the neighborhoods where the rich people live. We each pick out our favorite fantasy house—usually an imposing Victorian with wraparound verandas and a porch swing. If there's a college in town, we walk around the campus, get coffee in the student union, sit on a bench, and marvel at how the students get younger-looking every year.

And that's not all!

Sometimes we do what the locals do. We play bridge in small-town clubs, where our roaming lifestyle invariably causes a stir of amazement and envy. If there's a rails-to-trails bike path anywhere in the region, we ride it for a few miles. We went to a ball game in Denver and a golf tournament in Atlanta. One Fourth of July we watched the annual pet parade in Bend, Oregon, and at dusk followed insiders to a ridge above town for a perfect view of the fireworks extravaganza. If a town has a golf course with low weekday greens fees, we might stay an extra day to play nine or eighteen holes. (Golfers, is there any pleasure greater than walking onto a well-maintained, deserted course in the middle of nowhere on a Tuesday morning and playing eighteen holes for $15?)

We enjoy the Indian casinos that have sprung up everywhere across America: Turning Stone Casino in New York's Mohawk Valley, Lac du Flambeau in the North Woods of Wisconsin, and the Yakima Nation RV Park and Casino in Toppenish, Washington, are places where we've contributed many quarters to the tribes. One day, on a remote stretch of the Pacific Coast, we happened upon the annual Quillaute Days festival. The parade, carnival, salmon roast, and canoe races were all being held in a steady rain that none of the locals seemed to notice. Huddled under a tarp strung between trees, Mark and I ate delicious salmon grilled by an aged Indian man over an open fire that was magically staying lit in the storm.

In outdoorsy places, we go on serious hikes. At Pictured Rocks National Lakeshore near Munising, Michigan, we passed up the $44 tourist boat trip and took the land route, hiking for free through cathedral-like hemlock groves to an overlook with a perfect view of Lake Superior and the multihued cliffs. We hiked on the Oregon Trail near Hagerman, Idaho, wondering how the pioneers must have felt walking endless stretches of desert sagebrush, praying their ox-drawn wagons would make it up the next hill. Our most strenuous outing was climbing 2,000 feet up a rugged trail in the Swan Range near Bigfork, Montana. At the 7,300-foot crest, we got our reward. On one side, we looked over a huge panoramic view of the lovely Flathead Lake and Valley, and on the other, the so-called Jewel Basin, a deep valley dotted with fast-running snowmelt streams and tiny crystal-clear lakes in different shades of blue.

But wait—there's more!

Bookworms that we are, we love to go on self-guided literary odysseys, searching out the venues of some favorite books, songs, and movies. Hemingway's Big, Two-Hearted River in the wilds of northern Michigan. Cajun detective Dave Robichaux's New Iberia, Louisiana, and the lush Evangeline country along Bayou Teche. Archer City, Texas, the dusty and dying town immortalized in Larry McMurtry's *Texasville* trilogy. The Four Corners area where Arizona, New Mexico, Colorado, and Utah all meet, providing the dramatic desert setting of Tony Hillerman's popular Navajo police mysteries. Savannah's elegant squares and mansions as portrayed in *Midnight in the Garden of Good and Evil*. And U.S. Highway 45 running south from Kankakee alongside the Illinois Central tracks, racing the no-named trains that Arlo Guthrie sang about in "City of New Orleans."

We also love places where geography and history meet. We spent months criss-crossing the route of the Lewis and Clark Expedition. In Montana we took a boat ride on the remote, rock-walled stretch of the Missouri River that Lewis named Gates of the Mountains. We drove through Lolo Pass into the Bitterroot Valley of Idaho, where the explorers almost froze to death. And we visited a reconstruction of primitive Fort Clatsop near Astoria, Oregon, where the men spent a miserable, rain-soaked, flea-infested winter before heading back toward civilization.

Everywhere you go, there are historic forts, restored pioneer villages, and ghost towns that paint a picture of American history like it never was painted in school. Our first summer, after visiting a dozen such places, I made the mistake of muttering, "If you've seen one historic fort, you've seen 'em all." The very next night,

Mark and Cleo dragged me to an outdoor family edu-tainment program at Fort Wilkins State Park in Copper Harbor, Michigan. The headliner was a historical reenactor giving a lively one-man show about the explorers, French voyageurs, trappers, woodsmen, log rollers, lake sailors, and immigrant mill workers of the Great Lakes a hundred years ago. Before I knew it, I was singing sailor chants and hauling on imaginary ropes along with the rest of the audience, to pull the imaginary barge up the imaginary canal. I am here to tell you, folks, when you've seen one historic fort, you have not seen them all.

We left that beautiful place, like so many others, making mental notes of all the things we didn't have a chance to see and vowing to return some day "when we have more time."

15 Elkhart, Indiana
August 28

Well, the time to get the side of our RV hammered out finally arrived. We are spending an idyllic few days here in Elkhart at a nice campground near the Dutchmen RV factory. Yesterday, while they worked on the trailer, we toured the Amish countryside. At an interpretive center we learned the differences between the Mennonites, Hutterites, and Amish (all categorized as Anabaptists). And we've been enjoying the sumptuous Amish cooking, particularly their beef and noodle stew and heavenly cream pies. Getting here from Wisconsin was an adventure, however.

I knew it was time for us to leave the North Woods as Mark was getting sucked deeper and deeper into the Great Lakes Walleye Debate. It started innocently enough, the day I ordered the walleye lunch special at a small roadside café. "She'll have the walleye pike," Mark told the waitress. "Walleye is not a pike," she informed him.

Mark didn't believe it. We saw signs all over the place advertising walleye pike. Mark asked the campground owner, who told him walleye was indeed the largest member of the perch family, not a pike at all. Still incredulous, Mark asked a fisherman. That's silly, the man said. It's a pike. Soon Mark was polling everyone we ran into: Is walleye a perch, or a pike? We were told on great authority by half of our sources that it's really part of the perch family. The other half were adamant: It's a pike.

Pike. Perch. Pike. Perch. . . . So good-bye, cool days and crisp nights. Good-bye, sparkling forest lakes. I dragged Mark away to Minneapolis, just before I lost my sanity. In the Twin Cities we had dinner with Doug and Joyce Benson, old friends from Mark's Chicago days. Joyce gave us the final word on walleyes:

"Whatever it is, it's a delicious fish—but we don't get it any more because it all comes from Canada and it's $14.99 a pound!"

We are finding that visiting big cities is not easy, given our lifestyle. The bigger the city, the farther away we have to stop to find a campground. In Minneapolis we landed in the far southwest suburbs, at the Mystic Lake Indian Casino and Campground. At night, the place is visible at a great distance across the plains because searchlights beam light rays in the shape of a ghostly teepee up into the sky overhead. This was not only the newest and best-kept place we've been, but a fantastic bargain, as well. The nightly rate was $20, but each day we got a $10 coupon at the office that could be traded in for cash or chips at the casino. Mark did well enough at the blackjack tables so we ended up just about camping for free. Well, almost.

Our next-site neighbors were five carpenter-roofer guys from Texas who had been enticed north to work on storm-damaged neighborhoods with the promise of wages and "free lodging." The lodging turned out to be a tiny camper about a third the size of our rig, into which the foreman crammed all five of them. Around 6 o'clock every morning they poured out the door like circus clowns tumbling out of a tiny clown car.

The workmen spent most of their nonroofing time at the picnic table, drinking soda pop and beer, eating take-out chicken, and throwing the bones on the ground. This, of course, was all right with Cleo. I had to physically drag her away from their site for every walk. Eventually one of the guys (who had a truly amazing collection of tattoos, and seemed determined to become Mark's New Best Friend) told us that he was leaving the bones there on purpose for our dog. He got extremely huffy when Mark told him we didn't allow her to eat chicken bones. A dog not allowed to eat *bones?*

The really big excitement at Mystic Lake was the weather. On Saturday around sunset the wind grew furious, the sky turned several shades of greenish purple, and clouds boiled all around. The horizon looked like a bruise-colored cauldron. A van with a tornado warning siren drove through the campsites urging people and pets to seek shelter in the concrete block bathhouses. Mark and Cleo were the life of the party, walking around with our spiffy little hand-held NOAA weather radio turned up to top volume. Unfortunately, Mark didn't recognize any of the place names the announcer was talking about. (Next time we're in Kansas, Dorothy, remind us to memorize the names of counties and towns near our campground.)

Meanwhile, I stayed in the laundry room, calmly finishing up my wash. I was not going to leave damp clothes in the dryers, tornado or no tornado! We ended up with "no tornado," but it was close. One or two funnels touched down about five miles to the north of us, we heard later. Maybe we were protected by the magic mile-high teepee of light.

Aiming toward our appointment at the Dutchmen factory here in Indiana, we headed eastward via Iowa, one of the four states I have never been to (Alaska, Nebraska, and North Dakota are the remaining three). We made a reservation at a place in Dubuque, alluringly described as a "campground and yacht basin on an island in the middle of the Mississippi River." It turned out to be the waterfront equivalent of a truck stop, surrounded by rusty shacks and dockside machinery, piles of gravel, and boats in all stages of deconstruction, with nonstop barge traffic up and down the river and train tracks right across the way.

We thought that place was rock bottom until we got to LaSalle, Illinois, the next night, and stayed at an honest-to-goodness truck-stop campground about twenty windswept yards from I-80. Mark had to test about six electrical posts before he finally found a site with one that worked. And the clogged sewage drain was just too gross to describe. The bottom line here: You just never know how a place is going to be, based on the writeups and ads in the campground directories. Every day is a new adventure.

As I write this, we now have a fully repaired water heater, a new knob on our awning, a quieter water pump, and most important, a dent-free trailer that no longer bears witness to the Georgia diesel-pump debacle. This little bit of body work has made a new man of Mark. He says he feels a great stain has been lifted from his soul.

We head for the Chicago area over Labor Day weekend and the following week, to visit many old friends and relations. Then we plan to s-l-o-w d-o-w-n for a while, staying longer times in fewer places. We'll be taking from mid-September to mid-November to get from here to Orlando (scene of the national bridge tournament), spending most of the time in Kentucky and Tennessee. Anybody got any hot tips about places to visit, food to eat, or people we should look up while we're there? We're open to all suggestions.

Love to one and all,

Donia

16 Where Do You Find Campgrounds?

It's a great adventure, picking out an entirely new place to live every few days. There are some 16,000 RV parks in this country, all offering the same basic service—a spot to park your RV—but their differences are amazing. One day you can be parked in a hilltop campground overlooking the lights of a city, the next day in a tree-shaded site next to a stream or lake, and a few days later in the middle of a grassy field with mountain views all around. The differences in quality are even more surprising: Who would have thought that within a week's time we would go from our most luxurious park so far (at Mystic Lake, outside Minneapolis) to that dilapidated truck-stop campground in Illinois—and, ironically, pay $10 in both places?

When Donia and I first started out, we didn't worry about economizing too much. As rookie RVers we were mainly focused on finding campgrounds where we could maneuver our rig in and out easily, get utility hookups, do e-mail, and take a bathhouse shower without standing in a quarter-inch of mildew. If it was a big resort campground in the middle of the summer, we might spend as much as $35 or $40 a night—but these were rare. On average we paid $12 to $20 a night, for campsites that ranged from merely okay to surprisingly terrific, the quality in no predictable ratio to cost.

Several people have tried to talk us into joining a membership-campground organization, where you pay a yearly fee entitling you to stay at your "home park" for free and other campgrounds in the system at a large discount. There are several of these networks around, and we know many experienced full-timers love the bargains and other benefits they provide. But in our first year, Donia and I had some very specific sightseeing destinations, and we didn't know if we could find network campgrounds in the places we wanted to visit. So we decided to hold off on membership camping for a while.

If you asked us to name our top priorities for campgrounds, we would probably say something like: spacious sites, a good place to walk Cleo, and clean, pleasant surroundings. However, at the risk of sounding antisocial, I have to admit that our fondness for a campground nearly always depends on how empty it is. We love having the run of a place. A campground where we can exercise Cleo off her leash without ruffling anybody's feathers is our ideal. We like a place where our windows are looking out over open space, not straight into another RV's windows three feet away.

We know many people are perfectly happy parked cheek-by-jowl with other campers, but crowded places always made us uncomfortable, right from the start. Even if the facilities were minimal or run-down, we preferred small mom 'n' pop campgrounds over large, sophisticated RV parks bustling with recreational activities and vacationing families. And Cleo was definitely more relaxed in a less-populated place.

Many of the public campgrounds in national and state recreation areas are ideal in terms of wide open spaces and scenic surroundings. Without a doubt, our most beautiful campsites have been at state and national parks located on the banks of rivers, lakes, and streams—often with the bonus of majestic mountain views. The tradeoff is, this type of campground often has limited or no hookups, and the campsites themselves can be very small, or restricted by rocks and overhanging trees. Many older parks, and those located in more primitive wilderness areas, were designed for tent camping—definitely not with today's big rigs in mind.

It's hard to tell from guidebooks or tourist brochures exactly what the published RV size limitations mean in public campgrounds. A few times Donia and I have driven to a state park or one of the more remote natural areas managed by the Army Corps of Engineers or the Bureau of Land Management

(BLM), just to see if our thirty-four-foot trailer would fit in a campground with a stated twenty-two-foot RV limit. The answer was sometimes *no problem,* other times *no way.*

On a couple of occasions we had to fight our way out of the place we were investigating, creeping around tight curves on a narrow roadway lined with trees. Thus we learned the hard way that, in tight situations, it's best to park somewhere out of the way and check out the campsites on foot before pulling in. Venturing into a place you can't comfortably exit from is one of the more stressful experiences in the RVing life. I have also given up being a hero when the office assigns us a site that is too small or hard to get into. Now we just circle back to the office and request a different one. Luckily, we've always been given a second, more accessible site in these situations.

On the other side of the coin from the public campgrounds are the thousands of privately operated RV parks. The high end is occupied by luxurious, state-of-the-art resorts with pools, hot tubs, landscaped sites, and security keypad-locks at the front gate and on every bathhouse and rec hall door. At the budget end, you might find yourself in an oversized backyard that a local entrepreneur has divided up into RV sites with only fifteen- or twenty-amp electrical service, which is not really adequate for today's needs. We've stayed in campgrounds at both ends of this spectrum, but usually ended up midway between. Some of our best finds were parks with "seasonal sites," as noted in the guide-book blurbs. This means long-term spaces are rented to people who leave their RVs there year-round or for an entire season, but mainly use them only on weekends, holidays, and vacations. These parks tend to be wonderfully deserted during the week, even at the height of the season.

We were also surprised the first time we stayed in an RV park that had "monthlies"—more or less permanent residents who rent by the month—making it more like a conventional mobile home park. These folks may be older retirees living there out of choice or necessity, or younger men and women who travel from place to place following the job market. They often have older

"Thou Shalt Not" Campgrounds

Occasionally we're amused by a rules-crazy management that posts signs on every available surface telling guests what *not* to do. At one otherwise beautiful Idaho campground, whose owners probably should have retired long ago, the "hospitality guidelines" included (but were not limited to):

No Arrivals before 12 Noon
No Guests or Extra Vehicles Allowed without Permission
Checkout 12 Noon—$2 Per Hour after Noon, No
    Exceptions!
No Tents on Hookup Spaces
No Generators Allowed
Barbecue Grills Must Be on Legs! (whether on ground or
    tables)
No Washing of RVs, Vehicles, or Mechanical Work of Any
    Kind in Park
No Mats or Rugs on Grass
No Big Dogs Allowed
No Dogs of Any Size Allowed off the Leash at Any Time
Do Not Leave Pets Unattended in Your RV (they bark
    while you are away)
Pets Must Be Taken Directly to the Dog Walk and Back
    to Your Campsite
We Will *Not* Tolerate Loose Dogs in Our Park!
Laundry Room Use by Request Only
No Shoes or Unwashed Clothing of Any Kind in Dryer
Restrooms Are Locked from 9 p.m. to 7 a.m.
No Showers after 10 pm (?)
Young Children Must Be Escorted to Restrooms by an
    Adult
No Leaving Hair in Sinks

continued

Do Not Sit on Sinks
Absolutely No River Access to Anybody from Our
    Property!
This Bridge and Roadway Are Not a Play Area for Any-
    thing, Nor a Turnaround
All Mountain Areas Are Off Limits (private land)
Do Not Climb on or over Any of the Fences
No Swimming, Wading, or Playing in River Permitted
No Motorbikes, Bikes, or Roller Blades Allowed
Absolutely No Fireworks of Any Kind Allowed (this means
    sparklers too)
No Metal Detectors
No Frisbees or Ball Games of Any Kind

"Thank you for your cooperation—Have a nice stay and
come back soon."
(Fat chance!)

trailers or motorhomes, with a lot of miscellaneous gear arranged
outside their rigs: patio furniture, plastic coolers, cinder blocks,
scrap lumber, storage cabinets, cooking equipment, outdoor carpeting, clotheslines, plastic lawn figurines, and so forth. While
some private RV parks welcome this type of full-timer, others
firmly discourage them by limiting the length of time you can
rent a site.

Donia and I are both geography nuts, traveling with an array
of atlases and road maps, so we always know approximately where
we'll be when it's time to stop driving for the day. Sometimes
there's no choice in accommodations—we stay overnight at the
only campground available in that area, and drive on the next
morning. Other times, we need to find a longer-term RV park
at a particular destination where we plan to explore the region
or visit friends.

Campground guidebooks were our faithful companions at the
beginning of our travels, and we still use them frequently to see

what kinds of facilities are available in an area. We have the latest versions of the directories put out by Trailer Life and Woodall's. They both provide the same basic information on quantity and size of sites, types of hookups, amenities (laundromat, public phone, propane, dump station, convenience store, modem hookup, etc.), recreational facilities (pool, playground, horseshoes, fishing), prices, and reservation policy. Many parks also take out lavish display ads in the directories—another good source of campground information, although a biased one.

The best feature of the Trailer Life Directory is the helpful one-to-ten rating given in three categories: Completeness of Facilities, Cleanliness and Physical Characteristics of Restrooms and Showers, and Visual Appeal and Environmental Quality. Many times this rating has been the tie-breaker if there was a choice of two or more campgrounds in an area. What we like best about Woodall's is the brief phrase it uses to describe the general ambience of each campground, such as "secluded, lakeside, shaded campground adjacent to a full-service marina." This helps us know in advance whether we're headed for a place in the center of town or in the middle of a wheat field.

We soon learned, however, that guidebook writeups never tell the full story. The interstate is just beyond the back fence; that appealing-sounding "creek" turns out to be more like a stagnant drainage ditch; there's road construction just twenty yards from your trailer; an X-rated movie theater or auto graveyard is your next-door neighbor. And just as often, the campground is much nicer than the guidebooks convey, with lush lawns and towering trees, or a state-of-the-art laundry room, or ultra-friendly managers. The truth is, you never really know what a place will be like—or how crowded it is—until you get there.

After we discovered that a night or two at a lousy campground wouldn't kill us, and might actually provide some amusing story material, we loosened up and started winging it. We tried parks listed in RV pamphlets picked up at state tourist information centers, even though they were too marginal to be covered in our campground directories. We've chosen parks by virtue of a highway billboard, or the blue tent symbol at an interstate exit sign, or the RV Park sign at the gate as we drove by.

A word here about boondocking. I know there are many budget-minded RVers who regularly seek out free camping spots in rest areas, truck stops, shopping center parking lots, or other large areas that are not being used overnight. While this is widely accepted, it's something Donia and I have done only a few times— usually in a Wal-Mart parking lot. One time in Bend, Oregon, we were booted out of our campground by an influx of customers coming into town for a large quilt show. They had reserved every campsite within thirty miles, far in advance. During that week, the Wal-Mart parking lot where we stayed for two nights became an all-out improvised campground populated by more than a dozen RVers in similar straits.

We have also stayed at spacious, well-lighted Wal-Mart lots in Ohio, Tennessee, and West Virginia—each time at the end of a hard-driving day when we just wanted to park overnight and leave early the next morning. We always go to the service desk first and ask permission to park overnight. So far we've never been turned down. Experienced Wal-Mart boondockers have a custom of picking up at least one trash bag full of litter and debris from the parking lot and landscaped areas while they're there, as a small gesture of thanks for the famous Wal-Mart hospitality. Donia and I always show our thanks in another way, as well— by shopping in the store after dinner and usually spending twice as much as we would have paid for a commercial campsite!

In the end, campground selection is hardly a life-and-death matter, since we're always in our own comfortable, self-contained home anyway. And if we don't like the place, we can happily move on the next day. More often, we find the opposite is true: We like the place so much we don't want to leave it when the time comes to hitch up and go.

17 Champaign, Illinois
September 10

Dear Friends and Fans,
    Not complaining or anything, but my Humans keep whizzing around so fast I never get a chance to check out all the smells in one place before we're off to someplace else. Just since my last letter we've been to Wisconsin, Minnesota, Iowa, Illinois, Indiana, then back to Michigan for Labor Day weekend (more about that disaster later). Now we're back in Illinois again.

A Feather in My CAP

I know this is ancient history, but I've got to tell you about the new Canine Assertiveness Program I started back in Minnesota. CAP was launched the day we arrived at that Indian Casino campground, when my Humans immediately went trotting off to the Mall of America without me. To teach them a lesson, I decided to hide my dog bowl while they were gone. I pushed the bowl full of Purina Dog Chow underneath the edge of Mom's rocking chair, then stuffed my placemat-towel in front of the food bowl to hide it even better. Was this not an amazing feat? Except I did spill a little on the floor. Well, okay, I spilled a lot on the floor. So YOU try to push a bowl filled with dog food under a rocking chair with your nose.

Anyway, Mom and Dad didn't get my point right away. They just blamed it on the weather. Duh! Like, I would really hide my dog bowl because of a few thunderstorms. Then, a few days later, I heard them talking about going to see some guy named Saint Paul, and it was clear they were once again not planning to take me along. I knew I had to make a really bold CAP statement this time, so I gave both my bowls a super hard shove with my nose, which scattered food, and water, all over the kitchen. I got yelled at for a couple of minutes, but they finally

84

got the message, because the next thing I know I'm sitting up there between them in the truck, headed toward Saint Paul! Turned out it was a town instead of a guy. A town of good smells and very nice lawns, I might add, although no chicken bones.

I pulled my next CAP maneuver on Dad one night about 4:30 a.m., pretending I had to go to the bathroom. When we stepped outside the trailer without the leash on, I took a few steps on the grass and then made a dash up the hill to the parking lot of this Casino I'd been hearing so much about. There were lots of bushes and a real pretty pond there in front, so I just took my time checking everything out, while Dad followed after me in his pajamas. He was trying to act real casual, like we did this every night. But I know the whole thing made a deep impression on him.

CAP was also active in Iowa, the day Mom bought a paper plate full of "kolaches" at the farmer's market. These are little rolls with fruit fillings inside, some kind of special Iowa thing. It was the last batch of blueberry kolaches the lady had left, and Mom was really happy to get them. Well, then my folks go and leave these goodies right there in the truck while they unhitch and set up camp. (HELLO? Did they already forget about the doggy-bag incident in Michigan?) I really didn't mean to eat all six of those kolaches, but they were kind of small. And really tasty! Mom is hopping mad when she sees the empty paper plate, but she knows it's her own fault. So she rushes back to the market to see if there are any kolaches left. The lady has one plate left— they're not blueberry of course, they're "prune." But Mom buys them anyway and she and Dad each get three.

Cat Scam

Unfortunately, the CAP thing backfired on me a while later. Here's where we get to the part about the Labor Day weekend disaster. We were visiting with some friends of Dad's at this country house in Michigan, and I was placed under house arrest in the trailer the whole weekend.

But first, you have to picture us arriving at this place, where there was lots of lawn, but not one foot of it level. Dad pulls up the steep driveway and tries about eight times to back the trailer into the side yard where we're supposed to park. Mom is doing her usual part, stomping around in circles, wringing her hands. Between Mom and the trailer, our poor host's grass is getting a little chewed up. Finally, Dad gives up and just drives the trailer all the way AROUND the house, bumping up and down and around the trees in the guy's hilly backyard, and pulls into the spot frontwise.

Anyway, back to ME and my humiliating fate. I was confined to the trailer because it was feared that my assertive behavior would upset Morgana, the host's eighteen-year-old cat, who ruled that household with an iron paw. If you ask me, Morgana was just putting on a big act, making the Humans think she would lose her appetite and die on the spot if this big evil dog was allowed to run free around the thirty-acre yard. Meanwhile, I can see through a window as "poor, frail" Morgana is jumping up on the dining room table stealing food off plates, once even leaping onto the kitchen counter to rip open a brand new package of muffins. What a scam! As I've said before, I have nothing against cats in general—some of my best friends are cats. But here's my advice to all you kindhearted cat owners out there: Next time your cats pull this "I'm going to quit eating and die" business, call their bluff. They're probably just faking.

The Dog Biscuit State

In closing, let me just say, of all the states so far, Indiana was the BEST. This is because when we first drove across the border, the lady at the little highway booth gave Dad a "toll ticket" for him and on top of it she put a beef-flavored biscuit for me! I thought maybe this would happen at every toll booth, so every time we come to one now, I sit up real tall so the toll booth Human can see clearly there is a nicely behaved dog in this vehicle. But for some reason, no one else has been giving out dog treats.

So I'm requesting all my friends and supporters out there to write to your Congresshumans urging them to make all toll booths in America dog-friendly like that first one in Indiana. Together, we can make this wonderful country an even better place to live!

Love 'n' Licks,
Cleo

Oh, P.S. Forgot to tell you about the day we got our trailer washed. We were passing through a small town in Illinois, and there were all these cute teenaged girls in shorts and bathing suits jumping around in front of an old closed gas station waving "car wash" signs at everybody driving by. So Dad suddenly decides the RV is due for a good cleaning (which Mom has been telling him for at least a month). These girls nearly faint when we pull in with our humongous rig, but Mom gives them a bunch of money, which they are real happy about because they're trying to earn enough to buy new "pom-pom uniforms," whatever that means.

Soon, about ten girls are scrubbing away and crawling twelve feet up the ladder onto the roof, spraying water all over the place and squealing, you know how they do. Dad decides they need a little help with this big job, so he grabs a water hose and joins the girls up on top. Meanwhile, Mom and I are sitting in the shade, keeping a close eye on all this. When they're about halfway done, a good-looking young guy pulls in driving one of those little cars with no roof, and all the girls go ape. One by one they leave our job and drift over to work on the young guy's car, till Dad is the only one left working on us. Meanwhile, Mom's just smiling.

18 What's It Like To Drive a Big Rig?

When friends and relatives tell us on the phone, "Oh, you can park it right at our place, we've got plenty of room!" they usually don't grasp the full concept of a one-ton pickup truck towing a thirty-four-foot fifth-wheel. Learning to handle this monster rig was by far the most intimidating aspect of our new lifestyle—and I'll be the first to admit that I still get bent out of shape whenever we have to navigate in tight situations.

Our RV driving lessons, given by the salesman, consisted of about half an hour of practice in going forward, backing up, and making turns in the far end of a shopping center parking lot—twenty-four minutes for Mark and six minutes for me. Backing up and turning at the same time was the final exam, which I didn't even attempt. This is hard to do in a big motorhome, and even harder with a trailer. You have to pull way forward before putting it in reverse, so the truck has enough time to start pushing the trailer's rear end the direction you want it to go. The steering wheel turns in the wrong direction, intuitively speaking, and you need to start turning it back the other way much sooner than you would think, to keep from overshooting your target.

Mark struggled mightily with these alien concepts, and finally managed to back the monster into a designated parking space, more or less. The salesman said, "Great! You're ready!" He was eager to give us our diploma and get back to work.

Our maiden voyage was to the Front Royal cabin, where we were packing up and preparing to depart. At first, there was a startled, *Omigosh, there's a huge vehicle right on our tail!* reaction whenever we looked in the rear- and side-view mirrors. This comical reflex is surely common to all trailer-towing novices. The driving itself, thanks to cruise control, was as easy as driving a car, once we hit the interstate.

Ah, but there was a slight hitch awaiting us ahead: The one-lane gravel road to our place ended in a forty-foot-wide cul-de-sac lined with trees. Plenty of room to pull over and park the trailer there—but if we ever hoped to leave, we had to get the forty-nine-foot rig turned around and aimed back downhill.

Mark decided to try a U-turn, since there was no place to back into. Of course, the rig was much too big to turn around in one pass, so he was now stuck crosswise in the cul-de-sac with the front bumper right up against the trees. With unflappable patience and confidence—those qualities of his that continually amaze me—he began zigzagging in forward and reverse, pivoting the RV's backside a few inches at a time. Finally, with one last zag, he cleared the trees and backed into place, now facing the right way. The only damage was where a tree limb had gouged the thin fiberglass of the rear window shield. Mark happily covered the hole with a smiley-faced decal from the Good Sam RV club, which remains there to this day.

Many RVing wives say they don't drive their rig at all—sometimes because they're scared to try, other times because "*He won't let me.*" This was never an issue with us; Mark insisted we share the driving from the start. And I wanted to. Well, in theory, anyway. All the how-to books advise wives to learn how to handle all the tasks involved in RVing, from emptying the holding tanks, to hitching up the rig for departure, to driving on all kinds of roadways, to getting safely in and out of campsites, pull-through or otherwise. This is so you won't be totally helpless and stranded if your husband should break a leg or suffer some other dire fate on the road. So I've learned all these things—although I'm more comfortable with some rig-handling tasks than others.

There *are* a few things to keep in mind when piloting a hugely long, twelve-foot-tall box—especially if there are any other objects around. Most people are not attuned to vertical hazards while driving, but with a rig that high, you want to watch out for low-hanging branches in campgrounds, street lamps or awnings protruding beyond the curb, and overhead clearance at service stations and in other drive-through situations.

You want to start braking for a stoplight a lot sooner than you would in a regular vehicle. It takes a good deal more lead time to bring nine tons to a halt than it does to stop a small foreign car. You want to pull way forward into the intersection when turning a corner, so you don't cut it too close and clip a curb, street lamp, or mailbox. Mark and I still remind each other, "Wide turn!" whenever we have to go right or left, but especially right. Also, you want to be real careful changing lanes. It takes a lot of room to drag that long box sideways without running other vehicles off the road. And if you're me, you definitely want to get out and turn the keys over to someone else any time backing up is required. (I reassure myself that I could if I had to.)

In planning our route from one point to another, we frequently have the choice between an interstate and smaller local highways. Getting somewhere in a big rig is generally easier on an interstate. You'll get there faster and the rest areas are handy if you want to stop and park. But eighteen-wheelers and other fellow travelers go uncomfortably fast on these major arteries, and the route can be so monotonous it puts you to sleep. We often opt for the secondary roads, because it's fun to see the towns they pass through.

Plan Ahead is our key principle when navigating unknown roadways and turning into parking areas with a big rig. We heard one horror story of a trucker who took a shortcut through a winding scenic drive in the Black Hills, and ended up backing his tractor-trailer one and a half miles down the mountain because the rig was three inches too high to clear a tunnel. More common to RV drivers is the "box canyon" phobia. After all this time on the road, I still dread the possibility of wandering into a parking lot that doesn't give us enough room to turn around and exit.

Over time we developed the knack of looking ahead and eye-balling an area whenever we wanted to stop and park. Finding RV parking places is usually a challenge in a big city, because every square foot of space is already taken—or so it seems. But in small towns and rural areas, where real estate isn't so expensive, you can always find a vacant lot or boarded-up building, the parking lot of a large grocery store, or a long, empty curb to park the rig briefly while you use the bathroom, check the map, fix lunch, or eat in a local café. In places with diagonal parking on Main Street (yes, they still exist!), you may have to go a block or two down a side street to park, then walk back to town.

The thing that mainly gave us fits at first was getting in and out of service stations. Of course, refueling is easy at interstate truck stops. They're set up for big rigs. But pulling into small service stations is a different story, as our early catastrophe in Augusta taught us. We learned in time to spot diesel pumps by their telltale green handles (true most of the time, anyway), and discovered that diesel is sometimes separated from the gasoline pumps, located over to one side or around the back. We mastered the art of the passenger clearly directing the driver to the proper fuel island—"It's the middle pump on the far left island; leave the pump on your left." And of gauging whether or not we could safely exit past those pesky cars parked in front of the mini-mart. And the most important skill of all: We learned to buy diesel, whenever possible, while we were unhitched and driving around without our towed load following behind.

19 Eddyville, Kentucky
September 20

Here we are in a nearly deserted campground on the shores of Lake Barkley, about forty miles east of Paducah, Kentucky. Donia and I really hadn't planned to stay here ten whole days, but when we went into town to pick up our mail we found out Paducah's celebrated barbecue festival was scheduled for the following weekend. I had read that barbecued goat meat is big here, sometimes called "mutton" to confuse us *auslanders,* and I wanted to try some. So, what's the weary traveler to do? We re-upped through the weekend, of course.

Since our last e-mailing, we spent the Labor Day holidays with a group of Chicago friends at the rural retreat one of them owns in Buchanan, Michigan. It was the first time we've stayed in someone's yard rather than a campground. It turned out to be a white-knuckle adventure—finding a reasonably level place to park the big rig, getting it unhitched with the truck and trailer at different tilts, tripping circuit breakers when we ran too many appliances at once, and then rehitching when it was time to leave. We learned a lot about how strong a board has to be to serve as a ramp for one wheel of a 5,500-pound truck. Answer: stronger than the first two we tried.

Then, in the first week of September we started driving south along the Illinois Central Railroad tracks—humming Arlo Guthrie's "City of New Orleans" all along the way. It continued to be a lazy, gunking-around kind of week. The campsite we stayed in just outside Champaign had a great open field for Cleo to run around. We played par-three golf one day. Stuffed and roasted a chicken in our little oven the next. There was a movie rental shop nearby, so we finally got to see Albert Brooks's *Lost in America,* an RV comedy several of you recommended. We took a cigar walk around the University of Illinois campus, watched the U.S. Open tennis finals, and added a couple of latches on the outside of the trailer to keep compartment doors from banging down on our heads when we get things in and out. It was just like regular living in a real house!

Well, almost. We opted for no sewer hookup when we got to the campground at Champaign, to save $2 a day. Hence our stay was limited by the capacity of our three holding tanks. Oh, sure, we could have hitched up, gone to the dump station, and then circled back. But instead we made it a game to minimize putting water down the drains. Even after four days, our little holding-tank gauge showed all waste levels still in the yellow-light range, none of them flashing red for "full" yet.

One of the things we like best is meeting new people everywhere we go—often quite different from our white-collar, suburban crowd back home. In Champaign, we were parked next to Steve and Michelle, a sweet newlywed couple. Steve had landed a job as an electrician at the nuclear power plant nearby working "twelve/sevens," which means seven days a week, twelve-hour shifts. He gets every other Sunday off, because there's a law that says you can't work someone longer than thirteen days straight in a nuclear facility. (Sounds good to me!) So, with commuting to the job, he's gone from about 5 a.m. to 6 p.m. every day. It's grueling, but his take-home pay for a week is around $1,800, what with time and a half for every hour in a day over eight, and for Saturday, and double time for Sunday. They hope to save enough to pay off their truck and trailer, and still have enough to take next summer off, driving the trailer up to Alaska to visit with Michelle's mom.

We had another RV maintenance adventure en route to Kentucky. Somehow the plastic case of our rooftop air conditioner mysteriously broke apart, with one chunk catching against the chrome rooftop railing. We didn't know anything about this until informed of it by a trucker on our six [translation: behind us] who said over the CB radio, "I don't suppose the happy camper has his ears on, by any chance?" When I answered him back, the trucker told us about the A/C problem, which he was apparently observing at about eye level.

We found a replacement part at the third RV service place we tried on our way down the road, and as soon as we arrived at our current campground I climbed up on the roof and bolted on the new cover, so now we're all set again. Oh, and at the RV store I found a new gadget for flushing out our holding tanks! It has a clear plastic tube that fits between the drainpipe and the sewer hose. I call it Dump-O-Vision. I wish I could tell you all about it, but Donia informs me this is not a polite subject for correspondence.

Here in Kentucky, sightseeing has been a thorny issue. Donia insisted on going to the famous Paducah quilting museum; I insisted on waiting for her outside, strolling around Paducah's cool river-wall murals on the Ohio River waterfront, smoking a cigar. Another day I ventured across the river into Metropolis, Illinois, to visit a frontier fort, the world's largest Superman statue (and museum), and a riverboat casino (smoky and icky). Donia opted to stay home and rearrange the dishes in the cabinets, on the theory that, "When you've seen one antique musket (or riverboat slot machine), you've seen them all."

But we did both agree on making the 220-mile round trip one day, two states away, to do lunch at Lambert's Café in Sikeston, Missouri—legendary as the "throwed rolls" place. Like a mobile food bar, the waitpersons come around with kettles of all-you-can-eat extras. The star attraction is fresh rolls trundled out on a cart, still in pans hot from the oven. The waiter intones "Hot Ro-o-o-o-lls," and if you hold your hand up, he'll throw you one across the room. Another waiter circulates with a molasses pot, announcing "Sorghum for your ro-o-o-o-lls!" Other free pass-arounds that day were fried okra, blackeyed peas, macaroni and tomatoes, and fried potatoes and onions. Oh yes, and midway through lunch, a waitress came around putting dishes of banana pudding at everyone's place. All this in addition to your chosen entrée with two sides. A true test of stomach capacity, Lambert's.

I know I've talked about food a lot in this letter, but I feel compelled to report on that barbecue festival we stayed a whole extra week to attend. Unfortunately, it turned out to be a big bust. We made the mistake of waiting till late Saturday afternoon to go. Though there was still plenty of food for sale, most of the booths were already beginning to fold up their gear. Sadly, there was not one bite of goat to be found. We started out with one quick pork sandwich, but it was only so-so. We tried another from a different barbecue guru down the way; this also did not satisfy. In desperation we staggered from booth to booth, downing a riblet platter, a third sandwich, then a half-slab of ribs, with sides of slaw, cornbread and beans, and red beans and rice. In the end, we decided there was nothing here clearly better than the barbecue at Hogs on the Hill, back in Washington, D.C. On the way home we had a big fight over the last Rolaid.

So, friends, don't feel too envious about our candy-store life-style. We have bad days, too. . . . Although, the philosopher in me wonders, can any day that includes three pulled pork sandwiches, ribs and more ribs, plus beans and rice and cornbread, truly be called a "bad" day?

Love,
Mark

20 How Do RV Utilities Work?

When you live in a regular house, you don't have to think much about water, electricity, and sewer service. They're automatically there when you turn on the shower, plug in a lamp, or flush the john. Those of us who live on the road have to think about these things a lot.

Like most RVs, ours is designed to be self-contained for brief periods: We have our own twelve-volt electrical system, freshwater reservoir, and wastewater holding tanks. Still, Mark and I prefer to stay at campgrounds with utility hookups most of the time. When we do camp in a place with limited or no hookups, there's a good reason for it. Our lifestyle is adventurous enough without going out of our way to rough it just for the sake of roughing it. (More on this later.)

A full hookup consists of a water spigot, large electric outlet, and in-ground sewer drainpipe right at your campsite. Jacks for cable TV or phone may be added amenities, either included free or for a dollar or two more per day. Partial hookups, far more common, usually have water and electric at the site, with a central dump station for campers to drain their waste tanks on the way in or out. Some state parks and other public campgrounds offer only electricity at the sites, with community water faucets available to refill your freshwater tanks, if necessary.

Whenever we pull into a new campground, the hookups are always our first priority. We've practiced this two-person drill enough so that we've got it down to about twelve minutes for a full hookup and seven for a partial.

For a full hookup, we:

- Unlock the RV's electric storage hatch, drag out the inch-thick cable, plug it into the campground's outlet, and flip on the circuit breaker.

- Unlock the RV's water connection hatch, remove the protective cap, and connect our clean-water hose to the campground water supply.
- Drag the flexible, three-inch sewer hose out of its storage compartment, attach one end to the sewer drainpipe under the trailer, and stick the other end of the hose into the drainpipe in the ground, using one of our seals or adapters to smell-proof the connection.

I always go immediately for jobs #1 and #2, hoping to escape the icky task of sewer-hose connecting. In spite of the canvas bag full of fancy plastic coupling devices we carry with us, it seems our drain-hose diameter is never quite in sync with the diameter of the pipe in the ground. When all else fails, our last-ditch method of keeping our hose from slipping out of the drainpipe is to wedge it in using a small, wedge-shaped wood scrap we carry just for that purpose. (You never know when a piece of debris you find on the ground—in this case modified with a string "safety strap" to keep it from falling into the sewer—will become a prized piece of equipment!)

This sewer business is all very important to get right, because the sternest RV taboo of all is dumping wastewater on the ground instead of into a bona fide drain hole. It's actually against the law to discharge even sink and shower water on the ground in most states we've visited—Kansas being one notable exception. In horror, we once watched our neighbors at a Kansas state park open their valves to let gray water gush right out onto the grass beside their trailer. And perfectly legal it was.

Propane is a fourth utility of sorts, used to fuel our propane furnace, stovetop and oven, and sometimes the refrigerator, which automatically switches over to propane any time the electricity is disconnected. The water heater will also convert to propane at the flip of a manual switch. In a special compartment on the side of the trailer, we have two thirty-pound propane tanks that must be periodically refilled at a propane dealer, service station, or campground where propane is sold.

The tanks are used one at a time: When the first one becomes empty, which usually happens at 3 a.m. on a frigid night in the mountains, you go outside and twist the selector valve to the other tank. This is a foolproof maneuver that even I can perform, now that I've lost my initial fear of the whole trailer blowing sky-high as soon as I touch a propane valve. Once you've switched tanks, of course, it's important to remember to have the empty tank refilled in the next few days.

But I digress. Let's get back to the fine points of electric service.

Remember the old "word problems" in math class? It's a cold morning and Mark and Donia are running both electric space heaters. Cleo has tracked dirt and leaves all over the carpet, so Mark vacuums while the coffee is brewing. Meanwhile, Donia dries her hair with the hair dryer. At what point will they trip the thirty-amp circuit breaker on the electric post outside? And you thought junior-high math would be useless in later life!

I must point out that besides amps, there are also watts and volts, and they're all related. We generally have 120-volt electric service in the United States—the *force* of the current that runs through the wires. Amps refers to the *amount* of current available from any given circuit or hookup. And watts are the measure of the electricity that an appliance actually *consumes*. Watts divided by volts yields amps. This is a magic formula; don't ask me any more about it. Mark says our modern Western industrial economy is based on it. In practical terms, it means that a 100-watt bulb takes only 0.83 of an amp (100 divided by 120), whereas a 300-watt light bulb will eat up 2.5 amps, and a 1,500-watt hair dryer needs a whopping 12.5 amps.

It helps to know this stuff because, when connected to a campground outlet, you need to be aware of the combined amper-age requirements of all the appliances you're using at one time. The combined circuits in an average house amount to 100–200 amps' worth of electric service, with the washer, dryer, and kitchen outlets on separate heavy-duty circuits—plenty of power for most domestic uses. Typically, an RV campsite has a single 30-amp outlet. A few newer parks, or those located in warm climates, offer 50-amp service, which owners of large motorhomes find necessary to run their two air conditioners simultaneously. Only rarely are we limited to 20- or 15-amp service, as we were at that RV park in Illinois—or if we're camping in a friend's driveway and are plugged into a regular household outlet in their garage.

I made myself a handy list of all our plug-ins and the amps they consume (see box). On 50 amps, we can run just about every appliance we want at the same time. With 30 amps, we have to watch it a little bit but are usually okay. With 15 or 20 amps, we have to be very careful. The thing is, there are a number of "hidden amp-eaters" in the trailer: These include the electric water heater and refrigerator, which we can manually switch over to propane if need be. But there are also the battery charger, propane-gas detector, several clocks, and the VCR memory circuit, which all use small amounts of power at times we have no

Mark and Donia's Appliance Amperage Needs

Air conditioner	13.5 amps
Microwave	12.8 amps
Space heater, high	12.5 amps
Hair dryer, high	12.5 amps
Upright vacuum	12.0 amps
Water heater	11.7 amps
Iron	10.0 amps
Space heater, low	6.3 amps
Junior coffeemaker	5.2 amps
Refrigerator	2.7 amps
Rice cooker	2.5 amps
Electric blanket	1.5 amps
Computer	1 amp
TV	0.9 amp
75-watt light bulb	0.6 amp

control over. So we have to subtract a few amps for openers, when tallying up our available electricity. If we're on 20-amp service, this leaves only enough juice left to run one additional large appliance at a time.

Amp awareness becomes automatic after a while, once you've tripped a circuit breaker or two. Far more difficult, for me, is limiting water usage when we have no sewer hookup and have to collect all wastewater in our holding tanks. In these situations, our most valuable resource is empty space. The water itself we have plenty of, but if we run out of a place for it to go, we have to pack up and leave.

To make RV plumbing even more interesting, nearly every recreational vehicle in the world is equipped with a holding-tank gauge *that doesn't work*. Apparently, crud collects on the sensors in the tank, producing a red-light "tank full" signal even when you know the thing is empty because you've just finished dumping. You can spend endless hours flushing out your tanks with special solutions to try keeping the sensors clean . . . or you can stop worrying and just play it by instinct, as we finally started doing.

Our toilet holding tank, the so-called black-water tank, has a forty-gallon capacity and can go for a week to ten days without needing to be dumped. But the shower and kitchen-sink tanks, the gray-water ones, hold only about twenty-five gallons each. To conserve shower-tank space, we can always use the campground's showers, if available, or take Navy showers in the rig—i.e., wet down, turn off water, soap up, turn on water, rinse off.

It's the kitchen holding tank that gives us problems. Our cooking style involves a lot of vegetable rinsing, shrimp peeling, dirtying of every pot in the cupboard, and so forth. It doesn't take long to collect twenty-five gallons. Four days is about our limit, with ordinary use. When the campground has a bathhouse, we use that for showers, and move some of our kitchen operations like dishwashing over to the bathroom sink. I carry the dishes and pots back and forth to wash and dry a few at a time, since there's not a lot of space on the vanity top. (This is my idea of roughing it.) If we want to stay more than a few days, we switch our diet to things that can be eaten from paper plates.

In a pinch, of course, we could always tie everything down, put in the slides, unhook existing utilities, and haul the rig to the campground dump station to empty our tanks. But that's for holding-tank weenies! We just ration our tank space for as long as we plan to stay, then dump as we leave. Even with the Tank Gauges That Lie, we've had only one wastewater emergency that disrupted our day and sent us scurrying prematurely to the dump station.

Full-fledged dry camping, or "boondocking," without even having an electric hookup, is a subject all its own. Many RVers are gung-ho boondockers. They strategize ways to spend months on end without hookups. The vast desert encampments throughout the Southwest are favorite spots for them. They buy diesel- or propane-fueled generators, or install solar panels on their rooftops. They collect shower water in buckets to flush their toilets with, and dump their holding tanks into small plastic sewer wagons—called "blue boys" because of their color—to haul wastewater to the community dump station. Or they rely on the local "honey wagon" service, a tank truck that sucks out their wastewater tanks for a fee.

Some day Mark and I may try this, but for now our boondocking experiences are generally limited to two- or three-day stays at places we couldn't otherwise visit. Many lovely wilderness campgrounds have all the space and scenery you could wish for but no utilities. In these situations, we have to rely on our trailer's twelve-volt electrical system, which powers the built-in lamps and stereo, small ceiling exhaust fans, slide-outs, refrigerator controls, and furnace fan motor. In cold weather, the furnace fan depletes our twelve-volt batteries very quickly. Not only do we get chilly, but the lights get too dim to read by—the ultimate hardship for Mark and me.

Once they are run down, the batteries can be recharged only by hooking the trailer up to a regular 120-volt outlet, or by plugging the batteries into an outlet on the pickup truck to let the engine recharge them as we drive. Therefore, our "house batteries" are the primary limiting factor in how long we can stay in a place without electricity.

One April, we drove twenty-seven memorable miles across the New Mexico desert on a rocky, rutted road to reach the Chaco Culture National Historic Park, famous for its ancient Anasazi ruins. The park's primitive campground was picturesquely nestled at the base of a cliff. Out our back window, we could see the remains of someone's nine hundred-year-old home carved into the rock. We had hoped to stay four or five days in this enchanted setting, but the weather turned cold, and by the end of two days our batteries had run down. We had no choice but to hitch up and leave.

Later on, when we were boondocking overnight in a Wal-Mart parking lot outside Cincinnati, we went into the store and bought a propane lantern and small catalytic heater that both run on inexpensive, one-pound propane cartridges. I know Abe Lincoln did okay for himself using a fireplace and lantern light— but I'm sorry, these propane things hiss and smell bad and make my eyes water. For some things, you just can't beat good old electricity.

21 Lexington, Kentucky
October 5

A funny thing happened on the way to Lexington. About ten minutes after we headed east out of Eddyville last week, Mark looked at the map and said, "Wait a minute! We're going to miss *Mammoth Cave National Park???*" I mumbled something about "when you've seen one cave you've seen them all"—but since we had just bought a pricey Golden Eagle pass for free entry to all the national parks, we turned hard right and made a three-day detour to Mammoth Cave. Mark is reveling in this travel-by-whim, make-no-reservations mode, now that the peak summer travel season is over.

The bad news was, the park itself didn't charge an entry fee, and the tickets to the cave tours weren't covered by our pass. The good news was, those caves were totally awesome. At first we just planned to take a quick look, but when we returned from our two-hour Frozen Niagara tour and looked at the cave map, we realized we had only covered three-fourths of a mile, a piddling fraction of the thirty-some miles included in the seven or eight different tours they offer. (Over 350 miles of cave passageways have been explored and charted, in all.)

So we added another day to our stay and went back for the Violet City Lantern Tour, a three-hour, three-mile walk, with only kerosene lanterns for light—the way tourists as early as 1816 toured the caves. One guide, twenty tourists, six lanterns, and no handrails this time. The path wound up and down steep, slippery inclines surrounded by huge piles of rocky rubble. We saw the remains of a saltpeter mine that had provided gunpowder for the War of 1812. And, most incredible of all, we toured a group of abandoned huts that had once been a tuberculosis hospital, buried more than a mile from the cave's nearest entrance. Sending patients down to live in the damp, year-round chill of fifty-four degrees was the brainchild of a wacky nineteenth-century physician who happened to be a nephew of George Rogers Clark and his younger brother William Clark, of Lewis and Clark fame. No TB patients were cured in this facility, we learned. They all got bored sitting around shivering in dim lantern light with nothing to do and walked out after three months to spend their last days in the sun.

In our travels Mark and I are always discovering some fascinating tidbit of pioneer history—tales of amazing exploits and true grit in the face of hardship. Like the Revolutionary-era fort we visited in Vincennes, Indiana. There, in 1779, George Rogers Clark led a surprise wintertime attack against the British garrison, a victory that ultimately secured the entire Ohio Valley region for America. He did this by marching his ragtag group of 175 men across two hundred miles of flooded river valleys, some of the time slogging through forty-degree, chest-high water. The British, never dreaming anyone would try this, had sent their hired French and Indian mercenaries home for the winter to save money. Thus the small contingent of British regulars were sitting ducks for the Americans. What a country! You could take a dozen U.S. history courses and never run across all this wonderful stuff.

We finally got to Lexington the last day of September, just in time for the arrival of fall in these parts. After two weeks of record-high heat for Kentucky, we woke up on the first of October to a cool, crisp morning and felt that old seasonal urge to walk around a college campus. So we headed for Berea College, in a little town about forty-five miles south of Lexington that bills itself the "World Capital of Folk Arts and Crafts."

On the surface, Berea looks totally typical for a small southern college: grassy plazas, ivied brick buildings, tall trees, kids in tee shirts and backpacks all heading somewhere in a hurry. But this school has a unique low-income twist. Applications are not accepted from anyone with a family income above $44,000, and nobody pays tuition. Instead, students work ten to twenty hours a week at various jobs, most notably in crafts workshops, where they turn out items like wooden Skittles games and rustic hearth brooms made of twigs and grasses, all for sale at the local galleries.

Students also wait tables at the college-owned Boone Tavern Hotel, which we had heard was a fun place to dine. It was. The cuisine included spoonbread, lime Jell-O and pineapple salad, and "ruby punch," your classic wedding-shower beverage. And our server, Tiffany, turned out to be a sweet, freshman version of Mr. Magoo. We watched, fascinated, as she wove through a series of near misses with teetering trays full of platters that often turned out to be the pot roast special instead of the entrées the customers had ordered. I have to say, it was a totally memorable lunch. Maybe the servers get more competent and less entertaining as the semester wears on?

So here we are now in Lexington, where everywhere you look, the landscape is filled with majestic horses grazing. Even the local mini-mart is trimmed out like a horse stable. We're staying at a wonderful, modern campground attached to the Kentucky Horse Park, an impressive combination of horse farm, museum, and horse-show arena. Mark and I have never been horse fanciers, but we spent the entire day at the exhibition center yesterday, learning more than we ever thought possible about the history and lore of horses. There was a monument to Man o' War so lavish and laudatory you would think he was a U.S. president. They had a Parade of Breeds including a miniature horse about thirty inches high (Mark's favorite) and a Tennessee Walking Horse (my favorite). And a museum display that included an equine gas mask worn by some of the million-some horses the United States shipped over to Europe during World War I.

All weekend the park was holding something called Jump Start Horse Trials. We got to watch dozens of determined teenaged girls in black velvet riding hats and pearl earrings put their horses through paces, both in the show ring and cantering around a cross-country course of multilevel jumps. Cleo attended the cross-country event with us and was totally enchanted. Overnight, she has become a horse nut. (Mark remarked today, however, that all this rolling-meadow, white-board-fence beauty depends on the grimy, gritty world of horse-race gambling, and somehow the two don't seem to fit.)

Here's hoping your October is picture-perfect, and all your horses come in winners. Keep those e-mails coming We love hearing from you all!

Cheers,

Donia

22 How Do You Do E-Mail?

Without a telephone of our own, getting online with our computer to do e-mail is another constant adventure. At that Kentucky Horse Park in Lexington, the setup for RV guests was a relatively nice one: Mark was cheerfully shown to a desk back in the convenience store office, where he could plug our double-pronged cord into their phone jack to send and receive e-mail using the 800 number for our Internet service provider.

It wasn't always that easy! When we first set out, most campground managers not only didn't provide any kind of phone-jack access, they didn't even know what we were talking about when we asked. They would direct us to the pay phone. Or tell us sorry, their computer didn't do e-mail. Or simply shake their heads blankly. Over the next several months, however, a kind of revolution took place in e-consciousness. By the end of our first year on the road, everyone understood what it was we wanted, even if their office policy was no.

Mark looked at the e-mail issue as a chance to test his ingenuity, sort of an ongoing game. We still savor the memory of our ultimate e-mail adventure—trying to get online from a remote state park in Kentucky.

It goes something like this: Mark fools around for half an hour with the phone jack for the credit card machine in the campground office but can't get it to work. Half-crazed after ten days without e-mail, he goes back to the trailer and rummages through his stash of electrical gizmos, to try hot-wiring the pay phone circuit box outside the laundromat. He has mulled over this possibility for months; now the time has come. Amazingly, it works! (Warning: Maneuver performed by house-inspection professional. Do not attempt yourself.)

I'm the lookout for this caper, to make sure nobody picks up the pay phone and breaks Mark's connection. Despite Mark's reassurances, I'm also a nervous wreck. I'm convinced he will be electrocuted or arrested or worse. (He stresses that we are *not* ripping off the phone company, since the computer is calling its 800 number as usual.) Oddly, no one pays the slightest notice to the guy sitting on the laundromat steps with his laptop wired to the wall.

Late that day, flush with triumph, we go to the office to sign up for another night. "I'm sorry, I can only take cash," the new clerk on duty apologizes. "I can't get our credit card machine to work right now, for some reason."

Mark turns the little machine over; a look passes across his face. He swaps two jack connections he accidentally reversed earlier in the day. The clerk is dazzled. "I'm a house inspector," Mark explains modestly. "We can do all sorts of things."

The majority of our e-mailing efforts, however, have been far more conventional. For example, if the campground can't accommodate us, we try the public library. Some have computers with Internet access but no phone jacks for e-mailing. Many travelers can get their mail this way, but our Compuserve account has to be dialed into using our own computer and program. In large towns, Kinko's copy centers are a reliable option—except the one we visited in the suburbs of Minneapolis, which had a fancy internal phone system that blocked our laptop's automatic dialing function.

Other solutions are truck stops with phone jacks at their diner tables, dataports on airport or convention-center pay phones, or the elusive cyber-cafés. I say "elusive" because we never have found a genuine cyber-café with a working setup—though in one Wyoming town, the visitor's center directed us to a local pizza place to do e-mail. Sure enough, there on the counter was a gigantic computer terminal with adjacent phone jack. A cyber-pizzeria!

Once we borrowed the jack of a long-term camper with a phone in her trailer. Another time, a friendly bridge player we met at a local club game invited us home to use her phone. We also got very bold about asking tire dealers and other places where we were doing business to let us briefly plug into their wall jacks.

When RV park owners did start getting on board with e-mail access, the facilities they provided were all over the map. At a couple of public campgrounds we have found pay phones with built-in phone jacks on the front. The best setups have a dedicated phone line for e-mailers in the campground's office, laundry room, or recreation building, with a roomy shelf or tabletop to set the computer on. But these are rare. Typically, we ask the campground clerk to let us use the office phone or the auxiliary jack on the back of the fax or credit card machine.

Over time, we have carefully honed our phrasing to be as reassuring as possible: "Would it be okay if we hooked our computer into your phone jack very briefly, to dial an 800 number and get e-mail? The call is free for you, and it'll only take three or four minutes." More and more, the answer is, "Sure, no problem."

We have run across many campground clerks who've obviously been burned by phone-jack abuse—laptoppers who get online and surf the Net, or look up all their stocks one at a time, or tie up the line writing lengthy replies to e-mails. These wary clerks tend to hover over you while you're online, asking "Are you almost done?" every minute or so. Naturally, this will be the time when my children decide to e-mail me photos from their vacation, and in the largest possible format, so they take forever to download.

After a few of these nerve-racking experiences, we wrote to all our e-mail correspondents explaining our limited phone-jack access and asking them not to e-mail photos or forward Internet humor pieces to us on the road. Now we have an automatic "Please don't!" letter we send out to anyone who forgets this rule.

Of course, the ideal e-mail situation is to find an RV park with instant-phone hookups at each site. The ultimate luxury! You can send and receive e-mail, surf the Net, whatever you want to do online, any time you please, maybe four or five times a day.

You take a phone line for granted when you stay in a motel. Why aren't phones at sites standard for RV parks? Alas, in all our time on the road, I can still count on the fingers of one hand the campgrounds where we enjoyed this service.

A few years ago Pocket Mail hit the scene—a small, handheld device that lets you send and receive simple e-mail messages by clamping the device to the handset of any touchtone phone. It seems to work fine with most pay phones. Many RVers jumped at this chance to keep in touch by e-mail without having to bother with a computer. Other simplified, e-mail-specific gizmos quickly followed.

One of the enduring struggles of RVing computer users has been the search for a reliable cellular-phone-plus-modem setup that provides Internet access from anywhere, any time. We've seen many magazine articles, Web sites, and e-mail newsletters devoted to this quest. The technology is constantly changing, of course, but at this moment in time, Mark and I are far from convinced about wireless e-mailing. Those who've tried it complain of agonizingly slow transmission rates, uncertain reception, and costly roaming charges.

Maybe satellite phones or direct-dish television systems will prove to be the answer. For now, however, Mark and I are satisfied with the borrowed-phone-jack method. It's just a more *interesting* way to go.

23 Raccoon Valley, Tennessee

October 20

Dear Friends and Fans,

I am truly grateful for the continuing kudos on my column. My Uncle Rob in Maryland actually suggested that I be the designated writer for our whole family, but you can just imagine how far THAT one got with my Humans—the Charles Kuralt Wannabees. Anyway, thanks again for all the e-mail support!

Looking for a Gift Horse in the South

We are now in Tennessee but I never got a chance to tell you how much I loved that state called Kentucky, where the main animal is the horse. They had these neat kinds of trailers at the campground—the horses live in the back part and the people live in the front, and they all travel together to horse shows. I went to one of these riding shows with Mom and Dad, where the horses had girls on their backs, and they were jumping over little fences set up all over the field, and people with clipboards were keeping score. I really wanted to get off that leash and go hang out with the horses. But Mom and Dad were being poopy about it, and said, "Not now, Cleo. Maybe later." But they had a little smile on their face. This could only mean one thing: THEY'RE GETTING ME A HORSE FOR CHRISTMAS! I just know it. So I guess I better act extra good between now and Christmas. No more incidents like the dispute with that beagle at Lake BARKley.

The Great Dishrag Wars

I'm sure a lot of you have secretly wondered how long Mark and Donia could keep up their lovey-dovey relationship in an eight-by-thirty-four-foot RV. Well, already a few cracks are beginning to show. Here's the story. At the kitchen sink Mom has always liked to use those lightweight kitchen wipes that dry out really fast. Dad says they're about as absorbent as plastic wrap. He rants about them being "nonwoven textiles" like this was the work of the devil. He favors the old-fashioned rag dishrags, which, according to Mom, "never dry out and smell like a garbage dump all the time." Are you beginning to get the picture? Anyway, the other day while Dad was gone to the post office, Mom THREW AWAY the old, gray dishrag and installed a new pink kitchen wipe in its place. Dad is pretending not to care, like this dishrag thing is really far beneath him, but tension is simmering under the surface. Stay tuned.

Mom's Bad Hair Day(s)

I guess finding a good Human-groomer on the road is not so easy. A while back Mom got her hair cut in a shop in Indiana and it looked really silly—like she had a little tail going down the back of her neck. When we got to Kentucky, Mom says, "I can't stand this any longer, I'm walking into the first beauty shop I see." So she did. NOW it looks like the haircut of some eighth-grade kid on a skateboard, kind of floppy on top and shaved around the bottom. It's all Dad and I can do to keep a straight face. As for me, my summer crewcut has all grown out now, so once again people say, "Oh, what a beautiful dog!" I'm not bragging, just telling you what they say.

Six Poops a Day Keep the Diet at Bay

Some of you may have heard about the humiliating diet of low-fat kibbles I was put on a couple of weeks ago (Slogan: You Call This Dog Food?) after some fat guy at an RV repair place yelled out to me, "Hey Fella, you and me, we both need to go on a DIET!" What a bozo. Doesn't he realize long-haired dogs look heavier when they're growing in their winter coat? Well, okay, maybe I have put on a few extra pounds. What can you expect, with the sedentary job I have, lying around guarding the trailer all day while my Humans gallivant around playing golf, going to Wal-Mart, et cetera? Anyway, that diet didn't last long. Seems there's something in low-calorie kibbles that makes you poop five or six times a day, which didn't bother me so much, but bothered my folks a lot since nature frequently called at times like 3 a.m. So I'm happy to say, I'm back on my old favorite, Pet Chow for Dogs Who Do Not Have a Body Image Problem.

I Love a Parade

I've been working a lot of overtime this month, as you might have gathered, so it was nice to get a day off a couple of weeks ago. The folks took me with them to see this thing called a "parade" in a small town up in the mountains in Kentucky. This consisted of a bunch of weirdos marching down the middle of the main street THROWING CANDY at people watching from the sidewalk. I'm not kidding! They had girls in little bitty skirts and boots twirling silver sticks, and dressed-up kings and queens of this-and-that riding on the backs of convertibles, and old guys called "Shriners" in zany hats driving hay wagons and clown cars. My favorite part was when these teenaged girls rode by on horses! I saw the perfect horse for my Christmas present, a pretty Palomino the exact same color as me, and I started barking with joy. (Unfortunately this did not go over well with the crowd, who totally misunderstood my meaning.)

A Horse of a Different Color

A while later we went to this place called Pigeon Forge, where my Grandma and Grandpa Steele came from Atlanta to visit us. THEY stayed at a nice motel in town, but we had to stay at this grungy RV park way out in the country with a barnyard behind the office. They had goats and pigs and chickens, plus obnoxious roosters that strutted around the pay phone crowing all the time when people were trying to talk long distance. And yeah, they also had a horse. But obviously, this Tennessee barnyard nag was not the kind of sleek Kentucky thoroughbred horse I want for Christmas. So I lunged right up to the fence and barked in a very negative style, just so there wouldn't be any doubts about it. Mom got all upset and said, "Cleo! I thought you liked horses." Duh! Humans can be so dense sometimes.

The Tennessee Schmaltz

Right now we're at this place named "Raccoon Valley" where the campers are all in a club called "Escapees." Where did they ESCAPE from? That's what I want to know. I think to be in this club you have to sign a pledge to be, like, icky-gooey friendly to other campers and tell them all about your propane tanks and drain valves and diesel engine whether you've ever seen them before or not. I mean, these bearded, sinister-looking Escapees will just walk right up to your rig like they've been your neighbors for years. Since my job description includes barking at people like this, I'm kind of in a no-win situation. All of a sudden I'm getting all this grief for just doing my job. Dad grabs my collar and holds me back while saying stuff like, "Cleo! A stranger is just a friend you haven't met yet!" Oh, please. Where's my barf bag?

Dirty Dancing

One of these insanely friendly Escapees and his jolly wife invited my Humans to go to a place in Knoxville called "Cotton Eyed Joe" to try out country-and-western dancing. I gathered the dance thing didn't go so well when they came home around 11 p.m. and Mom is saying to Dad, "No, no, you did fine, you just need to practice some." So the next morning Twinkle Toes is up early, watching a show called "Dance Club" on cable TV and trying to do the steps right there in the RV in his pajamas—step shuffle, turn-two-three, bump into Cleo's water bowl, spill-it-all-over-the-kitchen-two-three, slide shuffle, wipe-it-up-two-three. If this dance craze keeps up, looks like we'll have to go back to those absorbent-type dishrags, after all.

That's all the bites I have for now. Take care, all you two-legged and four-legged pen pals, and keep those cards and letters coming!

Love 'n' Licks,
Cleo

24 What's RV Housework Like?

Once upon a time, back in the last millennium, I lived in a three-story suburban dream house complete with five bedrooms, sprawling kitchen/family room, large living room, and den/office. Our entire trailer would have fit into the master bedroom alone. Ah, but the cleaning and polishing in my dream house was never-ending.

I'll take the trailer.

Cleo's account of the Stinky Dishrag Debate captures a central truth about our sardine-can lifestyle: Little things loom large in a thirty-four-foot dwelling. The dishrag stays wet all the time because Mark and I hand-wash the dishes after every meal. In our kitchen we don't even have room for a wire dish-drying rack, let alone a dishwasher. We simply lay the wet dishes out to dry on a dishtowel spread on the counter, so they'll be ready next time we need them. It has to be this way, when you've only got four plates, four soup bowls, and so forth. But who's complaining? For a card-carrying neatnik like myself, our minimalist household has a clean, *Survivor*-like appeal.

In our little home on wheels, clutter is the biggest enemy. If we don't follow the "place for everything and everything in its place" rule, the tide of miscellanous items quickly rises and leaves us no place to sit, eat, work, or sleep. In a four-bedroom house, an unmade bed is no big deal. But it's a big eyesore in a tiny RV bedroom, where a queen-sized mattress goes nearly wall to wall and is the only furniture in the room. Moreover, a neatly made bed makes a handy work surface for things like sorting papers or folding clothes.

On the one-to-ten neatnik scale, I'm a nine-and-a-half married to a six. After listening to my laments about shoes and magazines left scattered around the place, Mark got creative and hand-crafted some wooden wall racks in the woodworking shop at our South Texas winter campground. Today, a rack next to the front door holds outdoorsy shoes, magazines, a small flashlight, and even outgoing mail. He put cuphooks on the wall to hang dog leashes, keys, caps, and gloves. We also have his 'n' hers bedside racks for books, glasses, hand cream, and so forth. As decor this arrangement is not elegant, but it gets things off the floor and does wonders for domestic tranquillity.

While clutter is a constant, actual dirt depends on the physical surroundings where our RV is parked. Campsites may be pavement, gravel, grass, dirt, sand, pine needles, compacted leaves, or a combination thereof. Concrete, blacktop, and gravel are the least scenic but definitely the cleanest, acting as a kind of natural doormat to knock off debris. Dirt all too often turns to mud, and grass, when fresh-mowed and wet, sticks to shoes and dog paws like glue. And speaking of man's best friend . . . a long-haired dog flat-out doubles the mess. This is true of dogs who live in houses, too, but in a house the dog hair is distributed over a far greater area and therefore is less noticeable.

Wind is also a major factor. In a high-dirt environment on a windy day, a perfectly clean interior can be covered with a fine film of dust in fifteen minutes. In time I learned not to agonize over the losing battle of dusting. I generally wait until a kitchen towel gets dirty, then—en route to the laundry basket—use it to take a few swipes at the dustiest surfaces. This feels wonderfully liberating to me, as I was raised in a household where my daily after-school chore was to completely dust all the surfaces in the living and dining room to my mother's white-glove-inspection standards.

On the bright side, the actual cleaning of a carpeted RV is a snap—provided you have the right tools. I make this distinction because full-timers often make mistakes when it comes to cleaning equipment. Storage space is so limited that they tend to choose small-sized, bagless, low-power carpet sweepers or vacuum cleaners at the outset.

Mark and I learned the hard way that the best tool for cleaning RVs is a full-powered upright vacuum. Our first choice was a pull-along, tank-type vacuum with a motorized carpet attachment. Because it had lots of handy wands and brush attachments, we felt it would be great for cleaning all our small spaces. As it turned out, we hardly ever used those wand attachments, and as the carpet wore thin in high-traffic areas, the tank-type grew ever-feebler at sucking up debris. Eventually I was stooping down to pick up lint and dog hair rolls by hand, and feeding them into the vacuum. Once we traded the tank-type in on a regular twelve-amp, bag-style upright, vacuuming the 90 percent of the trailer that's carpeted became the easy, fifteen-minute job it always should have been.

The other 10 percent—bathroom fixtures and kitchen—is even easier to keep clean. My favorite task is wiping up dog tracks and debris from our eighteen square feet of white kitchen lineoleum with a wet paper towel. It's amazing how much bang for the buck you get out of this simple, one-minute job—it gives the whole room a fresh-cleaned look. Ditto for the bathroom vanity and the toilet.

Mark's cleverest invention ever was devised to solve a delicate potty-hygiene problem: The floor-pedal flush method doesn't always have enough whooshing power to fully clean the sides of the bowl. The more expensive RVs have a built-in spray wand beside the toilet for this purpose, but not ours. So Mark bought a toy power-squirt water gun that now sits right beside the potty to take care of it. In fact, his invention was featured one month in *Trailer Life* magazine's "Ten-Minute Tech" column.

Doing laundry on the road is an adventure all its own. Some RVs have closets with built-in washer-dryers. Our hall closet came pre-wired and -plumbed for such a unit, but we prefer to use this valuable space instead to store linens, coats and jackets, and that hefty upright vacuum cleaner. For laundry, we go to laundro-mats. There are two ways to go here: a regular commercial laun-dromat with super-sized washers and dryers that get your loads done quickly and efficiently, or a campground laundromat, which has the advantage of being right on the premises.

Campground laundries are the most varied of amenities. They range from a single outdoor washer and dryer on the concrete porch of a shower house to a spacious indoor facility with ultra-modern equipment, sparkling clean floors and folding tables, rolling wire clothes baskets, comfortable chairs, and several recent issues of *Martha Stewart Living*. The typical setup falls somewhere in the middle—four washers and four dryers (one or two out of order at any given time), a small tabletop to fold clothes on, one plastic lawn chair, and an October 1994 issue of *Field and Stream*.

In a laundromat, though, it's the social life that counts. And campground laundromats definitely offer more interaction than a commercial place in town. While waiting on your clothes you can pick up tips about the fastest washers and hottest dryers, advice on great sightseeing attractions and campgrounds down the road, and sometimes the real lowdown on campground managers.

With limited facilities, laundromat protocol becomes critical. Particularly non grata are those campers who leave finished laundry sitting unattended in a machine while others are waiting. This raises the perennial question: Is it okay to remove the absent owner's clothes from a machine to put in your own? Then there are those touchy times when three ladies with wet laundry are all waiting, hawklike, to pounce on one dryer as soon as it stops turning. These are the moments when people's true natures are revealed, moments that are sadly missed by those who have their own washer-dryers.

Ironing is a chore that I do only rarely, as most of our clothes are no-iron knits and cottons. In the RV we carry an iron but no ironing board. For some reason, campground laundries never have irons, and only the best-equipped RV resorts have ironing boards. So, for my one dress and two cotton shirts that need ironing, I usually just make do with a folded towel on our kitchen counter.

There is one final cleaning subject exclusive to RVers, and that is washing the exterior of the rig. Some diligent folks seem to be forever washing, polishing, and waxing their units—especially those with new, high-end motorhomes. Mark and I get tired just watching them. In our first three years on the road, we had the trailer washed only four times (and this includes the pom-pom squad's carwash in Illinois, which hardly counts) and waxed once. Each time, it looked great for a few days, until we hitched up and moved on. By the time we arrived at our next destination, it looked just as dull and dusty as ever.

The same can be said of my early efforts to keep the louvered windows clean. No matter how sparkling I got them, they immediately took on another layer of road goo. Or, in the case of South Padre Island, Texas—where gale-force winds blew off the water every day—another layer of salt spray. The guy parked next to us on our glorious oceanfront row just shook his head when he saw me scrubbing the glass squeaky clean. "Why are you doing such a good job on that?" he said. "By tomorrow you won't even be able to tell you did it." And right he was.

Eventually Mark and I just accepted Mother Nature's cleaning system—free rain. We don't even feel guilty about it anymore.

25 Kingsport, Tennessee
November 3

I think I never want to be anywhere else in the fall for the rest of my life than here in the southern Appalachians. The colors are succulent, covering hills that roll on toward the horizon, making for layer upon layer upon layer of hue. Wow.

Yesterday Donia and I finally left the Escapees park at Raccoon Valley, just north of Knoxville. We went there October 13, planning to stay a few days, and we just stayed and stayed. For a few days during that time, we ran over to Pigeon Forge to meet my mother and father, up from Atlanta for a few days of touristy fun. Donia and my Mom went crafts shopping in nearby Gatlinburg and brought me a great present—one of those little wooden letter-holders that mounts on the wall. I can put it up next to my side of the bed and finally have a handy place to put my glasses so I won't step on them in the middle of the night. When you're living in such tight quarters, little things like a wooden letter-holder can do wonders for your quality of life.

Cleo has already told you about our foray to Cotton Eyed Joe, the dance palace, and our fun times with insanely friendly Escapees in Raccoon Valley. I, however, don't share her look-down-my-long-dog-nose attitude about these folks. I *liked* a place where it felt like you had neighbors you've known for years. One gave us a tip on how to get half-price tickets to a nearby singin' and dancin' show produced by The Grand Ol' Opry. Another steered us to an interesting museum in Oak Ridge (Motto: America's Secret City® Shhhhh®), where the uranium was produced for the A-bomb in World War II. I talked to several guys about some problems we've had with our trailer, and got good advice and help.

I was able to return the favors, helping several people get their Internet connections straight. We shared many thoughts about finding telephone jacks, signing up for cellular phone service, where to spend the winter, how to drive to Alaska, and the like. Oh, and yes we did trade ideas for keeping our holding tanks fresh and sweet. Plus, as Escapees members, we had rates that were about half what we'd normally pay for the same quality site and hookups.

You are told at an Escapees park that most of the work is done by volunteers, and are gently nudged toward volunteering for something. We saw a need and filled it. No one knew anything about surrounding golf courses, so we undertook to write a guide to all five courses within a thirty-minute drive of the campground. We printed it with our word processor, complete with fees, driving directions, and course descriptions, and compiled it all into a folder along with sample scorecards. Of course to do this accurately, we had to play all five of the courses. Well, it was a tough job, but somebody had to do it.

We also fell in with the local Knoxville bridge community, insanely friendly people of another sort, at two club games we played in early in our stay. They told us about their upcoming sectional tournament, which was to be held in their brand-new, city-built bridge center, and led us to believe that they would bite our ankles if we tried to leave before the event. These folks fixed us up with partners, fed us, and even let us win master points. The highlight for me was playing Saturday night and two sessions on Sunday with a bridge teacher and club director who had many, many master points. I got, in effect, a three-session, free playing lesson.

In between all the fun stuff we did as part of this day-camp lifestyle we lead, we found Knoxville a wonderful place to just "live." It's a manageable size. The weather was moderate. The traffic was okay. The shopping was great. We did our errands, walked our dog, read our newspapers, went to the mall, watched TV, enjoyed a lovely dinner at the home of some warm, wonderful cousins of ours who live here. All the stuff that people who live in real houses in real places do. The surroundings were pretty, with rolling hills all around and the Cumberland Mountains on the outskirts, and the fall colors creeping toward their peak during our three-week stay.

Today we're at a little campground in the tri-cities of Tennessee (Bristol, Johnson City, Kingsport), about eighty miles from Raccoon Valley. We've always heard the tri-cities were nice, and we're going to spend a couple of days checking them out. It's been said that the best barbecue in America is available in nearby Bluff City. Who knows, we might stay three weeks!

A quick preview of our upcoming plans: We head next to Wake Forest, North Carolina, just north of Raleigh, to visit with some old friends. Then it's a straight shot down I-95 to Orlando, for the national bridge tournament we're playing in during Thanksgiving week with seven of our bridge buddies/best friends from the D.C. area. We can't wait to see them! After that, we'll spend another week at Disney World. (What, you think we don't need vacations too???) Finally we will wander for three weeks on the Atlantic coast around Savannah and Charleston and Myrtle Beach before docking in Atlanta for Christmas with my family.

Hope this letter finds all of you well, and as insanely happy as we are.

Love,
Mark

26 Where Do You Shop?

People who live in one place don't have to think a whole lot about routine shopping—they know exactly where their favorite stores are and what they have to offer. We, on the other hand, are always starting from square one, in places we have never seen before or even knew existed. Seeking out the most basic needs, such as groceries and diesel fuel, becomes a kind of municipal treasure hunt. At the very least, it's a great way to explore a new area.

Blindfolded, I could stick a pushpin in a map of our travels and recall a shopping adventure in nearly any place it landed. Take Knoxville, Tennessee, for instance. We loved being in Knoxville because it seemed just the right size, and its northwest commercial corridor was a gold mine of big-name stores we hadn't seen for a long time. We spent most of a morning indulging in our ultimate luxury—going to a Borders superstore and getting a Starbucks coffee to sip while we walked around ogling the new books. We also browsed through a Bed, Bath and Beyond, and ate pho at a Vietnamese noodle house. But mostly, we just enjoyed the Oz-like vision of all that shopping opportunity in one place, even though there was nothing we really needed to buy.

Or maybe that pushpin lands on Eagle River, the Wisconsin vacation mecca where we bought our change-of-life Teva sandals that have served us so well. Or the mid-sized college town of Missoula, Montana, where I faced the paralyzing prospect of buying a dress to wear to my son's wedding. I fully expected the search to take all day, maybe two. Before heading to the mall, we wandered into a funky Main Street home decor boutique, which also happened to have a few oddball dresses on sale. While the salesladies were all in a dither over an imported ceramic lion whose head had broken off, Mark pulled a dress off the rack for me to try on. Within ten minutes I had found a perfect mother-of-the-groom frock, in that most unlikely of places.

Our needs are usually more mundane—no matter where we go, we can always find an excuse to drop by the local Wal-Mart. Why do we love Wal-Marts so much? I swear, Mark actually falls into a hypnotic state when he walks through the front doors into that wonderland of ballpoint pens and cotton undies, vitamin supplements and WD-40. I suppose the place represents a comforting oasis of familiarity in a sea of the strange and unknown. You know exactly how the aisles are organized, what products you're going to find, where the bathrooms are located—*and* that you can return items purchased at one store to another store farther down the road, if necessary.

Wal-Marts also hold a special place in our hearts because of their hospitality to RVers. We have stayed overnight in their parking lots a few times and always felt right at home. In fact, as we began to criss-cross America, Mark and I developed a hierarchy of towns pivoting on the existence or nonexistence of a Wal-Mart (see box).

In a category all their own are the tourist towns, large or small, that feature antique stores, gift and souvenir shops, art galleries, outdoor-outfitter boutiques, outlet malls, and other ways for travelers to spend their money. Nowadays these "Cute-ification of America" spots can be found everywhere—from the deserts of the Southwest to the North Woods of Wisconsin to the hollows of Appalachia. After our first summer on the road, I totally lost interest in visiting them. They end up all looking alike to me, and they're always filled with high-priced goodies that I want but don't need. On a fixed income, we lean toward places that have things we do need, at low prices. We're nomads, not tourists.

For grocery shopping, we go mostly to large chain stores. They're more likely to have the pine nuts, fresh salmon steaks, and decent fruits and vegetables that we can't seem to live without. With our limited storage space, we end up shopping fairly often. I'm always amused by the classic advice given by consumer writers: To economize, buy bulk items from warehouse clubs. Good grief—where do you keep all this stuff? If Mark and I bought paper towels in a twelve-roll bundle, they would have to live on the sofa until we used them up. Here's a shocking scoop: We buy the highly uneconomical eight-ounce jars of mayonnaise because they fit into the narrow shelves in the refrigerator door.

But we're great supermarket connoisseurs, so going often is no hardship. We love to see how the big chains differ from region to region. Grocery-wise, the East Coast megalopolis has nothing on the Midwest. Some of the stores we've shopped at in out-of-

---

 ## Where's the Wal-Mart?

For diversion on long driving days, Mark and I make a game out of ranking towns based loosely on their Wal-Mart quotients. Our 1-to-5 scale has the following categories:

1. **Large City, U.S.A.** With sprawl, population 1,000,000+. Freeway-girdled metropolis where several interstates connect. Suburbs stretch for miles in every direction. The old downtown may still be a vital center of banking and commerce, like Chicago, or transformed into a quaint historic theme park, like St. Louis. But in any event, most routine shopping is done in the suburbs. Enclosed malls and strip shopping clusters abound. In the big commercial corridors, it's hard to find a store or restaurant that *isn't* part of a national chain. Wal-Marts and Wal-Mart Supercenters are everywhere.

2. **Small City, U.S.A.** Population 500,000 or so. Several major highways intersect here, with primary shopping areas radiating out from the center along these routes. City center has a historic district plus a newer section, but most businesses are offices, banks, and restaurants, as

continued

shopping has moved out along the highways. Here there are numerous chain restaurants, big-box stores, and several Wal-Marts—take your pick. Has two or possibly three enclosed malls on the periphery, anchored by a wide variety of department stores.

3. **Large Town, U.S.A.** Population 100,000. Generally located near an interstate highway, if not right on one. Has a Wal-Mart Supercenter, with groceries, and maybe a smaller Wal-Mart or two as well in another part of town. Has many downtown stores and services, though they tend to be marginal businesses like used bookstores and local nonprofit agencies if larger stores have moved into strip shopping centers on the outskirts. The mall may be anchored by a Sears or J.C. Penney instead of a full-line department store.

4. **Small Town, U.S.A.** Population 25,000. Located near a major U.S. highway, maybe an interstate. Shopping evenly distributed between old downtown and newer commercial district around junction of highways. Includes at least one large supermarket, a few fast-food restaurants and other national chain stores, and many local businesses. *Whew, there's a Wal-Mart!* Might even see a small, closed-down Wal-Mart across the street from the large, new Wal-Mart built to replace it.

5. **Dot on the Map, U.S.A.** Population: Not many. Possibly no buildings left there at all, or maybe the two-lane blacktop widens briefly into Main Street, with diagonal parking, as it passes through town. Stores with turn-of-the-century facades—most still in business—might include a locally owned beauty shop, a lonely insurance agent, a thrift shop, a gift/knickknack shop, and a café or bar or two. The gas pumps are at the mini-mart. There might be a small, independent grocery store, maybe a fast-food restaurant or two, and a K-Mart or Ames store, out by the highway. But, alas, no Wal-Mart.

the-way Indiana and Iowa towns had far more impressive inventories than major D.C.-area chains. And wherever we shop, Mark signs up for a discount club card so we can get the in-store savings on featured specials. We now have a fat collection of cards—Kroger, Winn-Dixie, Shop Rite, King Soopers, Safeway, Smith's, Vons, City Market, Furrs, Giant, and Food Lion. We make a game out of buying the discount items of the week. Hey, it offsets those mayonnaise expenses.

Sadly, the presence of supermarkets and other big-box stores "out by the highway" often signals a semideserted downtown, marked by the boarded-up storefronts of local merchants who could not compete with the big guns. Like it or not, this is the American retail reality of the past few decades. The shift may not seem so dramatic to people living in one place, but it really hits home for full-timers, who see it played out over and over, in every state in the union. The worst was Cairo, Illinois, a once-vital Mississippi River port whose abandoned downtown resembled a bombed-out war zone. On a happier note, we loved seeing the wonderful restoration efforts of towns like Portland, Oregon, and Duluth, Minnesota, which have transformed flagging downtowns or grungy warehouse districts into attractive urban centers with offices, shops, and restaurants.

Despite our affection for large supermarkets and Wal-Marts, Mark and I do try to shop at small locally owned hardware stores, meat markets, bakeries, and vegetable stands every chance we get. We also never pass up a mom 'n' pop bookstore—that most endangered of retail species. Not only are we doing our small part to keep small, independent businesses alive, it's also the best way to get the true flavor of a region. A standout in this category was Larry McMurtry's multibuilding used bookstore in tiny Archer City, Texas.

In fact, sampling the local color in places we pass through is one of the things we love best about our roaming lifestyle. The most fun Christmas shopping we ever did was during our first year on the road, when we picked up food specialties all over the Southeast to package as family gifts. What a great excuse to go wild buying pricey items like Minnie Mouse-shaped pasta from Disney World, pralines and flavored cocktail peanuts from Savannah, taffy from Myrtle Beach, microbrew beer from Jacksonville, and four kinds of hot sauce from Charleston!

In addition to shopping for consumable items, we sometimes need to find specialized or personal services in the towns we pass through—a printer repair shop, a tax service, a beauty salon. Usually, we ask campground staffers to recommend local businesses. On occasions when we need to arrange things in advance, we use our travel-planning and phone-directory CD-Roms to look up services in a town we plan to visit and print out a map to get us to the place.

Naturally you feel a bit insecure at first, getting work done by strangers in unfamiliar places. Like the time I took a beloved needlework sampler I'd just completed and entrusted it to the owner of a frame shop in Paducah, Kentucky. She was to size, mat, and frame the piece, then pack it up and mail it to Travis and Amy in New York. And all of this, after we had left town. In the end, the woman did a beautiful job, but I couldn't know this for sure until I had a chance to visit the kids many months later and see it hanging on their wall. Over time, we found many such craftspersons and technicians in our travels—competent, reasonable, friendly, and relaxed. We just trusted our gut instincts in selecting them, and we were never disappointed.

Well, *almost* never. Hair care is the one exception. All good haircuts are alike, but each bad one is a unique boo-boo that just has to grow out with time. While Mark has gotten fairly consistent results from walk-in barber shops, I have found truly amazing variations in beauty shops across America. And satisfaction has nothing to do with price. I've walked in off the street and gotten wonderful trim jobs for $12. And, on a friend's recommendation, I've made an appointment at a high-priced salon where I paid $40 for a cut that looked like the stylist had put a bowl on my head and cut around it.

I once went to a salon in a South Texas mobile home park, where the owner kept up a heated critique in Spanish as her novice assistant was trimming my hair. The owner occasionally left her own customer to stomp over and pull up tufts of my hair that the assistant had missed. Somehow or other, though, it ended up one of the best cuts I ever got, and a bargain at $7.

Most memorable of all was the agitated young stylist in Georgia. She answered my polite "How are you today?" by telling me she was running late because she had recently stopped taking her medication for Obsessive-Compulsive Disorder, and had to make sure that all the screw heads on her light switches were lined up parallel before leaving the house. Whereupon she took out her razor and started briskly chopping at my hair.

Yes, indeed, all you folks out there who have been getting perfect haircuts from the same reliable stylist for fifteen years— you just don't know what you're missing.

27 Kissimmee, Florida
November 25

Incredible as it may seem, I've been incarcerated in a DOG KENNEL for the duration of this big bridge wingding in Orlando. My Humans must've felt guilty about sticking me in this place, because they said I could make my column this time as long as I wanted. Okay, they asked for it.

No "Pen Pal" Jokes, Please

So here I am in this so-called Bass Pet Motel. Fishy? Yeah, you bet. That's what I call it when people only get locked up when they commit crimes, but DOGS get put in the slammer for doing nothing wrong at all. Oh, sure, this is a country club-type joint surrounded by lawns and gardens, with spacious, combination indoor/outdoor cells for each inmate, and "personal play time" with the staff for only $2 more a day. But it's jail, nevertheless. So I've decided to go on a hunger strike to protest the kind of treatment dogs suffer while their Humans are off having fun.

Like, for example, these bridge fanatics I live with are staying in a fancy-schmancy hotel with palm trees and car-park guys, just so they can play bridge around the clock without having to worry about coming back to the trailer to walk me every eight hours or so. This bridge thing has been building up for months. You should see the e-mail. The bridge buddies exchange problems like, "Playing Standard American, not '2-over-1,' you hold S-AKXX, H-AXXXXX, D-KQ, C-X. You open one heart. Partner bids two clubs. What is your call?" My call would of course be, "Get a life!"

Kissimmee Deadly

Anyway, getting back to ME. I got major sand flea bites when we first got here, so Dad gave me a cortisone pill to stop the itching. Then we took a ride down the main drag in this burg called Kissimmee, and wow! Those drugs were giving me like, awesome hallucinations! I saw a Twistee Treet ice cream stand in the shape of a huge soft-serve cone with colored jimmies on top! Shell World, featuring a vintage Volkswagen totally encrusted with shells and mermaid paintings! The Arabian Nights shopping center with red neon minarets on every store and a laser-show skyscraper bungee jumping ride! Jurassic Putt Mini-Golf with scary dinosaurs guarding the holes! Al Capone's dinner show with gangsters and dancing flappers! AND the World's Largest McDonald's. So if you ever have a chance to visit this place, be sure to bring your drugs! (And a lot of money.)

Me-e-e-e-m-ories . . .

Now I have nothing to do all day but languish in this wire cell and think of good times past. Like in the beginning of November, when we stayed in our best campsite ever at our friends Pete and Robin's family compound in Wake Forest, North Carolina. We parked our trailer for a week on their beautiful grassy field next to some pine trees, and I got to run free the whole time! Pete and Robin are extremely cool dog people who have three dogs themselves, named in honor of Pete's Marine fighter pilot days. There's the old father dog, Company C, and his two grown sons, Alpha and Harley. This has something to do with birth order, I believe. They are of the "Yard Dog" breed, meaning they stay out on the porch all day and bark at anything they please.

While we were there we had to string together a bunch of extension cords to get electricity from the house of Pete's parents, who are both very old and have their own wheelchairs, but are also very cool dog people. Well, it rained one night, and one especially ratty old cord "made ground faults," whatever that means, which cut off our power. So Dad had to keep sneaking up to their house in the dead of night to "reset the circuit breakers." For us full-timers, the utility adventures are never-ending.

Mom tried out one day for a new career in nail pulling and brick cleaning. This is a job in the "house deconstruction" field, which is something Pete practically invented back in the 1970s. It means you take apart old nineteenth-century houses board by board, and reuse the lumber and bricks and stuff to build new houses, which makes them look like old houses. Plus, it helps keep good stuff out of our nation's landfills. Anyway, after twenty years this concept has finally caught on, and now the local papers are writing all these articles about Pete, calling him "the Father of Deconstruction."

Mom returned from her day of deconstruction looking just like Pig Pen from the Peanuts comics. She had dirt and bruises and scratches all over. But she was extremely cheerful, because, as the story goes, some twenty-two-year-old fellow deconstruction worker spent the whole day flirting with her with his thirteen words of English, even though she explained to him with her seven words of Spanish that she had children older than him and a husband who was probably arriving any minute. Apparently four of Ricardo's English words were, "Joo have beyooteefool eyes." Boy, middle-aged women get their kicks in weird ways.

Stayin' Alive on I-95

Everywhere you go in this country, in dinky towns you've never heard of, they have statues and plaques and museums devoted to Humans who were born there in total obscurity and later got famous. One day we found ourselves exiting the highway at tiny Smithfield, North Carolina, in search of the Ava Gardner Museum. Imagine our disappointment when the sign on the door said "Museum Open 12 to 4," and it was then only 10 a.m. Mom and Dad had to be content to peer through the flyspecked windows to see the faded publicity photos thumbtacked to the walls, and the dress Miss Gardner wore in *Showboat*. Now here's a trivia quiz for you: Can you name Ava Gardner's three famous husbands? (Answers at the bottom.)

But we had to be moving along, because Dad had just seen a billboard for the World's Largest Cigar Store just off I-95 in nearby Selma, North Carolina, and it was making him crazy. Never mind that he just ordered $250 worth of cigars from a catalog, to be shipped to Grandma and Grandpa Steele's place. Mom says when you're going to be at a relative's house soon for Christmas, you do all your mail-order buying for the foreseeable future. I know all you Humans in fixed-foundation houses take mail-order shopping for granted, but we can't very well have the Land's End delivery boy chasing our RV down the road, can we? Anyway, at the exit for The World's Largest Cigar Store, Dad suddenly remembered that he "forgot" he couldn't live without a box of La Gloria Cubana Robustos and a few others. So now he's got $387 worth of cigars.

Mom and Dad, Blowin' Smoke

Entering hour two of this pet motel hunger strike, I am cruelly reminded of our visit to a world-famous barbecue restaurant called the Georgia Pig, also just off I-95 at Brunswick, Georgia. The folks told me beforehand I could eat barbecue, too, but when they saw this place they decided it didn't look fit for a dog to eat in—mud parking lot, broken porch, burned-down woodshed, patched and tarred roof. Of course, that didn't stop THEM. I had to wait in the truck. They came back a long time later, looking giddy and smelling of smoked pork.

My Life As a Twenty-Pound Dog

When we first got to Florida, Mom wanted to visit the Tampa Bay area, which she felt nostalgic about because she once changed planes there in 1957. (Hey, don't ask me, I just live with these people.) So get this: When they call to make a reservation at this chi-chi campground in Palm Harbor, the lady says they only allow dogs twenty pounds and under. Mom says, "With all her long hair Cleo looks bigger than twenty pounds, but she's very well behaved!" Yeah, right, I'm twenty pounds of dog with fifty pounds of fur. Now I have to act like some Mexican hairless or toy poodle? Talk about pressure! I can't bark, I can't pee on this dame's precious shrubs, I can't poop anywhere on campground soil under pain of death—and then, even though my behavior was impeccable, this woman still booted us out after only one night. Something about a previous reservation for our site, was her excuse. Humph.

But like all setbacks in our new life, this one turned out fine in the end. We just moved over to the campground across the street, where the people were nicer, and it was cheaper, and they had a Rottweiler puppy for me to play with. We had great fun the rest of the time in the Bay area, driving around looking at all the rich people's houses in Saint Petersburg, and visiting this seaside town called Tarpon Springs where they have a gazillion fishing boats and Greek restaurants.

One of the old boat guys yelled at us from the sidewalk and even invited me to come on his sponge-diving tour boat—"Ten dollars for the dog, and the people can come for free!" But Mom and Dad were really more interested in getting carry-out from one of those Greek restaurants. I'm practically fainting right now, just thinking of those little pieces of bread Mom kept feeding me under the picnic table in the park. That Greek bread is the BEST.

Oops . . . The kennel keepers are coming around with the inmates' food. I guess they don't know I'm on a hunger strike. Well, maybe it shouldn't be a TOTAL hunger strike. A semi-hunger strike would make the same point, and still keep me strong enough to carry on the fight. I mean, what good am I to the cause if I'm dead? Okay, gotta go. Till next time,

Love 'n' Licks,

Cleo

(Oh yeah, Ava Gardner trivia quiz answers: Mickey Rooney, Artie Shaw, and Frank Sinatra)

28 Do You Eat Out a Lot?

Cleo comes honestly by her obsession with food. Just look at the Humans she lives with. As my son Travis once described our new lifestyle: "My folks have gone out to dinner—for a few years."

Full-timing is truly a movable feast for people who love food as Mark and I do. Lots of people who stay put love good food, too—but even if your home is surrounded by every possible kind of restaurant, there is no way to duplicate the experience of moving from place to place, enjoying distinctive regional specialties like Pacific Ocean Dungeness crabs, Amish shoofly pie, and Cajun *boudin*, right where they grown, caught, cured, stuffed, or spiced.

People are always asking us if we eat out more often since we hit the road, and whether we don't get tired of all those restaurants. The answer is, our ratio of dining out versus cooking in is about the same as it was back home in Virginia. We still shop for groceries a couple of times a week, cook something from scratch nearly every day, and eat 85 percent of our meals in our RV. The difference is, when we do go out, there's far more variety in restaurants than we ever had at home.

It was a grand stroke of destiny when a friend gave us a copy of Jane and Michael Stern's *Eat Your Way Across the U.S.A.* as a farewell present. This modest paperback, a revision and expansion of the authors' earlier classic, *Road Food,* quickly became our travel bible. Although the authors do mention a few of their favorite haute cuisine restaurants, their primary focus is on the same kind of down-home places Mark and I would choose—homey diners, crab shacks, hamburger joints, barbecue pits, funky lunch counters and cafeterias, and home-cooking meccas with cracked-vinyl booths where the same waitresses have served the same customers for forty years.

Thanks to the Sterns, we had fried green tomatoes at the original Whistle Stop Café in Irondale, Alabama; Chinook Eggs (poached eggs on savory salmon patties) for brunch at the Classen Grill in Oklahoma City; and cabrito (goat) tortillas at El Norteno in Albuquerque, New Mexico. We once spent two entire days in Memphis, trying out one barbecue place after another. Another time we drove two states away (a 220-mile round trip) to have lunch at Lambert's famous roadhouse in Sikeston, Missouri—"Home of the Throwed Rolls." You raise your hand, and a waiter standing halfway across the dining room throws you a roll warm from the oven. Honestly, how could you resist a place like this, when you're camped just 100 miles away?

We even planned parts of our travel route according to *Eat Your Way* restaurants that we wanted to try. We learned the hard way, though, that it's best to call ahead. When we detoured through Decorah, Iowa, specifically to try two eateries, we found that both of them had gone out of business. Boy, did we feel stupid, standing there on the sidewalk. But all was not lost, as we ran across a fantastic farmers' market in town that had every late-summer vegetable you could name. And we got a spacious, tree-shaded campsite for only $10 in Decorah's city park by the river.

This is not to imply that Mark and I can't find restaurants by ourselves. In fact, we have our own list of favorites we'd like to tell the world about. Mark's time-tested method for restaurant selection in a strange town is the Full-Parking-Lot Rule: Always go to the restaurant that has the most vehicles in its parking lot, even if it's surrounded by places that look better on the outside. Trust the locals; they know where the good food is. Thus did we discover gems like the wonderful Onate Basque supper club in Boise, a place of heavenly food and timeless ambience. And the Main Street Diner in Buffalo, Wyoming, a Naugahyde-stool joint where we lunched on world-class burgers, home-cut fries, and made-from-scratch tomato soup. And the Bluebonnet Café, a no-nonsense eatery in Marble Falls, Texas, where there are always so many customers lined up for the chicken-fried steak and banana cream pie that the staff has taken to seating singles and doubles at large shared tables in the middle of the dining room.

Sometimes it's the ambience that attracts us, as in the case of the Legs Inn in Cross Village, Michigan, where we were drawn by the goofy sight of wood-stove legs forming a railing around the gabled roof. And the soup-to-nuts Polish feast we ate there wasn't bad, either. Then there was the inimitable Ajax Café on the waterfront in tiny Port Hadlock, Washington. We had heard about this place where guests are offered a selection of zany accessories to wear as they dine. But until you try it, folks, you can't imagine the silly fun of eating dinner in a General Patton helmet and polka-dot clip-on tie (Mark) or a fluffy chicken hat with long yellow feet dangling down like pigtails (that would be *moi*). And of course, you're surrounded all the while by other guests laughing at each other in French Foreign Legion caps, Abe Lincoln stovepipes, fifties-style pillbox hats with veils, and sweeping lavender feather boas.

In those inevitable stretches between restaurants, there's always the pleasure of buying foodstuffs an area is best known for—buffalo meat in Wyoming, *nopalitos* (cactus leaves) in South Texas—and taking them home to experiment with. We are suckers for anyone selling produce or seafood on a dock, out of a roadside lean-to, or off the back of a truck. A standout here was lamb stew and fry bread that Navajo women in New Mexico sell from battered cookware off beat-up truck tailgates in dusty parking lots. But this is not to slight the smoked salmon jerky we got on the Oregon coast, or the fresh Texas peaches, Michigan cherries, Washington apples, and other fruits obtained at the peak of their in-season ripeness.

In our travels we are always running across recipes for local specialties like the great recipe for baked potato soup on a postcard in an Idaho potato museum, and several recipes for crawfish étouffée picked up at a Cajun cooking presentation in Louisiana. We once stopped at a South Carolina welcome center where visitors were greeted by an entire table of freebie print materials, courtesy of a local literacy campaign. For some reason, there was a major emphasis on Louisiana cooking. We left with a small, spiral-bound New Orleans cookbook that has been a mainstay of our kitchen ever since.

By now you're probably getting the idea that full-timing is tough on waistlines. No question about it! We always plan to get a grip as soon as we leave the delicious region we're in, but it never seems to work out. *We'll eat light when we get to Michigan.* Except for a few different kinds of Cornish pasties at that pasty shop. Where else are we ever gonna get Cornish pasties? *Well, it will be easy to diet when we get to Indiana. What does Indiana have, anyway?* Yikes, forgot about that heaven-in-every-bite raspberry cream pie at Das Dutchman Essenhaus. *Okay, then Kentucky. For sure, we cut down in Kentucky.* Wait a minute—Kentucky has barbecue!

I say "we," but actually Mark doesn't spend a lot of time thinking about waistline control. His motto is, I'm not overweight, I can read the charts, I'm just eight inches too short. But I—a Weight Watchers veteran several times over—need to keep focused on the key question: Can I still button my jeans? Living in an RV, I really don't have room for two entire sets of clothes, size 12 petite and size 14 petite.

Of course, there is an obvious solution here—and it is Exercise. Some RVers claim they get a lot more exercise naturally, including all the physical work they do around the rig. Lots of RV parks have swimming pools, tennis courts, and exercise rooms with workout equipment. The large winter-resort parks even offer organized calisthenics and water aerobics programs. Some campgrounds have marked off walking trails around park roadways or through adjacent woods. Others are located in an urban or residential area where the surrounding neighborhood is available for an early morning power-walk or bicycle ride. I wish I could say that Mark and I are conscientious about exercising, but I'm afraid our typical workout consists of walking the dog. We will choose serious eating over serious exercising any day.

RVers just love to eat, period. They love Sunday-afternoon ice cream socials. They love sitting around the picnic table eating hors d'oeuvres while they cook out on portable grills. They especially love going out to restaurants. At Texas Trails the retirees kept talking about a place some fifteen miles distant that served giant hamburgers for $8.95. One day we drove out there to see for ourselves. Nothing we'd heard had prepared us for the eye-popping hamburger, twelve inches in diameter, that the waitress brought out on a plate the size of a pizza pan. At home, it took us three days to finish off the doggy bag.

Even when the focus is on a totally non-food-related activity, RVers will happily turn it into an excuse to eat. In South Texas I took part in a twice-weekly quilting bee, where one Tuesday a woman brought along some fabulous homemade cookies to share. Now the race was on. Everybody had to try to outdo last week's snack with her own irresistible baked goodies. One quilter had diabetes and couldn't eat the sweets; she started bringing deviled eggs.

Campground potlucks are another beloved tradition where campers try to outdo one another with a staggering smorgasbord of dishes that must average sixty-five calories per bite. Yummy creations laden with sausage, sour cream, hamburger meat, pasta, cheddar cheese, or condensed mushroom soup are the norm. Don't be fooled by the potluck variation known as a "salad luncheon," either. The typical salad is a molded gelatin dish made with whipped cream, fruit, and nuts—and half of the total array is desserts.

Naturally, Mark and I are big fans of campground potlucks. We invested in one of those insulated carriers with handles, which Mark calls our "Rio Grande Valley briefcase." It's indispensable for keeping a 9x13-inch casserole dish warm en route to the rec hall. Also, like many other RVers, we bought ourselves some large partitioned plastic trays to take to potlucks, because—let's face it—no regular plate is big enough.

29 Orlando, Florida
December 7

You just got to love a place where one big sign on the interstate points to Tampa and the other points to Magic Kingdom.

The bridge tournament in Orlando was wonderful and intense. Both Donia and I played mix-and-match style with a group of our friends who traveled down from Washington for the event— seven days straight, two or three sessions a day, each session demanding three hours or so of intense concentration. Then, when you play three sessions in a day, the rushing out for meals and finding time to sleep only adds to the stress. *We love it!*

When the tournament ended, we hitched up and hopped over to Fort Wilderness, the campground at Walt Disney World. Friends, the World still shines. *Warning:* Anyone who is not a lover of Walt Disney World might as well stop reading right here. Trekkies got their Star Trek. I got my Disney. I can't get enough! Fortunately, these weeks between Thanksgiving and Christmas are the least crowded of the entire year, with virtually no lines to stand in, so I actually *can* get enough.

As an illustration, here's what we did on Monday, our first full Disney day: Took our friend Bob to the airport (6:30 a.m.), bailed Cleo out of jail, got lost driving to Magic Kingdom and were waved through to a "backstage" area (I guess with my boss truck, they just took me for a plumber), found the right parking lot, rode the tram and then the monorail (Whoosh!) to the park, met our friends Ken and JJ. Then we rode Space Mountain, Walt Disney's Carousel of Progress, Buzz Lightyear's Space Ranger Spin, Tomorrowland Transit Authority (stopped to eat a smoked turkey leg), the ExtraTERRORestrial Alien Encounter, Mickey's Toontown Fair, Mickey's Country House, Cinderella's Golden Carousel, and "It's a Small World After All" (yes, we put our sanity on the line and survived). Next we watched the Snow White's Friends Characters Parade, drank bottled water, and toured the Haunted Mansion, Pirates of the Caribbean, and the Enchanted Tiki Room Under New Management. Whew. Then we rode the monorail and tram and our truck back to camp. Walked Cleo. Took the monorail to EPCOT (Experimental Prototype Community of Tomorrow), ate a great Moroccan dinner in "Morocco" and rode the Norway Maelstrom in "Norway," watched the laser-and-fireworks show (narrated by Walter Cronkite), spent forty minutes at Guest Relations straightening out a minor ticket mix-up . . . went home, walked Cleo, and went to bed!

We haven't kept up quite that pace on the following days, but by the time we leave tomorrow, there won't be much of the World that we haven't seen. Sure, some of Disney is a bit tarnished by time. The moving walkways and monorails are familiar features in many airports now. The reduced-scale architecture of "Main Street U.S.A." is on view at many other tourist venues. Even the computer-controlled drip irrigation system, touted as "agriculture of the future" in EPCOT's The Land exhibit, is standard equipment in the gardens of many of the larger houses I inspected before I retired.

But these are exceptions. Mostly the magic still shines, and the best of it sparkles in Disney's whimsical, witty way. My heart still was gladdened by the dancing fountains and twinkle-lit paving stones at EPCOT, Cinderella's Golden Carousel and the Peter Pan ride in Magic Kingdom, and the gently satiric handbills (pasted over the Post No Bills notice) on the stucco walls of Africa Land at the new Animal Kingdom.

Two changes in the World are clearly Signs of our Times. The script of the entertaining Jungle River Cruise (where Nixon's press secretary Ron Nessen got his start!) was altered last April when Animal Kingdom opened. No longer does the pith-helmeted boat driver pull out a pistol and shoot the ear-wiggling hippos that are threatening our boat. She just shoos them away.

Well, disarmed she may have been, but disarming still. And EPCOT's Exxon-sponsored World of Energy attraction is now hosted by Ellen "Bet-you're-surprised-to-see-*me*-here" Degeneres. Yes I was, and mightily heartened as well.

Finally this trip we have had time to explore the World beyond the parks. The new resort complexes are spectacular. Each is designed with a different look that extends to the architecture, interior decorations, restaurant menus, even the employee uniforms, or "cast costumes," as they are called at Disney. There is the Wilderness Lodge (great hewn beams and American Indian artifacts); Old Key West (date palms and wide, slatted porches); Dixie Landing (riverboat landing, straw-hatted desk clerks); and so on through Grand Floridian, Polynesian, Contemporary, Caribbean Islands, Boardwalk, Yacht Club, and Beach Club.

Donia has been having a real time-warp experience. She brought Curry here in 1975 (and was seven months pregnant with Travis) soon after the park opened. At the time, Disney World consisted of only the Magic Kingdom and the Contemporary and Polynesian resorts. All agog, she has said approximately 439 times, "This part is all *different* now!"

Ah, but all good things must come to an end—especially with campground fees over $35 a night. Tomorrow we hitch up and head north, visiting Savannah and Myrtle Beach again en route to Atlanta.

Here's hoping your holidays are filled with cheer and all the lights around you are twinkling.

Love,
Mark

Tybee Island, Georgia
December 13

ERRATA!

Our eagle-eyed friend Bob Schwenk promptly pointed out to us that Nixon's press secretary was Ron Ziegler. Ron Nessen was Ford's press secretary after Jerry ter Horst quit.

Moreover, our California friend Bob Doyle informed us that Ron Ziegler did his hippo shooting at the original jungle ride in Anaheim, "not that ersatz place in Orlando."

We regret the errors, and any embarrassment it might have caused any of you who've been casually dropping names of past presidential press secretaries and their Disney connections into holiday dinner party conversations.

Cheers,

Mark

30 Don't You Miss Real Vacations?

If you define a vacation as taking a break from your job to travel somewhere new and different and have fun, then the notion of retired RV full-timers going on vacation might seem a bit strange. Instead, think of a vacation as taking a break from your ordinary life routine. Since our ordinary routine is traveling, this means that sitting still for a while is our idea of a great vacation.

Yes, Donia and I did spend nearly a week at Disney World during the Christmas season. But just as big a thrill was our stay at an Orlando hotel—a big Quality Inn that offered an amazing $45 rate for bridge players—during the previous week's tournament. This spared us the hassle of commuting from an outlying RV park at 8 a.m. and midnight every day, and paying pricey parking fees for the truck. It also gave us more time to socialize with our friends from the D.C. area who met us at the tournament. As an added bonus—sorry, old girl—sending Cleo to the Bass Pet Motel for the week gave us total freedom from dog walks.

The Quality Inn folks couldn't have been more accommodating when we explained our situation. At no extra charge they allowed us to park our entire rig in a large bus-parking area behind the hotel, and they put us in a room on the back side so we could keep an eye on it. We loved having our stuff close by. If there was a special shirt we had forgotten to "pack," we simply went out to the RV and got it. Same for our coffee maker, midnight snacks, special pillow, and wool blanket. These trips to the rig gave us a chance to check on our refrigerator, which we had switched from electric to propane. After a few days without an electric hookup, the electronic ignition on the fridge got a little squirrelly and needed to be manually restarted from time to time (a problem that was easily fixed at the next RV shop down the road).

It was also a treat having our own phone in the hotel room for a week. We could catch up on e-mail, do our banking, order books online, talk to parents and children—all without standing at a public pay phone. Having maid service wasn't bad either. After all these luxuries, spending five days at Disney World was just frosting on the cake.

The following year the fall bridge tournament took place at two huge Copley Square hotels in the heart of Boston. We knew there was no way we were going to get close to downtown Boston with our big rig, so we worked out our travel so we could park and plug in at Donia's cousin's farm outside Corpus Christi, Texas, and fly to Boston like regular people.

Another year, we went on a ten-day sailing trip to the South Seas with my sister Kathy and her husband, David, who had long planned this once-in-a-lifetime vacation to celebrate Dave's fiftieth birthday. This time, we would have to find a commercial storage place for our RV while we were gone, but our first few calls to Atlanta-area storage companies had not been encouraging.

As we were trying to figure it all out, we stayed overnight at a small rural campground about two hours south of Atlanta. On an impulse, I asked the friendly owner-manager if he offered storage. From the guy's expression it was clearly not a regular feature—but he quickly agreed to keep the trailer there for us, parked on the grass along the back fence, for $2 a day. "Mammaw sits in her mobile all day long looking out the window," he said. "She'll keep an eye on it. Nothing gets past her."

The following day we maneuvered the trailer into position under Mammaw's watchful eye and prepared to leave it sitting with no electric hookup at all for two weeks. This was too long for our batteries to hold out, we knew. So we drained our plumbing and put anti-freeze in our drain traps in case of a hard freeze. We also had to remove all perishables from the refrigerator, turn it off, and leave it propped open to air out for the duration.

I must admit I felt some qualms as we drove away in the truck leaving our home and possessions sitting there on the grass in that out-of-the-way place. But when we returned at the end of our trip—it turned out we were gone closer to three weeks than two—our gear was shipshape, just as we had left it. In fact, the interior of our fifth-wheel looked incredibly spacious to us after the cramped quarters of a chartered sailboat.

With a nod to Mammaw we hitched the trailer up to the truck and hauled it a short distance to a campsite with a water and electric hookup, where we plugged in and stayed for one more night. We needed this time to recharge the batteries, restock the refrigerator, unpack our sailing laundry, and get ready to hit the road again.

There is another type of vacation Donia and I occasionally enjoy, and that's taking solo trips. One of us goes away somewhere on a plane, and the other one stays home with the dog and trailer. So far we've never soloed to some exotic locale like Yucatan or the French Riviera; it's usually a bargain-ticket deal to a Midwest bridge event, or to visit Donia's children in the Northeast or my family in Atlanta. Since this break in the routine applies to both of us, it's just as much fun for the one who stays home as the one flying away. Though we love each other dearly, sometimes it's nice to take a breather.

But of all the routine-busters for full-timers, the ultimate is spending winters parked at an RV resort someplace warm. By now Donia and I have tried several of the so-called snowbird parks, and every one—whether in Florida, South Texas, or Arizona—has had the same go-go atmosphere as a kids' summer camp. At Winter Camp for Seniors, the activity schedule begins with 7 a.m. free-weight workouts, then continues with water aerobics, square- and round- and line-dancing, billiards, woodworking, Spanish lessons, ping-pong, golf outings, shuffleboard, tennis, quilting, arts and crafts, card games, and more. When the water aerobics ladies get to wisecracking and teasing the bald guys and shrieking with laughter in the pool every morning, they sound for all the world like a bunch of teenagers. *We're working on eighteen-inch waistlines. . . . Ha ha ha ha ha! Yes, and I'm already halfway there! HA HA HA HA HA HA!!!*

The park's main hall is transformed into ye olde camp dining hall for regular pancake breakfasts, hamburger cookouts, ice cream socials, and potluck suppers. There are also dances, variety shows, visits by musical entertainers, blindfold golf cart races, sometimes even campfires with singing and s'mores.

Best of all, you're there long enough that you can make friends with the couple a few spaces over, because they are staying the whole winter, too. And you get a phone hookup right in your RV, so you can call up your friends on your phone and see if they want to come over and play bridge, or go out to eat, or whatever. This may sound like no big deal to normal people, but for those of us whose primary lifestyle is roaming from place to place waving goodbye, it's sheer delight.

Then suddenly it's the first of March and what RVers call "hitch itch" sets in. The winter Texans with homes up north start packing up and moving out. (Is it just a coincidence that "March" and "move" begin with the same letter? I think not!) Donia and I look around the fast-emptying campground and ask ourselves, what are *we* still doing here? We've been lazy and comfortable long enough! With the secret relief that vacationers so often feel heading back to their real lives, we disconnect the phone, wind up our cords and cables, drag out the maps, and hit the road again.

 RV Having a Merry Christmas?

Staying in Orlando over Thanksgiving week gave us time to catch up on Christmas preparations—like getting our favorite Steeles on Wheels snapshot made into holiday photo-greeting cards. To accompany the card, we composed this poem celebrating our first exuberant months on the road:

continued

'Twas the year of retirement, and all through the house
All the creatures were stirring, plus laptop and mouse.
The trailer was hitched up and filled with our gear,
Which the Ford's diesel engine could haul anywhere.
In the roomy back seat rode our faithful dog Cleo,
We're the Eight-Legged Steele Family Traveling Trio!

On a perfect June day we waved Virginia good-bye
And headed southwest to give Freedom a try.
At our first dumping station we got a great fright:
Seems our black-water tank was not sealing right.
Yet the worst came in Georgia, where that small service
station
Wedged us tight in the pump lane, to Mark's consterna-
tion.

Ah, but what's a few scrapes to brave retirees?
Eastward we turned toward the sea's balmy breeze.
From Myrtle Beach to Cape Cod, we did the Atlantic,
And when weather grew hot, we didn't get frantic.
We just headed north to the Great Lakes' shore,
Huron and Michigan and Superior to explore.

In Wisconsin's North Woods Donia turned fifty-five
And said, quote-unquote, "I've never felt more alive!"
Mark's favorite campground was an Indian casino,
He cleaned up at blackjack (and steered clear of Keno).
Early autumn found us in the southern Midwest,
Touring Illinois, Indiana, and Kentucky with zest.

Tennessee we loved, and we lingered there long,
Lured by Dollywood, barbecue, and campgrounds for a song.
Then we hustled to Orlando for some tournament bridge.
(Holed up in a hotel room! Without our own fridge!)
Playing three sessions a day, Mark racked up some points,
And also made time for the best dining joints.

continued

After this tough week of cards we needed a vacation,
So off to Disney World for a quick celebration.
From Epcot to Magic Kingdom to the theme park MGM,
The bright lights of Christmas and gay sparkling trim
Have swooshed up our spirits in a holiday mood—
And we're wishing the same for you and your brood!

But last night in Florida we glimpsed a strange sight
As Santa soared overhead on his first warm-up flight.
Could the Clauses be contemplating retirement themselves,
With pink slips for the reindeer and all of the elves?
'Cause we saw Santa clearly above that palm tree,
And instead of a sleigh, he was driving an RV!

Happy Holidays
   from
    Mark
     Donia
      & Cleo!

31 Cordele, Georgia
January 1

HAPPY NEW YEAR to all my two-legged and four-legged friends! I'm sure you've all been waiting for the answer to the big holiday question: Did Cleo get that Kentucky thoroughbred horse of her dreams for Christmas???

Cutting right to the chase here: The answer is NO. Unfortunately, a few more negative behavior issues came up in the final month, like when I darted away from Mom and Dad and goosed a high-class lady walking across Savannah's fancy Oglethorpe Square. (It's so much fun when they jump and scream!) And the Gingerbread Incident in Myrtle Beach, when I took a couple of tiny bites out of the dessert just before Mom's friends arrived for dinner. (Well, okay, maybe seven or eight bites. Big deal. There was still plenty left.) And the Broken Leash Incident, when I took off after a squirrel and my leash snapped, leaving Dad holding the shredded end.

Anyway, instead of a racehorse for Christmas, I got the canine equivalent of a lump of coal: a package of those fake-bacon dog treats. Do they think I was born yesterday? I must say, though, they taste pretty good for something made of ground wheat and corn gluten meal, glycerin, hydrogenated starch hydrolysate, and bacon fat preserved with BHA. In the end, I decided to be philosophical about horses. They're high-strung and they poop a lot. So who needs them?

A Real Cliff-Hanger
While we were in Atlanta visiting Grandma and Grandpa Steele, we stayed at that same campground by the lake, except this time it was winter instead of June. It was the first time we ever had to move into a campsite after dark, and the site we got was right on the edge of a cliff and we had to back in. Dad was acting all cool about it, but Mom was freaking out because the ground

was real uneven, a lot higher in the front than the back, and she was trying to put leveling boards under the tires but she couldn't see anything except the water down below. AND it was freezing cold. Dad hustled around and got us set up, growling at Mom for being a Nervous Nellie. But the next morning when he went outside, he laughed and said, "Glad I couldn't see this last night!" The RV's butt was sticking out over the water and looked like it was going to slide right into the lake any minute. But you know what? It never did!

Had a Holly Jolly Christmas

This was the first time I ever got to come to Christmas at Aunt Kathy's house (that's Dad's sister), and boy was it ever fun! On Christmas Eve Dad decided he was going to cook for the whole family, so he spends all day shopping at the Farmers' Market and then just marches in and takes over Aunt Kathy's kitchen. He's loving it, this big kitchen with a regular stove and every kind of pot and pan you could want. I am authorized to tell you that the menu consisted of Cornish hens (plus a few of Uncle David's quails from the freezer from hunting season last fall), wine-poached fruit, braised baby bok choy, and endive-and-walnut salad. Unfortunately, I was not authorized to eat any of it.

The next day, at present-unwrapping time, Mom and Dad had a surprise for everyone. For a couple months they had been buying little ritzy food treats everywhere they went. They wrapped each one up in tinted plastic stuff so you could see what it was. Then they spread out all these packages on the dining room table and gave everyone a little basket with a ribbon on it, and told them to go "shopping" for their gifts. You should have seen this Shopping Spree, with everybody scrambling around that table! The only thing left over at the end was a jar of icky "tomato preserves" that nobody took. Mom finally put it in her purse and said, "Oh, goody, I really wanted to try this, anyway."

Of course the presents included dog goodies—such as the aforementioned fake-bacon treats. There was one for my Uncle Spike, who lives with Grandma and Grandpa Steele. He's an elderly shit-zoo, pardon the spelling, and he leaves his dog biscuits lying all over the rug, holding out so Grandma will give him little pieces of steak. Now THAT old boy knows how to manage a hunger strike. Luckily, I'm around to clean up all those extra biscuits. Also, Aunt Kathy has a humongous Newfoundland puppy named Sophie, and Kathy's daughter Jenny has a mixed-up black Lab puppy from the dog pound named Trouble. Christmas day was a gas, with all us dogs running circles around the living room, plowing through the piles of wrapping paper. That is, until Sophie and I had a little spat over a rawhide bone and nearly turned over the coffee table.

Once during the holidays, Dad says, "I'm beginning to think Cleo is a high-maintenance dog." Then Grandma says real nice, "Cleo, would you like to come live with me?" You know, like relatives are always saying, but they don't really mean it. And Mom looks at Dad over the top of her glasses and says, "Quick, get a pen, I want to get this on paper."

Plains-Clothes Police

Now the holidays are over, and Mom and Dad have decided to keep me after all, and lucky for them that they did. The place where we're staying this week is near a town called Plains, Georgia, where a guy named Jimmy Carter lives. He used to be president of the United States and, I gather, was famous for stuff like carrying his own suitcases. Now he goes around solving world crises and building houses for poor people and teaching Sunday School. Mom and Dad actually got dressed up early one morning and went to his Sunday School class.

Anyway, we all had a close brush with death in Plains trying to get an up-close look at Jimmy and Rosalynn's house. We went down this little street by a tall fence and sign that said "Restricted Area—Keep Moving." All of a sudden, this guy comes running toward us, yelling and tucking his shirttails in at the same time, and I spotted a funny kind of belt across his shoulder. He looks like one of those punks in shades who leans on the cars in gangster movies. He also looks like we interrupted his nap. He tells us we have to GO BACK, no one can walk down THIS street, so we do what he says. Sure, pal, you got it. No problem. Anyway, I'm sure I saved Mom and Dad's life that day. You gotta figure, no Secret Service guy is going to blow you away when you're walking a fluffy white dog on a leash.

Off-Season, Schmoff-Season

This campground where we're staying is the best yet! It's called the Georgia Veterans State Park, because up at the visitors' center they've got all kinds of old World War II airplanes and tanks and artillery parked on the lawn. (No pooping on the grass, OR ELSE.)

Our rig is set up right on the shores of a big lake, with open fields and piney forests all around. There's hardly anybody else here, so I get to run around off the leash. Mom says, "We should always try to stay at campgrounds like this, beautiful and deserted." Dad says, "Yeah, we've found the trick. We go places in the winter where it's cold, and in the summer where it's hot."

Today we had a perfect New Year's Day, all of us doing what we like best. First we slept extra late, since Mom and Dad were up past midnight watching some big TV whoop-de-do, all because a bunch of people dropped the ball in a place called Times Square. Humans are so weird!

It was thirty-four degrees when we woke up, but soon it warmed up to sixty, so Dad went to play golf. Mom cut up a bunch of vegetables and cooked a beef bone and made vegetable soup and cleaned the house and did three loads of laundry and watched a "rose parade" on TV. Except it didn't look like much of a parade to me. Nobody was throwing candy.

Later Mom gave me the beef bone, and I took it outside and buried it somewhere near the trailer (that's all I'm going to say). Then I sat and watched how the sunlight was shining on the lake and making little sparkles, and the way it looked like a bunch of sparkle-fish having a race when the breeze rippled the water.

I hope everyone's new year started off as peaceful and relaxing as mine, and that YOU also get a chance to run around off your leash every now and then.

Love 'n' licks,

Cleo

32 Can You Get TV in All These Different Places?

Back in our preretirement days, when we subscribed to a 120-channel cable system and could tune in anything we wanted any time we wanted, Mark and I hardly watched TV at all. Then we began traveling full-time, and reception became an iffy proposition. Wouldn't you know, *that's* when TV became important to us. At the end of a long day filled with unknown places and strange faces, turning on the tube was like going into a familiar bar and relaxing with old friends. Dan Rather. Ally McBeal. Regis Philbin. And of course, that old ex-barfly himself, Dr. Frasier Crane.

It was such a pleasure, our first New Year's Eve on the road, to be able to tune in to the annual Times Square pandemonium, then leave the TV on throughout the following day for the parades and bowl games. Even though we were spending the holiday completely by ourselves in a remote Georgia state park, thanks to television we had these cultural rituals to connect us to the world at large as the new year rang in.

In order to tune in TV programs on the road, we either have to be close enough to a broadcasting city to pick up signals with our RV's built-in antenna, or be parked at a campground that offers cable hookups at the sites. Cable, of course, is how we were able to watch the Rose Bowl Parade from the wilds of Georgia—although that was just plain luck, as public campgrounds hardly ever offer cable. In fact, it's hardly universal even among private campgrounds.

Hooking up is simple: We plug one end of our cable cord into a receptacle on the side of the RV, and the other end into the campsite's cable box, which is usually located somewhere near the electric post. Inside, with the TV's remote controller, we call up the programming menu and do a cable "Auto Search" for channels in the campground's system. If everything's in working order, we can then tune in to the various stations by pushing the Channel Up and Channel Down arrows. This process is available to virtually everyone with a TV and a remote, but in a fixed house you usually have to scan for channels only once, when you first get cable service. We need to do it each time we hook up to cable in a new RV park.

Campground cable service usually includes local network affiliates, PBS, and a few cable basics such as CNN, ESPN, TNT, WGN, and A&E. You might get six cable channels, or you might get three dozen. Our favorite is The Weather Channel—"MTV for Seniors," as one campground wit called it. Geography nuts that we are, we never tire of seeing those big colorful maps with the highs and lows and snowflakes and radar patches sweeping across America. And somewhere down below, there *we* are!

Often, we are at a campground with no cable, so TV reception is limited to the broadcast stations we can pick up with our antenna. The antenna is attached to the trailer rooftop; we raise and lower it with a crank located on our bedroom ceiling. A disk surrounding the crank allows us to manually twist the antenna around in a 320-degree arc to position it in the direction of the broadcast signals. Also in the bedroom is the small button that switches *on* the antenna, which we didn't even know existed for our first couple of months on the road.

Wherever we camp, we crank the antenna up, switch her on, and try to tune in whatever we can get, starting with the first strong station we land on. One of us mans the antenna-twister in the bedroom, identifying the different positions military-style, keyed to the face of a clock. The other one stands in the living room watching the screen and calling out status reports: Yes! No! Worse! Go back to seven o'clock! Better! and so on, until we pull in the strongest signal we can for that station. Then we do an Auto Search with the antenna in that position, to see what other channels come in. If other broadcast signals are coming from different directions, we may have to do several Auto

Searches, and change the antenna position each time we switch
to a different channel.

It's an all-new grab bag each time we camp, seeing what we
can pick up with our antenna. It may be one or more local
affiliates of NBC, CBS, ABC, Fox, and PBS. It may be a powerful
independent station like UPN, or a local indie devoted to religion.
Or it may be nothing at all. Near a big city, we normally have
the luxury of half a dozen or so broadcast stations—although
mountains can create havoc with reception, even if the transmitter
is close as the crow flies. The farther we are from civilization, the
more likely we are to get snow, static, interference from airplanes
flying overhead, double images, no color, and so forth.

On a few occasions, when there was a show scheduled that I
just didn't want to miss, I've ignored Mark's *tsk*-ing and called
ahead to campgrounds to do some TV scouting. The campground
clerks will invariably say something like, "Sure, we get channel
6 real good, and 8 and 13 also come in OK." Of course, this
means nothing to us nomads, who think in terms of ABC, Fox,
etc. When I ask, "Is one of those channels ABC?" the clerk will
usually draw a blank. People who live in one place don't have to
be as network-sensitive as we are. Every now and then I just have
to deal with it when the only networks we can tune in are ABC
and CBS, and part two of that *West Wing* cliff-hanger is going
to be on NBC. Mark mocks, "Life is full of sadness."

RVers who are truly serious about TV subscribe to satellite
service, which goes with them everywhere. Their dish is mounted
on top of their rig or set up on a tripod on the ground nearby.
They have to adjust it when they first arrive, but then they can
get most anything they want on dozens of cable and network
channels. Oddly, they have to watch or record a show at the time
it's being broadcast in the time zone where they first subscribed
to their system.

Mark and I, of course, must keep track of which time zone
we're in as we travel, so we don't find ourselves tuning in to a
much-awaited program just as the closing credits roll. In general,
a 9 p.m. show in the eastern time zone also plays at 9 on the

West Coast, but comes on at 8 in the central time zone. And it's anything goes, apparently, in mountain time. For whatever reason, those stations practice schedule anarchy.

Since it's a bit haphazard trying to look up TV schedules in daily newspapers when we're traveling, I buy a *TV Guide* during the new fall season and other periods of high TV interest. However, *TV Guide* schedules are extremely location-specific (Denver edition, South Texas edition, North Dakota edition), and we may be several states and a couple of time zones away by the time we reach Thursday.

Evening news broadcasts are particularly inconsistent around the country. The network news will come on any time between 5 and 7 p.m. If we're busy around those hours, we may go for days without watching a national news show. But that's okay, because we have really developed a fondness for local news programs around the country. Their newscasters are a lot more varied and human than the national celebrity anchors; we like their regional accents and less-than-perfect hairdos. Their stories convey the authentic flavor of the region, along with the grassroots concerns of people who live there. It may be a city water supply crisis, or antilogging legislation, or coverage of last weekend's Potato Salad Festival.

We especially love the locally produced commercials, filmed on a shoestring and starring the real folks who work down there at the café or car dealership. Or their kids. Taken all together, local TV creates a heartwarming portrait of a lively, diverse population out there across America—down-home characters who don't need slick TV executives to tell them how to be. Our new lifestyle has put us squarely in their midst, and we couldn't be happier.

33 New Orleans, Louisiana
January 18

Now we know why people go south—*way* south—for the winter. Donia and I and, especially, Cleo really did love that state campground in Georgia. But twenty-eight degrees overnight is a bit much. We got the southern tail of some megastorm that was making a mess of the Midwest, and one night our water hose froze solid. We turned on the bathroom faucet in the morning and *nothing came out*. RVs like ours just aren't built for subfreezing weather. Not enough insulation. So we hightailed it out of there, headed for New Orleans via the Gulf Coast of Alabama and Mississippi. I mean, "Gulf Coast" has a warm ring, doesn't it?

Before the cold snap, luckily, we had time to visit Andersonville, site of the infamous Civil War prisoner-of-war camp. The day was appropriately dank and gray and cold. We stood in the rain, looking at the sticks and brush and bits of tattered cloth from which the prisoners tried to fashion some kind of shelter, and we could only begin to imagine their misery. From what we read, it was even worse for them in the summer's heat, with only one polluted stream running through the camp for all the drinking water and sanitation needs of 45,000 men. Although the prison was open only one year, more than 13,000 Union prisoners died of exposure, infections, dysentery, malnutrition, measles, and untreated war wounds.

Besides preserving and interpreting the prison site, the National Park Service has also built a museum devoted to all American prisoners of war throughout history. It's a grim subject, but the museum is very well done, and well worth a visit next time you—well, next time you find yourself in the far reaches of southwest Georgia.

Maybe it was the rain and cold, or some kind of sympathetic

illness inspired by those poor soldiers, but in any case I came down with a horrible case of the flu the following week. I had never before appreciated having a faithful family physician back home who would see us on an hour's notice whenever we needed care. Donia stood at a campground pay phone calling area doctors for what seemed like hours, but had no luck finding anyone in our health care network who could see me.

Finally, by default, we ended up at a hospital emergency room—not the most comfortable place to be waiting on a cold hard chair for two hours when you've got a fever of 104 degrees. Anyway, eventually I was sent home with some medicine, and Donia was rewarded for her faithful nursing service by coming down with the flu herself, two days later. The moral of this story: If you're a full-timer, just don't get sick in the first place.

By the time we arrived in New Orleans it was apparent we were both going to live. We stayed at a great in-town state park right on the banks of Bayou Seignette, and took it easy for a few days. From the park we made side trips to Houma and Thibodaux, and down to the mouth of the Mississippi River seventy miles south of the city (not much to see except oil-drilling equipment, but we felt a need just to do it). While we were in the area, we also took walking tours of the Garden District and French Quarter, looked at Mardi Gras gowns in a museum, and so forth.

But you know us. What we mainly did in New Orleans was *eat*. Here's my daily log:

Monday
   Lunch: Rosy's Lunch and Seafood, in Venice, at the mouth of the Mississippi—Red beans and rice, smoked sausage, crawfish pie, beets. Donia is the only woman in the place, except for the help. Everyone else is a male oil-rig roustabout.
   Dinner: Joey K's Restaurant on Magazine Street in the Garden District—Fried boudin balls, Shrimp Magazine on angel hair pasta (large butterfly shrimp lightly floured and pan-fried, then sautéed in olive oil, garlic, artichoke hearts, tasso ham, and green

onions), soft-shelled crab with veggies and new potatoes, Ms. Cathy's pie (chocolate glazed brownie, ice cream, whipped cream, and chocolate sauce in a fancy drizzle all over the very large plate).

Tuesday
Lunch: Casamento's, a hole-in-the-wall on Magazine Street where walls, floors, every surface are covered in beautiful 1930s ceramic tile—A dozen oysters on the half shell, gumbo, deep-fried oyster loaf on pan bread, Barq's root beer (served in a long-necked bottle, a short glass, no ice).

Dinner: Mosca's in Avondale, billed as "The most famous Creole roadhouse in America"—Chicken Grandee (a whole bird is "oven sautéed" and perfumed with enough olive oil, thyme, oregano, rosemary, and garlic to sink a ship. The garlic cloves, nicely caramelized, are left in the pan to munch on along with the meat. All the other humans we came near for forty-eight hours got a funny look and averted their noses). Spaghetti bordelaise, salad dressed in blue cheese and studded with gardenaria. Chianti.

Wednesday
Lunch: On break; ate home.

Dinner: Late afternoon coffee and beignets at Café du Monde on Decatur Street in the heart of the French Quarter, then four dozen oysters and a very cold bottle of Red Stripe beer at Felix's Oyster Bar on Iberville Street. Felix's is the only "negative option" restaurant in the country—just like a book club that keeps sending you books until you tell them to stop. At Felix's you stand at the terazzo-topped bar and the shuckers start opening oysters and sliding them in front of you. They keep shucking and sliding *until you tell them to stop.* Then they count the shells and give you a check. Soda crackers, ketchup, fresh grated horseradish, hot sauce, and lemon wedges are on a tray at the end of the bar so you can mix your own sauce.

Thursday

Lunch: At Bubba II's in Thibodaux, billed as "The most famous sports bar in America"—Crawfish étouffée, baked spaghetti, spinach soufflé, grilled red snapper.

Dinner: At Kim Son's in Gretna (on the "west" side, which is actually the south side, of the Mississippi)—Spring rolls, salt crabs (two hours of picking and sucking on hardshell crabs that have been stir-fried in a wok with oil, onions, and pepper), charcoal beef with lemon grass (make-your-own rice paper wraps!), and a bottle of Miller's even colder than the Red Stripe at Felix's.

Tomorrow we head westward, into the heart of Cajun country. Donia wants to visit New Iberia—home town of Cajun detective Dave Robicheaux, main dude of the down 'n' dirty murder mysteries by James Lee Burke (every one of which Donia has read, at least twice). I do believe she thinks Dave is for real, and secretly plans to break a few laws in New Iberia, in hopes he will show up and arrest her.

As for me, I plan to conduct some rigorous taste tests of boudin and crawfish étouffée. Scientific research is tough. But somebody has to do it.

Love,
Mark

34 Where Do You Find Doctors?

Finding reliable medical care on the road is one of the thorniest issues RV full-timers must deal with. Granted, the current health-care situation is filled with hassles for everyone, regardless of how or where they live. But when you are constantly moving from place to place, coping with logistics alone is enough to give you high blood pressure.

The best strategy for twenty-first-century nomads is never to get sick at all. Mark and I are both blessed with overall good health. I like to think of this as our reward for the handfuls of vitamins, minerals, bone-mass builders, and other preventive pills we pop every day. Mark credits barbecue.

Luckily, for those rare times when we do need a doctor, we have retiree medical coverage carried over from my job. Our only significant problem to date, knock on wood, has been that flu attack during our first winter on the road. And that was more uncomfortable and frustrating than anything else.

Living in Alexandria for over fifteen years, Mark and I never had to think twice about medical care. Our insurance made it totally seamless. We had a longtime family doctor who was our PCP (primary care provider), a few specialists like my dermatologist, and a neighborhood drugstore—all members of our health plan's "network." We paid a flat $15 co-pay fee per doctor visit, which covered most routine medical treatments and lab work. We also had hospital inpatient and emergency room coverage, plus a pharmacy card that got us prescriptions for $5 or $10 in participating drugstores. For chronic medications like Mark's arthritis pills, we could a order a prescription from the mail-order pharmacy for a three-month supply, with three refills, which would cover us for an entire year.

When we hit the road full-time, this comfortable setup changed. Now the process was full of seams. I would have to pay a monthly premium of about $200, which would provide the same network coverage as before—if we could find network providers. They were numerous in large urban areas, but not to be found in smaller places. Going "out of network" for doctors would be much more costly, involving an annual deductible and coverage for only a percentage of "allowable" charges. As an added wrinkle, the health plan for company employees and retirees living in half the states, including Virginia, was administered by one insurance firm; the other states were administered by a different firm.

Before leaving, I made an appointment with our employee benefits counselor to discuss the ins and outs of finding health care on the road. It was apparently the first time anyone in the entire corporation had done a weird thing like selling their house to travel full-time in an RV. The fact that our new Texas address was just a mail-forwarding service, not really where we were located most of the time, left the benefits people scratching their heads for a while. Texas was in one group of states; Virginia was in the other. The benefits people finally decided to leave us categorized as Virginia residents for the time being, since we still had the cabin in Front Royal.

Sure enough, we ran into a lot of confusion and rejected claims when we first went to doctors for annual checkups in other parts of the country. Apparently we could go to any family doctor or specialist in the network, as long as we had a medical complaint such as a sore foot or sinus infection. But an annual checkup was supposed to be done only by our PCP back "home" in Virginia. Eventually, we discovered that we could *change* our PCP as often as we wanted. Ah, ha! Now each time we went for a physical, we just needed to remember to call the customer service number ahead of time and designate the doctor we would be visiting as our new PCP. The best news of all was, the urban-area networks seemed to operate independently of the split-state division, so we could go to a network doctor anywhere we could find one. Who knows why? Never mind; it's a mystery we can live with.

However, trying to connect with network doctors for urgent care can be a tortuous process, as I learned during Mark's bout with the flu. Standing at an outside pay phone, I had to call our insurance's customer service number and wend my way through an endless telephone tree until I got a service rep who gave me some names and phone numbers. If I'd had a telephone jack at my disposal, I could have used the computer to look up network physicians on their Web site. But I didn't.

The rep on the phone asked me what zip code we were in, and from her computer listings gave me ten names in that area for starters. I began calling them, and one after another, the doctors' assistants said sorry, we don't take new patients, or sorry, we can't see you till a week from Thursday, or sorry, we don't participate in that network anymore. One candid receptionist told me I might as well just take Mark to the emergency room at the big downtown hospital, as that was going to be our only chance to get seen today.

By now Mark's fever had reached 104 degrees, so I said *let's just do it*—no more messing around on the pay phone. I had always heard about down-and-out people who went to emergency rooms for routine illnesses because it was their only clear option. Now we were joining them. During our two-hour wait we sat next to a woman who rocked back and forth loudly groaning in drug withdrawal pains (though she staunchly denied using drugs when the doctor asked about the needle tracks on her arms). At one point a bleeding woman was brought in by her scary-looking biker boyfriend.

Mark's turn came, in time, and he was examined by a competent and pleasant doctor who did not chastise us for being there. An X-ray was taken, to rule out pneumonia, and after only two more hours we finally escaped with prescriptions for an antibiotic and an industrial-strength expectorant. All I had to do now was call the insurance's 800 number and justify going to an emergency room for flu treatment. It was an experience. It was an adventure. It was a place I hope to heaven I'll never find myself in again.

Two days later I started coming down with the same bug, and dragged myself back out to the pay phones once more, feeling like Marie Antoinette heading for the guillotine. This time I gave the rep a slightly farther-out zip code. This got me a different batch of doctors from the network listing, and I promptly scored an appointment with the first number I called—a nice, bright, efficient medical group in a nearby suburban mall. Go figure!

 Other Lessons Learned

- Know the rules of your medical and dental plans. Read the policies and benefits booklets until you practically know them by heart. It's amazing how often you need to "remind" benefits representatives about what they should have known in the first place.
- When looking for a provider in a strange area, start with the suburbs. We've had better luck in small cities and in the suburbs of large cities than in rural areas or large cities proper.
- Get copies to go of X-rays any time they are taken, particularly dental X-rays. Many dentists won't treat you without a set of reasonably current X-rays, and health plans usually limit the number of new X-rays they'll pay for within a given time frame.
- If *all* you need from a new doctor is prescription renewals for drugs you already take, make an appointment to be checked for one of your conditions, rather than for a general physical exam. Take a list of all the drugs and their dosages, or bring along the bottles, to give the doctor. Try to arrange for all your prescriptions to come due for renewal at the same time.

My turn on the rack came later, however, when I took my prescriptions to the same network pharmacy where Mark's prescriptions had just been filled. The clerk tried for twenty minutes to enter my prescription card number into his computer. After several unhelpful phone calls to the insurance company, the senior pharmacist quietly took my prescriptions to the back and just filled them, at the network rate.

Dental care is a simpler story, though it costs us a little more out-of-pocket. Our plan works on the same arrangement as out-of-network medical care: We can go to any dentist we want, and, after paying an annual deductible, the plan pays a percentage of allowable charges. Our first on-the-road dentist experience was in Minneapolis, when one of Mark's inlays fell out and he needed to find someone to cement it back in. He got a recommendation from the friend we were visiting there, and the dentist saw him right away.

But most of our visits are not for emergencies, merely routine checkups—tune-ups and oil changes, Mark calls them. In a town where we don't know anyone, we've been known to just walk in off the street and inquire about his 'n' hers teeth-cleaning appointments. This was how we met the Humming Dentist of Georgetown, Kentucky. We both got immediate appointments, one after the other. The dentist carefully checked our teeth and expertly performed the entire cleaning process himself. And hummed the whole time. Hummed show tunes, opera arias, Beatles songs, jazz classics—one after the other. About halfway through, I began wondering why the dentist, and not a hygienist, was cleaning my teeth. Then it occurred to me that there *was* no hygienist in the office, not even a receptionist—just the humming dentist. Oh yes, and *the front office had no furniture.*

In the end, there was a perfectly logical explanation: Once a year, the dentist told us, he gave his staff two days off while he had his furniture sent out and the entire office, including the carpeting, thoroughly cleaned. He just happened to be in the office doing paperwork when we wandered in. Sorry, no explanation given for the humming.

The eccentric doctor award goes to my Rio Grande Valley dermatologist, who wore fancy hand-tooled cowboy boots under his lab coat and greeted me on my first visit with, "Sorry about my rough hands, I was tattooing calves all day yesterday." Turns out he'd been an animal doctor before becoming a people doctor and had both med-school *and* veterinary diplomas hanging proudly on his office wall.

We are forever grateful for the good doctors and dentists we've found all across the country who cheerfully agree to see us on short notice. We always wonder why they say yes to a couple of no-fixed-address types like ourselves, people who will obviously never become regular patients. Why do they bother, especially in this age of serious malpractice concerns, bad-debt risks, and burdensome paperwork? But see us they do, and give us the same conscientious care and attention that their hometown regulars receive. And they obligingly make us copies of our medical treatment records, so we can carry them with us when we move on down the road. I once had a sun-spot on my face biopsied by my Texas vet/dermatologist, removed via laser surgery by a dermatologist in Colorado, and checked six months later by my old doctor during a swing through Virginia. All three treated me as though I were going to be their patient forever.

As a daring alternative to U.S. care, some RVers we've met seek out the abundant, low-cost medical and dental services available in Mexican border towns. Many who spend winters in south Texas, New Mexico, and Arizona rave about the well-trained Mexican dentists they have found who do teeth cleanings, fillings, crowns, and bridges for one-third of what they would cost in the States. Not to mention the discounts of 50 percent or more they get on prescription medications in the Mexican *farmacias*—without even needing a prescription.

And finally, there are the full-timers who return at least once a year to a home base, where they can get routine checkups and major work done by providers they know and trust. It may be the place they used to live, or it may be a certain area they go back to each year for the winter or summer season. Mark and I sometimes do this, too: He likes to go to his new PCP during winters in the Rio Grande Valley, and I return to see my old doctors in Alexandria whenever I'm back there visiting friends and family. Certainly, the "home base" arrangement makes sense for those with geographic limitations on their health care plans— or for anyone who prefers peace of mind over medical adventures.

35 Odem, Texas

January 30

Dear Friends of all Species,

First of all, I want to thank my loyal fans from all over the country, and I'm talking California, Illinois, and the entire Eastern seaboard, who e-mailed Team Steele impatiently wanting to know when my next column was coming. Things have been extremely hectic in my life over the past month, and if I hear the word "Cajun" one more time I'm going to SCREAM.

But finally I've been able to get a paw on the keyboard, and now it is my proud privilege to report our family's top news story of the year:

". . . And She Can Even Keep Her Monogram!"

By now some of you have heard that my big brother, Travis Mills, is officially ENGAGED to his girlfriend of two years, Amy Miley. The monogram observation was made by Mom, who is like, mega-excited about this. Except, Hello—Earth to Mommy! Girls do not exactly embroider their initials on linens any more! Before I forget, I'm supposed to give Curry full credit for introducing her little brother to Amy back in Austin, when they were all hanging out together doing whatever it is that "theater and film students" do. Anyway, Amy is extremely cool. She and I have had a very close relationship ever since we shared the backseat last summer all the way from New York to Cape Cod, and she let me use her lap as a pillow. Is this a great gal, or what?

Down on the Farm

Right now we are in a little bitty town called Odem, Texas, where Mom's ancestors started a big cotton farm a long time ago. Our trailer is parked on the driveway right outside the farmhouse her grandmother and grandfather used to live in, except now the old folks are gone and Mom's cousin Darrell and his wife Jan live there. I take it the place used to be a lot different back in the olden days, with a barn and a chicken yard where Mom used to go hunting for eggs in the nests when she was a little girl. She talks about that chicken yard all the time like it was some kind of sacred site. Now the place is all modernized with a fancy bathroom and walk-in closets, and no more barn or chickens. But they still grow cotton in the fields all around the house— except this time of year it's just rows and rows of black dirt, stretching out on all sides as far as you can see.

The way it works with these big farms is, when the old people get put to sleep, the land is divided up among their kids, and then they divide the land up to give their kids, and then some of these kids buy up the land from their brothers or sisters or cousins. Anyway, Mom somehow ended up with fifty acres of this cotton land all her own, and you can tell she's just tickled pink about her acres, even though they look just like all the other black dirt out there. She says things like, "I never in a million years would have believed that I would some day be parked here in an RV, and Darrell would be farming MY cotton!" And she tells how Darrell used to tease the "little" cousins when he was a teenager and she was eight years old. Now Dad teases Darrell about the stereo in his John Deere tractor, and the cell phone in his pickup truck, and Jan's computer where she runs all the farm numbers. Then they all get into Jan's Lincoln Town Car and go eat barbecue.

To This Valley They Say We Are Going

Tomorrow we have to leave Odem because we're heading south to a place called the Rio Grande Valley, which is famous for being warm when everywhere else is cold, and famous for having lots of "snowbirds." Mom and Dad heard about this place from some other RVers they met in (excuse the phrase) Cajun Country, and they have been hot to check it out ever since. Apparently there are a gazillion different RV parks to choose from, and if you stay a whole month it doesn't cost as much. And they all have stuff like square dancing and potluck suppers for the Humans and "pet sections" for the dogs. Humph. Sounds like discrimination to me. Let's turn that around, I say. Potluck suppers for the dogs and "Human sections" for the people!

Love 'n' Licks,
Cleo

36 How Do You Decide Where to Go?

Even as a child, I was a big-time geography buff. My favorite board game was Game of the States, in which players were long-haul truckers crisscrossing a colorful map of America. You would pick up a load of potatoes in Idaho, say, and deliver them to Georgia, then draw a card to see where to go to pick up your next load. For the life of me, I can't remember what you had to do to *win* this game. I just delighted in hopping around the country with my cargo, learning about the crops and manufactured products of all the different states.

For Mark and me, planning where we'll go next and what route we'll take re-creates all the fun of Game of the States, and we keep the process just about as easy. We enjoy it so much we would never dream of having a professional travel organization like the AAA, or even a travel-planning CD-Rom, chart a course for us. We love poring over the maps and atlases and guidebooks and brochures ourselves, spreading them all out on the kitchen table and plotting our next few days—or months—over a second pot of coffee.

Some day we may decide to un-retire and take on-the-road jobs—like maybe hauling a load of pig iron from Pennsylvania to Arizona. If so, our travel plans will be dictated by work assignments. Or we may be blessed with grandchildren living here and there, and travel a yearly circuit to visit them, as so many full-timers do. But for now, we are free to roam anywhere we want, and we don't have to be in a hurry. We can take off-roads just for the fun of it, and stop to read as many historical markers and hit as many barbecue shacks as we like on the way.

We were not always so easygoing about traveling. Like many RV novices, when we first started out we were pressuring ourselves to move way too often. We planned out all our stops in advance and were so eager to see new places that we rarely stayed anywhere more than two days. Sometimes we wanted to stay longer but had to stow our hoses and cables and move on because we had already made plans to visit friends or pick up our mail in some town down the road. It took us more than a year to begin slowing the pace so we could stay put for a week or longer in a spot we enjoyed. We realized that the people and places we missed this time would still be there next year.

Nowadays, our big picture is like that of most full-timers. We generally head south to keep warm in the winter and north to stay cool in the summer. Beyond those broad guidelines, there is no single way we plan our travels. Often, part of a season is anchored by a major event that requires us to be in a certain place on a certain date. For instance, when Travis and Amy announced their engagement during our first January on the road, it lent structure to the rest of our year. Immediately we made plans to travel to Austin in March to meet Amy's family and get the wedding plans rolling. Then we would enter the "head north" mode, aiming for Montana to camp out for two weeks in July/ August with our friends Pete and Robin at their pioneer cabin. From this northernmost point in the loop, we would begin a leisurely southward journey to end up in Austin again for the October wedding. Aside from the three fixed commitments, though, our schedule was open-ended.

Graduations are another family event worth planning around. One spring, we routed our travels to be in Atlanta in May for Mark's nieces' graduations. Another year, we learned via e-mail that we were in central Texas at the same time our RV mentors and eight-year pen pals, Ron and Barb Hofmeister, were scheduled to be in nearby Seguin for a week getting some major motorhome work done. I was so thrilled at the prospect of finally meeting this couple, whose book and newsletter had inspired us and so many other full-timers, that we made a beeline for Seguin. We spent a delightful three days parked next to them in the back lot of the RV repair shop—"celebrity stalking," Mark called it—and then continued on our way.

And of course, American Contract Bridge League tournaments are a constant magnet for Mark. They come in three sizes: sectionals, regionals, and the three-times-a-year nationals. We could literally do nothing all year long but travel from one tournament to another around the country. Luckily, Mark's urge to sit for hours on end playing cards in windowless convention halls is usually outweighed by our yearning to see new places and learn about America. The travel planning for much of one summer season consisted of following the routes of the Oregon Trail and the Lewis and Clark expedition through parts of Montana, Wyoming, Idaho, and Oregon, and of visiting all the related museums and historic sites we could cram in.

When arriving in a new place, we usually stop at the welcome centers and pick up brochures for local attractions and historical sites. Mark and I go through the racks independently, then compare our two stacks of brochures. If we've both picked up the same one, it's a keeper. We add it to our list of Places to Go. We have an accordion file of magazine travel articles and other info sheets we save, filed by state. Also in this file we put notes about places that fellow RVers or local townspeople have recommended. (Tip: When someone you meet starts telling you about must-see spots, always take special note of the first one or two top-of-mind places mentioned. These will be the best, no matter how much longer he stands there dredging up more recommendations.)

To make or not to make advance reservations is another question we have turned around on since starting out. During our first months on the road, we called ahead to reserve campsites for nearly every stop, even for a one-night stay in the middle of the week. Often these would be confirmed with a credit card. In some areas with a high demand for camping space, campgrounds will charge a deposit to your card and will not issue a refund unless you notify them in advance of your changed plans—usually forty-eight hours in advance, but sometimes a week or more prior to your arrival date.

After a while these restrictions became a drag, and we got bolder about just winging it. When driving the rig, we usually travel no more than six hours or 250 miles in a day anyway, which leaves time for the adventure of finding a place to camp. We carry the campground guides with us in the front seat and pull them out when we start feeling tired. Or maybe we'll come to an area that looks like it's worth exploring and stop even if we've only driven two hours that day. Another comforting thing we learned: There are always campgrounds along the way not listed in the directories. They may not be country-club quality, but they are just fine for an overnight stay. And there are Wal-Mart parking lots and highway rest areas you can use in a pinch.

I can only recall a few instances where our nonplanning got us into a bind. The most memorable one happened during our first year, when Mark was entering the loosey-goosey stage but I was still fussing about advance reservations for weekends. We pulled into a Corps of Engineers facility in Grapevine, Texas, about 4 p.m. on a Friday with no reservation and were told that all the sites were taken by a large Boy Scout group that would be coming in that evening. But the super-friendly registration clerk said we could park the rig at the top of the boat-launch ramp and plug in to the 20-amp electric outlet at the fish-cleaning station, and maybe there would be a cancellation. I was in a bit of a tizzy about all this, but just about the time we were hooking up our water hose, the clerk zoomed up in his runabout golf cart and directed us to a regular campsite that had just opened up. It was all by itself on a hillside overlooking the entire lake—easily the best spot in the park. After this episode, it was hard to make a case for automatic weekend reservations any more.

Vacation travel in America moves in highly predictable seasonal patterns, and in time you learn which dates to beware of and which dates to cheer. The winter holidays are not a big camping phenomenon, in general, but watch out for spring break—especially anywhere near a beach. Memorial Day weekend brings the first big surge of the summer camping season, and by mid-June, when school is out, the resort-area campgrounds and state parks are filled with family vacationers toting kids, dogs, bikes, scooters, motorboats, boom boxes, barbecue grills, big tents and little tents, jet-skis, and all-terrain vehicles.

There's an abrupt back-to-school dropoff in mid-August, and then, after one last burst over Labor Day weekend, we have the campgrounds all to ourselves again. Well, except for crisp October weekends in areas with noteworthy fall colors to attract the leaf-viewing hordes.

Not so predictable are strictly local events that catch us unawares. For example, don't try to get within 150 miles of Greensboro/High Point, North Carolina, during the October furniture show. The Sisters Quilt Show fills Bend, Oregon, campgrounds every July, while the Sturgis, South Dakota, motorcycle rally means no room at the inn in the Black Hills for a couple of weeks each summer. Even Mark now agrees that if we absolutely, positively have to be in a specific place at a specific time, we are better off calling ahead for a reservation.

Climate and weather are also elements we try to plan around, but exceptions seem to be the rule in this department. Some of our nicest venues have been resort-type campgrounds that we visited during "unseasonably warm weather" in the off-season. The flip side is, we often get nipped by unexpected cold spells. Our low record so far was twenty-four degrees overnight near a lake on the Georgia-Florida border in December, a time of year when it was usually in the forties. It's especially hard to predict spring weather in the high country. One April we planned our route through the scenic mountains of northeastern New Mexico but had to bypass Chama in the San Juan Mountains because they were still snowed in. But that was okay, because we knew Chama and the San Juans would still be there some July and August of another year.

Once you loosen up about travel plans, there's no end to the wacky things you may end up doing. Mark and I might change course and go two hundred miles out of our way to pass through a state we're missing on our U.S.A. sticker map. We get to a place thinking to stay a night or two and like it so much we sign up for two weeks. We check the old atlas map on which we trace our route with colored markers, and decide to take a different highway from one we already traveled, just to avoid marking over the same highway again in a different color.

One summer we were intrigued by a flyer advertising the annual National Old-Time Fiddlers Championship, held in June in Weiser, Idaho. But we figured we'd already be far past Weiser by then, en route to the Pacific Northwest. Then, a day or so west of Weiser, we got bogged down and ended up in Baker City, Oregon, for more than a week getting some mechanical work done. On the morning we were finally ready to hit the road

---

 Sex and the States

Talk about *game of the states!* During our first week on the road, Mark and I carefully attached our U.S.A. sticker map to the rear panel of the RV and began adding the little colored stickers each time we traveled into a new state. It wasn't until a couple of months later that we discovered we'd been doing it "all wrong," at least according to a couple we met at the Indian casino campground in Minnesota. "We *never* put on a sticker until we've had sex in that state," Dave and Jerri informed us earnestly. "That would be cheating."

Mark and I sheepishly surveyed the places we'd passed through so briskly in our frantic first months. Uh, oh, there were six states alone—Virginia, West Virginia, Maryland, Pennsylvania, New Jersey, and New York—added after just one day of heavy-duty driving. All had stickers. But clearly, some were not earned! Since we met Dave and Jerri, we have faithfully followed the No Nookie, No Sticker rule. And vowed to return eventually to each cheater state from our first year, to make our sticker map legal.

again, Mark remembered our brochures and discovered that the timing was now perfect for us to attend the fiddlers' contest, only sixty-five miles behind us. At first the idea seemed absurd. We were now going to *backtrack* to Idaho on our way to Seattle? To boondock with hundreds of other RVers on the elementary school grounds, walking back and forth to the high school gym for five days of nonstop fiddle competition by grownups, teens, even toddlers?

"Hey, why not?" I said. We turned around and headed for Weiser.

37 Pharr, Texas
March 3

✉ Howdy, friends and neighbors! Did y'all think Mark and I just dropped off the face of the earth? It's hard to believe we haven't written in over a month—but life has seemed so darn normal (meaning stationary) since we became winter Texans. Not only are we staying warm for a change, but we're loving the perks of parking in one spot for a while—like a reduced monthly campground rate, a telephone hookup right in our rig, our own mailbox here in the park, and regular golf and bridge partners in the local community. It's quite a contrast to the frantic travel pace we kept up for our first half-year on the road.

In fact, Mark is so enchanted with this lifestyle I fear he's ready to chuck the RV full-timing and settle down right here to a contented life of bridge with Little Old Ladies who have zillions of master points—including the one who happens to be a real estate agent.

DANGER*DANGER** I gotta get him outta here, fast!

In all seriousness, the Rio Grande Valley is a delight at this time of year, a place where temperatures are in the seventies most days, and oranges and grapefruits grow on trees. It's a strange mixture of suburban sprawl, orchard and farm land, and Mexican border town, with a strong bilingual flavor. (I studied French and German in college; fat lot of good they're doing me here.) Our surroundings are so flat you can stand in one spot and see the municipal water towers of four or five neighboring towns, each decorated with the mascot of the local high school's team. My favorite: the Mighty Red Ants of Progreso. The only other items poking up from the horizon are the distinctive Valley palm trees, tall and skinny with a small pom-pom of fronds at the top, always blowing in the breezes that sweep relentlessly across south Texas.

From our campground near U.S. 83, known as the Express-way, little towns are lined up to the east and west like beads on a necklace, from Mission to Harlingen—bedroom communities where the main industry is retirement. Hundreds of health care facilities and medical specialists cater to the senior population. Houses range from tile-roofed mansions to mobile homes (lots of those) right on down to packing-crate shacks. There are a couple of malls in the area, nothing spectacular, plus an abundance of chains like Wal-Mart, Office Depot, Circuit City, and Applebee's.

The locally-owned mom 'n' pop restaurants tend to be Mexican, and Mark and I have naturally sampled our share. Our favorite, close to the Elks Lodge in Harlingen, where you can play duplicate bridge three days a week, is Vela's—asphalt tile floor, Formica tables, rickety chairs, and spectacular blackboard lunch specials. A typical $2.99 plate of pork and squash stew comes with chips and salsa, vegetable soup, guacamole salad, refried beans, rice, and dessert pudding with fruit and marshmallows. Oh yes, the price also includes iced tea with unlimited refills.

One weekday we drove about twenty miles down to the Mexican border town of Nuevo Progreso, a place that exists expressly for American tourists to come shop for cheap trinkets, dental care, and prescription drugs that need no prescription. Since it's not prudent to drive your vehicle into Mexico without special insurance, most everyone parks in lots on the U.S. side (all day for a dollar) and walks across the short Rio Grande bridge into the town. The shopping district is ten blocks long and fifty yards wide; just half a block off the main drag, the sidewalks disintegrate into rubble and the pavement becomes a dirt road with chickens wandering about. A Corona beer at a sidewalk table costs 75¢.

The town was packed with other winter Texans bargain-hunting like us. We saw dozens of dentists, many trained in the United States and advertising "English spoken here," who charge $9 for teeth cleaning and X-rays, $25 for fillings, and $100 for crowns. We passed these up and headed straight for the *farmacias*, where drugs from name-brand companies could be had for a fraction of U.S. prices. Oh, the thrill of walking into a store and buying all the cephelexin we wanted, without a prescription! Who cares that the package insert is in Spanish? We can read the English version on the drug company's Web site. All we have to do now is wait for bronchitis or a sinus infection to strike. Before leaving Nuevo Progreso, just to prove we were not totally drug-crazed *gringos*, we purchased a tiny wooden folding table ($3) for our RV, gaily painted with a big pink flower. Now Mark has a place to put the remote when he's lying on the couch watching *Who Wants to Be a Millionaire*.

Another day we left the truck parked on the U.S. side and rode the last remaining hand-drawn ferry across the Rio Grande, at Los Ebanos (translation, "The Ebony Trees"). It's a three-car ferry with standing room for passengers, and it travels back and forth, a distance of maybe sixty yards, via a bright yellow cable stretched across the river. Four strong guys stand along the side rail and pull on the cable hand over hand to propel the ferry. It loads up three cars, plus pedestrians, goes across to Mexico and offloads, immediately loads on three more cars and pedestrians, brings them back over to the U.S. side, and continues on this way from 10 to 4 every day. Once across the river, you can walk or take a taxi a mile and a half into the tiny town of Diaz Ordaz (translation, "This or That") to shop or eat in one of the no-English-spoken cafés on the main drag. But you better be back before the last ferry leaves at 4 o'clock! Those who miss it are out of luck. They have to hire a taxi to take them the long way around via the closest bridge—or else swim across.

Lots of folks do just that, as we noticed from evidence at a state park in Mission that we visited yet another day. Littering the river bank on the U.S. side were deflated inner tubes, sodden trash bags, and wadded-up underpants. Apparently the hopefuls strip down to their shorts, put their clothes in plastic bags to keep them dry, paddle across the Rio Grande on the inner tubes, then put their dry clothes back on and head toward their goal in the United States. The park ranger told us the illegals *always* get caught and sent back, thanks to a sophisticated network of sensors the Border Patrol has placed amidst the underbrush along the river. But I wonder.

Texas Trails, the park we've been staying in for the past month, has over nine hundred RV and mobile home sites and probably three total miles of impeccably paved roads. The activity center boasts everything you could want in a winter camp for grownups: indoor and outdoor swimming pools, a hot tub, sewing room, billiard room, domino and poker parlor, tennis and shuffleboard courts, square dances, potluck suppers, ceramics and woodworking shops—you name it.

The RV sites are tidy and identical, and the mobile homes are landscaped in one of two motifs—either living bougainvillea, oleander, hibiscus, and dozens of cactus varieties whose names I couldn't tell you, or else your basic no-maintenance tinted gravel and yard art. (My favorite: a large ceramic goose dressed up like Little Bo Peep.) The regulars who return year after year have fancy wooden name signs carved in the shapes of their home states: Michigan, Wisconsin, Iowa, Missouri, North Dakota.

The winter Texan season doesn't really last all that long. Apparently the snowbirds start pouring in the first week of January, as soon as they finish spending the holidays with the grandkids. "When did you get in?" everyone asks. Then, around the first of February, the tide turns. The question starts changing to, "When are you heading back?" The campers will nearly all be gone by mid-March. And so will we—that is, if Mark's soul doesn't get snatched away first by the bridge gods of the underworld.

Here's hoping your soul is safe and snug in your home state, and that the merciful weather gods send you an early spring.

Love to all,
Donia

38 Is It Hard to Live In Close Quarters?

There are two kinds of space for people living in tight quarters: physical elbow room and psychological distance. Physical space is far easier to talk about—and when it comes to RVs, size really does matter. Mark and I started out looking for one in the twenty-eight-foot range, and ended up nervously buying a thirty-four-footer. It gave us the extra length required by amenities such as spacious kitchen counters, a platform rocker, a walk-around queen-size bed, roomy closets, and a bedroom vanity shelf that became our computer desk. We pay for these extra six feet every time we have to maneuver into short or narrow camp-sites, but they have been well worth it for the livability they give our home on wheels.

Once, when touring a reconstructed pioneer village, Mark noted that the typical 12-by-15-foot frontier cabin had 180 square feet of living space for an entire family, a bit more if there was a sleeping loft above for the children. Our 8-by-34-foot RV is luxurious by these standards, giving us a whopping 327 square feet when we are parked with the two slide-outs extended—nearly double the room of the pioneer homestead.

In our winter quarters at Texas Trails, we met many full-timers and "Persephone campers" (six months in a house, six months on the road) who were making do with far less space. We've seen rigs where the owners had to crawl in and out of the bedroom area, and one spouse had to squeeze around the other every time he or she got out of bed or passed the narrow spot between the sofa and dinette table. Add a dog or two underfoot and you're really talking about sardine-can living.

Even with our oversized living area, Mark and I have space issues. The kitchen may be big by RV standards, but it's not big enough for us to work at the counter together, performing the cooking duets we enjoyed so much in our old life. Since we both like to play with food, it's now either a Mark meal or a Donia meal, and the other one's job is to stay out of the way. The bathroom door gets entangled with the adjacent hallway door, and I have to announce "coming through!" when I want to pass behind Mark as he's brushing his teeth at the sink or sitting at the computer. Some days I call him "Visa," because he's everywhere I want to be.

You would think having a roomy sofa bed in the living room would mean friends and family members could join us for camping adventures around the country, right? Wrong! Mark is a restless sleeper, up and down half a dozen times in the night to get water or a snack, use the bathroom, read a magazine. In extreme cases he may even defrost the refrigerator. If someone were asleep on the sofa bed, it would leave him no place to wander. When my daughter flew to Las Vegas to join us for Mother's Day week one year, we had it all settled beforehand that she and I would sleep back in the bedroom, leaving the living room-kitchen area and sofa bed to Mark. This turned out fine, though the arrangement obviously wouldn't work so well with other visitor combinations.

Clutter is perhaps the biggest space foe—not exclusive to RVing couples, but certainly more annoying when there's only 327 square feet to spread stuff around in, as opposed to the 2,200 square feet of a typical suburban house. In our house, there's no place for clutter to go except the dinette table, countertops, sofa, bed, or floor. Mark never seems to notice the stacks of books, dog leashes, castoff shoes and socks, needle-nose pliers, un-put-away shopping items, paper bags, and credit card receipts, all accumulating here and there around the trailer. Or the piles of magazines, snail-mail, eyeglasses and eyeglass cases, bridge-calendar problems, and small pieces of paper scribbled with numbers, creeping across the kitchen table like a rising tide. But I can only take it for so long; then I have to straighten up and put away.

Here is where Mark's handyman abilities have been a blessing. Over time, using a combination of homemade shelving and plastic baskets, he's converted several odd spaces around the trailer into his 'n' hers cubbyholes all referred to as "my Place" or "your Place." (Mark: "Where's my June Bridge Bulletin?" Donia: "It's in your Place—no, in your *other* Place.") Even more of a marriage-saver are the slim wooden wall racks he made in the woodworking shop at Texas Trails. These are now mounted next to our bed, front door, vanity-desk, and kitchen table, adding even more ways to stash clutter out of the way.

Far more vexing than physical space problems are the psycho-social stresses that arise when two people without jobs are living a nomadic lifestyle, twenty-four/seven, in a rolling fiberglass box. What a huge adjustment it is from the preretirement life we led in our four-bedroom ranch house in Alexandria—each with an independent career, activity schedule, and car to get around in. Not only are the two of us together constantly, but we now have only one vehicle between us, which means outings must be negotiated and planned in advance. It gives a whole new meaning to the term "full-timer."

Living on the road instead of in a fixed place with a familiar routine, we are faced with niggling decisions to be made every time we turn around. Shall we dump the tanks here, or wait till tomorrow and get a full hookup? Do you want shelving in that cabinet, or plastic baskets? NBC news tonight, or would you rather Dan Rather? In the beginning, we were drowning in petty decisions. Mark and I both love to be in charge, so we were doing everything together and quibbling over the stupidest details imaginable. ("Do you really need grapes and oranges *and* kiwi fruits?" "*Yes.*") At one point we decided to alternate days on minor decisions, Mark making all the judgment calls one day, and I the next. This lasted only about a week; we could never remember who was Decision Boss on which day. And besides, what's the definition of a "minor" decision?

As the newness wore off, I'm happy to report, these petty control issues mostly evaporated. "Anything's fine with me; you decide" is how we keep the domestic tranquillity now. For this to work, though, the designated decision maker needs to *make the decision.*

Because full-timers spend so much of their lives together, arranging for some time apart is a true necessity. At first I felt guilty saying, "No, I don't want to go riding on the bike trail today; I really want to stay home and write letters." I had the nagging feeling I was going to miss something wonderful and regret it forever. But this phase, too, passed. No longer do I feel the need to accompany Mark on every sightseeing tour, bridge tournament, or grocery shopping expedition. So what if he brings home zucchinis with blemishes? (Which he does. Even though I've showed him a million times what to look for.) (Mark: I do not.)

On these occasions I'm always delighted to have the time alone to do my own thing, even if it's just puttering around the trailer making all the decisions myself. He loves his solo time, too. The perfect Mark day consists of playing eighteen holes of golf with a pick-up foursome, going to McDonald's for a couple of burgers, and wandering around window shopping for an hour on the way home. I can be perfectly happy just staying home doing the vacuuming and four loads of laundry. Or I might take the truck out by myself to explore country roads that look intriguing on the map, leaving Mark home to dog-sit in a lawn chair and smoke a cigar. As the quilting ladies at Texas Trails were fond of saying: "Love, honor, and obey—but not lunch every day."

On really bad days in the sardine can—and everybody gets that smothered feeling from time to time—I can always retreat to my favorite fantasy of running away from home. There I am, tooling along in my sparkling little twenty-foot, all-in-one Class C motorhome with its comfy cab-over bed and cute curtains. I can drive it and park it and even back it up all by myself, and I don't need any advice on how to do the hookups, thank you anyway. I'm on my own, watching any TV show I please, picking out perfect zucchinis at the farmers' market.

Once, when I was really steamed up over some nitpicky comment Mark made, I furiously blurted out my RV getaway fantasy to him. Great move—now he wants his *own* Class C bachelor rig. And wants to keep in touch by e-mail, so we can meet for hot dates whenever our paths cross.

39 Austin, Texas
April 4

Bulletin: Donia and I are now official Texans! Don't be confused by the fact that we don't really live anywhere. Minor detail.

Let me explain. Leaving the Rio Grande Valley, we headed northward to Livingston, just above Houston, where the Escapees' home campground and national headquarters are located. We wanted to see this so-called Rainbow's End RV park firsthand, and some time ago we had decided to establish ourselves legally as Texas residents. Escapees, it turns out, has elevated that bureaucratic chore to a high art, complete with a handy how-to pamphlet called "How to Become a Real Texan." (Donia points out that she already *is* a real Texan—born in Beaumont in 1943, and proud owner of those fifty acres of cotton land in Odem.)

Our first step was to sign up for the Escapees mail service, so we would have an address in Polk County. We were having some problems with our original mail-forwarding service, so this seemed an appropriate time to make the switch. (If you didn't get our new-address announcement, let me know. I'll send you another copy.)

Armed with an address, we could now tackle steps #2 through #8: truck and trailer safety inspections, vehicle registrations and license plates, Texas driver's licenses, and new insurance for our truck, trailer, and cabin in Virginia. The vehicle part of it was a cinch. The Polk County folk love Escapees for the most part, and they have done this paperwork many times. Before we could say "Howdy," we were Texans—though no taller, unfortunately. We were so delighted to be virtual residents of this friendly, efficient little town that we immediately went and got cards at the public library. We could have registered to vote, too, but decided to wait a while on this one. First we need to find out what happens if you get summoned to Livingston for jury duty from somewhere like Maine or Montana.

The insurance steps (#6–#8) were trickier. Luckily, the Escapees parks are extremely telephone-friendly. I parked myself in one of the comfortable phone cubicles and started dialing 800 numbers for insurance quotes. The vehicles proved no big deal, but trying to get insurance on vacant property in Virginia was like running my head into a brick wall over and over. We had sewed up our Livingston residence-change business in less than three hours total, but it was several days before I finally got all the insurance stuff worked out.

Of course, this meant getting to hang out with the insanely friendly Escapees! I quickly became a regular in the 25¢-limit poker game and rediscovered poker-playing skills I haven't used since high school in Highland Park, Illinois. The Escapees played some games I was unfamiliar with, including Three-Two, Oklahoma, Fiery Cross, and some three-card-flop pyramid game whose name I forget. My first two evenings were marked by heavy losses as I learned the ropes. Luckily, I won more than I lost the next few nights and was able to dig myself out of the $14 hole I started in.

Donia and I also played bridge on three of the evenings. The games were basic rubber bridge, and we drew for partners after every six hands. The socializing was the important thing here, and we met and mingled with many nice people. We also enjoyed two potluck dinners, an ice cream social, and lots of hugs—the hugging of strangers being a trademark Escapee activity.

The Escapees club is big on volunteerism, so one day Donia volunteered to do a "couple hours' worth" of grunt work in the mail-forwarding building. Some 25,000 pieces of mail pass through this facility daily—far more than is handled by the post office in many small towns. Being a diehard workaholic, my beloved wife came back high as a kite after eight straight hours of mail sorting. She bragged that she had been steadily promoted through four levels—junk-mail sorting, second class (magazine) sorting, correcting addresses for mismarked pieces, and finally, filing second class mail in member "boxes," which are actually fat file folders lined up on row upon row of tables. I suspect Donia stayed all that time just to work her way up to this prestigious fourth level, so she could sneak a look at our own brand-new box and make sure it was 100 percent okay. It was, though it had no contents yet.

And so with our mail folder personally inspected and our fiscal house in order, we were off to Austin, seventy-five miles west. Here we had a long-planned date to meet the family of Travis's fiancée, and start the ball rolling on the whens, wheres, whats, whos, and hows for the upcoming wedding. Travis and Amy flew down from New York. There were Escapees-type hugs all around when we met Amy's mom, two sisters, brother-in-law, and little nephew Zachary. Cleo cordially sniffed important body parts with their family dog, Sebastian. The visit was wonderful in a big, new, extended-family way, and certainly set the stage for happy times in October.

While in Austin, we stayed in literally every RV park in the metropolitan area for a few days apiece, to pick the one we'd like to come back to in the fall. These ranged from the $14 per night in-town park that was too cheap to put toilet paper in the bathrooms and where you had to deposit 35¢ to make a toll-free call, to a heavily oak-treed park in the northeast suburbs, to the luxurious Lone Star RV Resort south of town, which boasts a $100,000 air-conditioned bathhouse, a brand new laundry, and a modem hookup complete with private work desk. Guess which place we'll stay in for the wedding? Oh, yes, and Donia and I *personally* tried out every restaurant on Trav and Amy's list of potential rehearsal-dinner sites. Heck, being the groom's parents is a tough job, but somebody has to do it.

After Trav and Amy returned home, I went and had my eyeballs fixed by the best doctor in Austin and his miraculous laser machine. I'm free of eyeglasses for the first time since fourth grade. Well, that's not entirely true. As a trade-off for getting good distance vision, I now have the same need for up-close reading glasses shared by everybody else over forty. No problem, I just went to Wal-Mart and got myself a mild-strength pair for $8. I wrote a detailed description of the operation and recuperation in a separate letter. If you have a strong stomach and want a copy, let me know. Or did I send it to you already? Hey, the laser fixed my eyes, not my brain.

That left income taxes as the remaining item on my Household Business To-Do List. This is a process that I had actually pre-planned since we ran away last June, and worried about on and off since. It turned out to be no different from past years, before our house had wheels. First, as always, I bought the current year's edition of Turbo Tax. This is the best computer program—nay, the best product of any kind—in the universe. Why didn't the IRS ever think of putting personal taxes into a step-by-step, easy-to-understand, logical computer program? Oh, don't get me started!

Anyway, here is my method: First, spread all the papers from the whole year out all over the bed and floor. Yell at the dog for stepping on them. Feed last year's tax data into this year's program (seamless, thanks to Turbo Tax). Question Donia closely to see if her records are all up to date. Yell at Donia about her records. Buy Donia dinner in a fancy restaurant. Start feeding numbers into Turbo Tax. Curse the IRS, everyone who sent defective 1099s and 1098s, and various other entities who failed to send them at all. Send e-mails and make phone calls demanding immediate action.

Go out and audition a few more Austin eateries for the re-hearsal dinner. Check e-mail and voicemail for responses. Feed new numbers into Turbo Tax, including estimates for the still-missing ones. Push the button to finish and print the taxes. Swear at the printer. Receive actual numbers for the estimates. Push the button and swear some more, and then file form number 4868 for an extension of time to file.

Well, it works for me.

Finally, with a big lump in my throat, I left Donia comfortably parked at Lone Star and made a quick round-trip flight to Virginia for one more item of business: listing the Best Revenge for sale with a Front Royal real estate company. It is becoming clearer and clearer that we like this lifestyle for the time being, and it's unlikely that we would ever settle on Front Royal as a permanent home base. Renting a storage room for the family keepsakes and few pieces of remaining furniture will be cheaper than keeping the house, and we will be freed from the responsibility of owning a vacant home that we don't use. It gives us a sad, scary feeling to think about giving up our cabin. It's the last link to our old life, and it's been such a big part of our lives together. But it simply makes no sense to keep it any longer.

So here we are—taxes paid, cabin up for sale, rehearsal-dinner restaurant selected, and a space in Austin's finest RV park reserved, six months in advance, for our October return. To celebrate, Donia, Cleo, and I went and joined hundreds of other folks on a grassy hillside next to the river bridge in downtown Austin to watch the famous bats fly out of their roosts at sunset. Yes, you heard me right. They didn't fly out of my belfry; they live in the tiny spaces under the bridge supports. Every night at sunset millions of them fly out from under the bridge and pepper the evening sky with their little furry bodies, eating insects. Tons and tons of bugs they eat, mosquitoes and everything else they can get their little mouths around, every night. So, bats are *good*, okay? And I don't want to hear any more derogatory bat remarks from anyone out there.

Wishing you all a bug-free sunset, wherever you may be,
Mark

40 Where Is Your Legal Residence?

Whenever we meet new people on the road the first question is always, "Where are you from?" For full-timers, this can take a while to explain. At the beginning we would try to get by with, "We used to live in Virginia." Whereupon our new friends would fire back, "And where do you live now?" Let me tell you, this dialogue could really slow things down at the bridge table. You would have thought we were from Mars, when they found out we lived nowhere—and everywhere.

Now we simply say, "We're full-timers. We live and travel full-time in our RV." More and more these days, people understand what the phrase *RV full-timer* means. When the year 2000 census takers swept through our campground in Las Cruces, New Mexico, they didn't bat an eye as we explained our nomad status.

Even us nomads must have a legal address somewhere, however, so we have to pick a state to claim as our "domicile." For full-timers who no longer own a residence other than their RV, the choice of a state is wide open.

Carol Richards, a lawyer who lives right up the road from Escapees headquarters in Livingston, Texas, gives an excellent seminar on domicile issues at RV gatherings around the country. She defines domicile as "the one true and fixed place to which you plan to return any time you are away." For travelers (a definition that may or may not fit full-timers at any given time), Richards says legal domicile means "the last fixed place you lived and considered your home." Many full-timers would interpret this to be the place they camped last night. Obviously, the domicile issue is full of gray areas and bears careful examination.

Experts, including Carol, advise full-timers to (1) choose the one best state for your circumstances, (2) get all registrations and other legal paperwork switched over to your adopted state, and then (3) *follow its laws* as though you really lived there. You can even file an "affidavit of domicile" with the state, to make your intentions perfectly clear.

So, how do you decide which state is best? The items most full-timers look at are:

- state tax structure (income, sales, inheritance, etc.);
- license and registration fees and renewal requirements, such as annual inspections;
- vehicle insurance rates;
- any state-required special driver's licenses for operating a large vehicle;
- health care availability, especially financial coverage, through HMOs or insurance providers;
- mail-forwarding services.

I have to confess, Donia and I did not do a lot of in-depth study of this subject during our preretirement research phase. We focused solely on mail-forwarding services in states that had limited or no state income tax (see box). We decided at the outset to become residents of whatever state our chosen mail service was in. This is not a necessity, by the way. Some people use the Escapees mail service in Texas, yet are legally domiciled in some other state. We just figured it would be easier to consolidate everything in one place. Imagine a scenario in which you have an Oregon mailing address because of your mail-forwarding service, but you're trying to get a driver's license and vehicle tags in Florida. This could lead to a lot of explaining.

Surely the reason so many full-timers choose Texas residency is the existence of the friendly and helpful Escapees in Livingston. Their pamphlet on becoming a "real Texan" was our bible for the few days we spent there getting our life in order. The town, in fact, is known in RV circles as Mailbox, Texas, because of the many full-timers and frequent travelers who use the mail-forwarding service there.

Incidentally, the Rainbow Drive address assigned to mail-service customers was actually declared a legal domicile address in a court ruling some time back. This is because the Rainbow's End park is a place where people can and do actually live year-round, and because of the wonderful elder-care facility set up there for full-timers who cannot travel any more.

Our state-residence business in Livingston started with vehicle inspections at a garage in town, an easy process that came with a warm welcome when the clerk recognized us as Escapees from our address. The next day, we took our safety inspection paperwork to the county motor vehicle department. Again we were welcomed as Escapees, and had license plates and registration for our truck and fifth-wheel in less than half an hour.

On a roll now, we went around the corner to a state office to get our Texas driver's licenses. Denise, the super-efficient clerk, promptly photographed us, tested our eyes, thumbprinted us (on a nifty, inkless pad that fed our whorls directly into the computer), took our money, confiscated our Virginia licenses, and issued our temporary Texas licenses. I balked momentarily when asked to turn over my old Virginia license. I guess in that moment it hit me that there was no turning back—we really were going to be *Texans* now. But Denise was firm. I could not keep the Virginia license, not even for a souvenir. She promised our permanent licenses would arrive in the mail shortly, which they did. Unfortunately, the computer camera put a fleck of virtual spinach between Donia's front teeth; she will just have to live with it till 2005.

It dawned on us during this process that Polk County has a nice little arrangement here—lots of vehicle registration fees to swell their coffers, more "population" for counting toward state grant apportionments and voting census, but no burden on the schools, fire department, or other municipal services. No wonder these folks are so friendly to Escapees!

Getting our insurance policies switched over to Texas was not as straightforward as getting Texas licenses. The truck and trailer presented no major problems; this was just a matter of looking for full-timer insurance ads in the RV magazines and calling the various companies to compare coverage and rates. But I spent hours and hours on the pay phone trying to find an insurer for our cabin in Virginia. Several places I called flat refused to write insurance on an empty second home. Virginia companies would no longer deal with us because we "lived" in Texas. Texas companies wouldn't insure property in Virginia. One agency said they would be happy to insure the second home if we bought our primary homeowners insurance from them, but the conversation ground to a fast halt when they learned that our primary residence had wheels. Such is life for those of us who don't fit into neat pigeonholes, residence-wise.

Finally I found a Virginia agent who was interested enough in our situation to plead our case with her underwriters. Curiously, they were most concerned that the vacant second home was on an unpaved road. We got our coverage, but going through this arduous process made us think hard about hanging onto faraway property that we were not planning to use in the foreseeable future. It was a major factor in our decision soon after to sell the Virginia place.

For those interested in gritty fiscal details, the net effects of our switch to Texas residency included a hefty increase in vehicle license fees and a slight decrease in truck insurance premiums. The latter was offset by an increase in trailer insurance, mainly due to the addition of personal liability coverage, which formerly was part of our homeowners policy. (Are you reading over my shoulder, Cleo? That's in case *you* bite someone, or trip them down our trailer steps.) However, the increases paled in comparison to what we would be saving on state income tax and personal property tax, as Texas has neither. Texas makes up for this with an 8.25 percent sales tax on everything except groceries—but then, we're only rarely in the state to spend money buying things.

Many people ask about voting procedures for RV full-timers. This works the same way it does for anybody else: You register to vote in the state where you claim residency and obtain an absentee ballot by mail if you are out of state at election time. Donia and I were offered voter registration cards at the Livingston

Prime States for Full-Timers to Call "Home"

One of the tasks facing would-be full-timers is to narrow their residency options to a few states, and then do some research and comparison. Trailer Life Books has a publication entitled *Selecting an RV Home Base* that summarizes taxes and other residency requirements for all fifty states. (See Information Resources, page 280.) But laws may change, so it's important to confirm facts with officials in your chosen state.

Since state income taxes are probably the single biggest financial consideration, many full-timers choose as their domicile one of the handful of states that do not tax income. The ones that tax *no* income are:

- Alaska
- Nevada
- South Dakota
- Texas
- Washington
- Wyoming

Florida, New Hampshire, and Tennessee do not tax salaries or pensions but do tax the value of some investments or income from interest and dividends. Interestingly, Uncle Sam doesn't give a hoot about your residence status as long as you file and pay federal income tax. If you don't, he'll find you no matter which state you pick as your domicile.

One thing that experts caution full-timers *not* to do is switch state residency around to sidestep specific taxes. We've heard several horror stories about people who bought expensive motorhomes in one state to avoid sales taxes, then tried to register them in a different state to avoid high registration fees. The result for some of them was prosecution, fines (in one case, $132,000!), and months of community service.

continued

In general, the potential "trouble" state is not the one you're trying to become a resident of, but the one you're moving out of—*if* they have reason to believe you're trying to skip out on taxes by changing your residency to a new state that you don't really live in or have any legitimate ties to. Moving as many aspects of your life as possible into your new state is a must if you want to avoid legal hassles.

motor vehicle office the day we got our tags and licenses. At the time, we decided to hold off until we had had a chance to check out possible jury-duty complications, but this was just our personal reservation. A great many Escapees do register to vote in Livingston as a routine step in their switch to Texas residency. It's another helpful piece of evidence that they are genuinely committed to their new domicile state.

It must be noted that Livingston full-timers—who account for a whopping 24 percent of registered voters in Polk County— encountered a political firestorm just before the 2000 presidential elections. A group of local residents legally challenged the voting rights of full-timers registered in Livingston, apparently motivated by a couple of tight Texas state legislature races that could have determined the majority party. The Escapees organization swiftly took up the fight on their members' behalf, and ultimately obtained a federal court ruling that allowed full-timers to vote in November 2000. Escapees has vowed to stay on top of the issue for future elections, as voting is a most fundamental right for all citizens—even those who live in homes on wheels.

41 Kerrville, Texas
April 20

I was born in Texas, and nearly all my relatives live here. All my life I've heard about the Hill Country with its famous bluebonnets, the Texas state flower. So why on earth did it take me fifty-six years to finally visit this gorgeous place? For the geographically challenged among you, the Hill Country is a large plateau in central Texas about a hundred miles in diameter, rising just to the west of the line that connects Austin and San Antonio. I love the names of the tiny ranch towns scattered here and there: Driftwood, Dripping Springs, Wimberley, Blanco, Bandera, Twin Sisters, Llano, Marble Falls. The land rolls in soft hills to the horizon, layers of fainter and fainter blue-gray. The tall, deciduous forests of east Texas have given way to scrubby live oaks, mesquite, and other waxy-leafed species that can stand up to drought. Picturesque peach orchards, sheep farms, meandering creeks, longhorn cattle, and wildflowers abound.

Mark's former house-inspecting boss, who knew just about everything, always said the Garden of Eden was seventy-two degrees Fahrenheit with 38 percent humidity. That's exactly what we have here. (This April, at any rate.) There's a sensuous pleasure just being outside in the heavenly air. Our timing was perfect, because April is prime bluebonnet season. The roadsides are blanketed with these distinctive Texas lupines, plus Indian paintbrush, coreopsis, wine cups, and cactus flower. One day we took a much-recommended scenic drive called the Willow City Loop, and stopped to gaze down into a broad valley at what we thought was a bright blue pond. Instead, we realized, it was a sea of bluebonnets. Wow!

We spent a couple of days in Fredericksburg, a town founded by German immigrant families in the 1800s. The area still retains a strong German flavor—dominated by antique shops, bakeries, and German restaurants that offer delicious sausages and schnit-zels, which you *know* Mark and I have dutifully sampled. I've never exactly been an architecture buff, but the rustic style of buildings here just knocks me out. Lots of nineteenth-century, frontier-type structures featuring log beams, wood siding, and square-cut limestone or rough stucco. Many of the old houses, cabins, barns, and mills have been remodeled into bed and break-fasts. There are some two hundred of them in the Fredericksburg vicinity alone.

We are here too early for the peaches to be ripe, but it's lambing season—a nice tradeoff. The fields are full of Cleo-sized kids and lambs, frolicking about as cute as puppies. Once, out for a Cleo walk near our campground, we wandered up the lane of a farmer who uses llamas to guard his flocks. He told us that Cleo was not welcome ("due to dogs presenting the danger of preditation, Ma'm") but that Mark and I could wander around his farm as much as we liked. We did that several times—but please don't tell Cleo. When we returned from our lamb walks, we always told her we had "gone to the store."

This part of Texas is also where Lyndon B. Johnson returned to recharge his soul (Mark: What soul?) when the pressures of Washington got too intense. The other day we toured the much-storied LBJ ranch, aka the Texas White House, on the banks of the Pedernales River. It turned out to be a sharply sentimental journey for us fifty-somethings, bringing to mind the entire tu-mult of the 1960s. Fascinating factoid: LBJ's favorite song, which he blared at top volume while driving visitors at top speed around the ranch in one of his two Lincoln convertibles, was "Raindrops Keep Falling on My Head" by B. J. Thomas. (Well, you didn't think it was going to be a number by Country Joe and the Fish, did you?)

I haven't spent a lot of time yet thinking about the dream house we might eventually build somewhere, but when I saw the reconstructed "dogtrot cabin" on the banks of the Pedernales where LBJ was born, I immediately knew this was what I wanted for my future retirement pad. A dogtrot cabin has two symmetrical sections of about two rooms each, joined by a covered breezeway eight to twelve feet wide (which the dog trots through on his way from the front porch to the back porch). In hot summer climates like that of the Hill Country, these pioneer cabins were oriented so prevailing winds would blow through the dogtrot and cool the whole house.

I have brought up the dogtrot-cabin-on-a-riverbank concept at least three times a day for the past week, despite Mark's grumbles about inefficient heating/cooling and resale value. I told him he could have his own half of the house and could even smoke cigars inside his private wing any time he wanted, but the old poopie is still not convinced. I guess he is holding out for the golf-condo-with-golf-cart-garage-and-no-exterior-maintenance concept. That's okay. I have plenty of time to work on him. We have miles to go before we settle down to a retirement pad of any kind.

We are currently camped at the state park in Kerrville, the Hill Country's largest town and shopping hub. The park is smack on the banks of the Guadalupe River, a swift-flowing ribbon of amazing emerald green that cuts through the Hill Country from west to east. What makes one river blue and another green? Nobody around here seems to know. But in any case, the Guadalupe would be a great river to build a dogtrot cabin on. Kerrville doesn't have the quaint touristy charm of Fredericksburg, but it does have an active bridge club with three games a week. They play in a meeting room at Kerrville's ritzy Y.O. Ranch Hotel, the lobby of which has cathedral ceilings, massive wood beams, and walls covered with trophy heads—deer, elk, bobcat, antelope, buffalo, you name it, it's staring down at you with glassy, accusing eyes. (Hey, this is *Texas*. Get over it.)

Turns out there is an actual Y.O. Ranch as well, a combination cattle ranch, convention center, and exotic game preserve out in the boondocks about forty-five miles west of Kerrville. They give bus or jeep tours of the ranch, complete with a lavish chuck wagon lunch, so we drove out there one day to check it out. We arrived just as the morning bus tour was discharging its dozens of chattering foreign tourists at the bunkhouse for their chuck wagon lunch. Again, our timing was perfect: Mark and I turned out to be the only customers for the afternoon tour, so our private cowboy guide took us in the open jeep, fitted out with benches in the back. This allowed us to get up close and personal with the animals and even feed some of the tamer ones food pellets out of our hands.

It was like going on our own mini-safari, winding through the open ranchland on bumpy dirt roads past herds of African gazelles, dik-diks, zebras, many varieties of endangered deer, and one ill-tempered ostrich that followed us around the ranch, taking wily shortcuts to head us off at the pass. This bird was just after food pellets, like everyone else on the tour, but he had been known to kick tourists on occasion, so we stayed in the jeep when he was around. Mark had his camera going a mile a minute, taking fabulous pictures of the animals, including his very favorite—a photo of me reaching way up over my head with the bucket of food pellets to feed the giraffe. Except it dawned on him about halfway through the tour that he had forgotten to put *film* in the camera. Meanwhile our friendly driver was bumping the jeep ever deeper into the rocky backwoods to find more great animals to photograph, so Mark kept pretending to take pictures, since he did not have the heart to tell the guy the camera had been filmless the whole time.

We had to hang around central Texas long enough for Mark to return to the laser center for a final eye checkup, so we looped down to San Antonio for a couple of days, arriving just in time to catch the tail-end of Fiesta, their annual Mardi Gras-like cele-bration. We joined the revelers at several street fairs and attended a colorful *charreada* (Mexican rodeo, to you *gringos*). And of course, sampled yummies from all the food booths. We strolled along San Antonio's famed River Walk, one of our very favorite urban spaces, and also visited the Japanese Sunken Gardens in the city park. Built in the 1920s on the site of a used-up rock quarry, the garden features koi pools, trailing vines, flowers, wil-lows, and serpentine walkways. The historical marker noted that after the attack on Pearl Harbor in 1941 it was renamed the Chinese Sunken Gardens—and remained that way until 1978, when revisionist history was re-revised.

But the best thing we did in San Antonio was buy a new mattress! All our lives we have heard that hard mattresses are best for your back, so we have always slept on rock-hard mattresses, including the foam job that came with the trailer. But if hard is good, I wondered, why did I toss and turn all through the night, and get up with an aching back every morning? Then we remembered we had also heard that stiff-bristled toothbrushes were good, real butter was bad, and if you wore sneakers instead of sturdy Oxfords as a kid your feet wouldn't develop right.

So we shopped for a soft bed. We didn't like the (expensive) air bed we tried at the mall or the foam pad that a friendly foam-pad dealer lent us for a one-night trial. Then at Mattress World we found a soft mattress that felt just right. We took delivery the very next day on our way out of town. Mark was delighted at the idea of reversing the usual delivery process—bringing our house to the store, rather than having the store bring the mattress to our house. The salesman and his helper simply carried the mattress out to the parking lot and maneuvered it into our little bedroom. Ever since, we've been sleeping like babies.

As we prepare to head northward, we wish you all heavenly spring days and comfy sleeping at night, on the mattress of your choice. We miss you all, so keep those e-mails coming.

Love,
Donia

42 Who Services Your Rig?

In the world of serious RVers, no subject is as intensely personal and hotly debated as rig maintenance. Some people spend hours on end washing and waxing their RVs, servicing their twelve-volt batteries, adjusting tire pressures, reading volumes of passionate advice in magazines and Web sites about other maintenance musts, and discussing all these things endlessly with fellow campers.

Mark and I are close to the opposite extreme on this one. The only thing we are passionate about is getting regular oil changes for our engine—at whatever quickie-lube place we can find when the mileage-reminder sticker tells us it's time. We have run across several different quick-lube chains around the country and, as far as we can tell, they all know what they are doing.

Aside from these oil changes, plus an occasional checklist item from our Ford manual, our approach is, *If it ain't broke, don't fix it.* If it does get broke, there are plenty of competent repair places around the country who can get you up and running again.

Although this program has worked fine for us, we certainly don't recommend it to anybody else. I admit, we probably would have gotten better service from our twelve-volt trailer batteries if we had cleaned the terminals and added water to the reservoirs a little sooner. But there's so much technical preventive maintenance advice floating around out there—much of it contradictory—that you could go crazy trying to sort it all out. We usually wait till something becomes obvious before we take action. And as far as we know, none of our vehicle problems has ever been the result of lax maintenance.

Living full-time on the road presents some interesting twists in the maintenance-and-repair department. For one thing, you have the option of driving your home back to the factory for any major work that needs to be done. When Mark accidentally

Zen and the Art of RV Maintenance

Donia originally said I could write the chapter on vehicle maintenance because I'm a guy, and vehicle maintenance is "guy stuff." But she didn't think my rough draft was serious enough, except for the part about oil changes. So I got demoted to writing this little box.

Apparently, from what I've observed in campgrounds, if you have a motorhome as opposed to a trailer, it's important to wash it—or at least rub it with a cloth or brush—every night.

The maintenance schedule for most other jobs becomes clear if you just keep your eyes and ears open. You're sure to be talking to your insanely friendly neighbors in most campgrounds, and many of these conversations start like this:

Neighbor: Nice day, huh?

You: Yeah!

Neighbor: Boy, am I pooped. Had to get off the road early today so I could shoot some graphite lubricant into my compartment latches. But I'm finished now. Where you from?

The first few months I would foolishly ask my New Best Friend what graphite lubricant was and why it needs to be shot into my compartment latches. That generally led to about a four-hour explanation of absolutely essential vehicle latch maintenance regimens. Now I know better. I tell him I'm from Delaware, which is the only state that nobody seems to have an opinion on, and I sneak off to ask some other neighbor what graphite is:

Me: Nice day, huh?

Other neighbor: Yeah!

Me: Heylemmeaskyousomething. What's graphite lubricant?

continued

Other neighbor: You talking about that Locktite stuff you get for 79 cents on the auto parts aisle at Wal-Mart? I think you spritz it into your compartment latches if they get sticky. Never had to use it myself. You?

So there you have it. That's my method for coping with RV maintenance. If you relax enough about it, but keep casually alert, you are bound to hear from a fellow camper about something that might need attending to on your rig.

By the way, I'm writing this in the customer waiting room of an RV shop in Idaho while getting my wheel bearings repacked. And to think, a week ago I'd never even heard of a wheel bearing!

scraped our door and side panels against that diesel guard post in Georgia, we waited until our travels took us near the factory in northern Indiana to get them repaired—the advantage of factory repairs being that the parts are available right on site, so the work is finished sooner and everything matches exactly.

One thing to bear in mind when getting major RV work done: It's your *home* that's in the shop, so you have to be prepared to spend the days out killing time in your truck or automobile until the repairs are complete. In our case, the factory finished in one day, during which we explored the Amish countryside, feasting on pie and other goodies until 5 p.m. But sometimes RVers end up camping out at the repair place for as long as it takes to get the work done. Many large RV shops actually have a few campsites out back with full or partial hookups, for just this purpose. *Movin' On* authors Ron and Barb Hofmeister wrote about staying for several days in their motorhome at one RV facility, literally locked inside the fenced enclosure each evening when the shop closed and the staff went home.

Another full-timer challenge confronted us during a heavy travel period one summer in the Pacific Northwest, when we started trying to remedy a leak in the truck's air conditioning. We first took the truck to a Ford dealer in Oregon, who spent one day fixing the leak and another day testing it. So far, so good. We paid the bill and moved on, only to discover—a week later and three hundred miles down the road—that the A/C was blowing warm again. After paying a second time to have the leak fixed, in Washington state, we moved on once more. This time the cool lasted nearly a month before it gave out.

Finally we reached Atlanta, where we would be visiting with Mark's family and could stay put long enough to see the job done right. In each case, the repairman had to start from scratch to diagnose the problem and try various solutions. We ended up spending about triple what it would've cost to fix if we had been living in one place—not to mention the aggravation of the whole rolling trial-and-error process. This is undeniably one of the downsides of being always on the move.

Most educational of all, however, was what we went through with our trailer tires. The first incident happened as we were driving through the town of Conroe, Texas, and a fellow driver pulled alongside us, frantically waving and pointing back toward the trailer. We pulled into a shopping center parking lot and discovered (with much distressed flapping about on my part) that the right front trailer tire was shredded right down to the rim, putting a dangerous double load on the rear right tire. This got fixed.

Two more tires failed before The Big One occurred one day at sunset, as we were steaming eastward on I-40 across Tennessee with a steady stream of tractor-trailers whizzing past us at 80 mph. This was probably the most perilous single moment in our travels to date. I happened to be driving when we heard the loud *pow* of a tire blowing out from the right rear side. Mark remained calm, Cleo remained calm, even I remained calm as I eased the rig onto the shoulder and helped change the tire. We'd had a bit of practice by now.

Eventually we replaced all our C-rated tires with heavier-duty D-rated tires. But we still had regular tire failures, and difficulty finding our chosen brand in different parts of the country. The tires we bought in Tennessee were unavailable when we were in

New Mexico and needed to get free warranty replacements. The hard lesson we learned as full-timers: Buy only nationwide brands of vital products that may need replacing.

Eventually we came to the realization that our heavy-duty fifteen-inch wheels and tires, despite their high load rating, were simply not capable of carrying the weight of our rig. Higher-priced trailers of our size and weight mostly had sixteen-inch wheels, which could wear much heavier-duty rubber. Problem: Our trailer's existing wheel wells were not tall enough to accommodate larger-diameter wheels. Solution: Raise the trailer's entire body three inches by installing four three-inch metal blocks on top of the axles.

This job was accomplished by a farm equipment repair yard in Oregon. Of course, *now* we needed an additional step to climb in and out of the trailer. Mark quickly made a wooden step box, similar to those that porters on passenger trains use to help passengers step down from train to platform. And, I am happy to say (knock on wood), we have been blessedly free of tire problems since we switched to sixteen-inch wheels and tires.

In addition to major items, little things occasionally need to be fixed. For instance, the engine's tendency early on to stall out in the middle of traffic was due to a faulty solenoid (whatever that is). Once we got it replaced—for free, under the Ford warranty—we had no more of those scary moments. Then there was the time the plastic casing on the trailer's rooftop A/C unit self-destructed and parts starting flying all over the place. A friendly trucker driving right behind us informed us of this problem over the CB radio.

We have also had little metal parts on the trailer give way. For example, both the support brace under our fold-down trailer steps and the slot that the crank-handle fits into to lower our rear leveling jacks broke as a result of metal fatigue. Getting these fixed was a matter of finding a welding shop with a big enough area to park our trailer. In our typical hit-and-miss fashion, we found just the place as we were passing through the dusty little town of Marfa in southwest Texas. I was excited about being in

Marfa, which is famous for mysterious lights flickering over the distant hills after nightfall. Tourists come from all over to see this eerie phenomenon. Unfortunately, the welder finished our two little jobs in twenty minutes, charged us $10, and had us on our way long before it was dark enough to see the Marfa Lights.

Collectively, these mechanical mishaps were wonderful growth experiences for us. Especially for me, since I tend to fret over the possibility of things going wrong. Things *always* go wrong; you can take that to the bank. But there's always someone who can help, just when you need them.

When we look back on our vehicle war stories, the problems fade into the background; we end up remembering the people who fixed them. The alert truck drivers, the guy in Georgia who freed us from the diesel guard post, the friendly and competent repairmen in little towns all over America. Often, the solutions they find are way simpler and cheaper than Mark and I—who are long on book learning but short on mechanical know-how— can possibly imagine. They reinforce the sublime lesson we keep learning over and over in our life on the road: Don't sweat it, everything is going to be all right.

43 Fort Cobb, Oklahoma
May 22

Donia wants a house by the water. I yearn for a golf course villa. We both got our wish this weekend. Site #8 in Area 3 of Fort Cobb State Park is twenty-five paces from Fort Cobb Lake and fifteen paces from the tenth green/eleventh tee of the golf course. Yesterday we took advantage of both. We strolled up the tenth fairway, signed in and walked eighteen holes, then strolled back down the tenth to our trailer. I had a beer, then a swim in the lake. The place is only about 10 percent occupied, so Cleo can play around off the leash, except when the park rangers are looking, and we have a real feeling of space and quiet.

So why is this place empty on a pretty May weekend? It could be a pre-Memorial Day calm, before the storm of summer family campers hits the parks and campgrounds. Or it could be that the whole state of Oklahoma is emptying out. We noted very little traffic on the roads. McDonald's on the highway was empty at lunchtime. The few towns we passed coming here seemed closed for repairs, or otherwise evacuated. And the newspaper this morning had a long story about closing schools and consolidating rural districts.

Come to think of it, west Texas might be emptying out too. We stopped at Archer City—the real-life "Thalia" of Larry McMurtry's *The Last Picture Show* trilogy—and found it to be practically a ghost town. The only employers left seem to be the county courthouse and McMurtry's used book store, Booked Up. The store is actually housed in four separate buildings all around the town square. We got lucky and spotted Larry himself as he walked in for breakfast at the local Dairy Queen, the one mentioned in the books and featured in the *Texasville* movie. As he stood at the counter trying to order his sausage gravy and biscuits, we acted like crazed teenage fans, shamelessly ambushing him into signing our copy of *Duane's Depressed,* the final book in his trilogy.

After breakfast I took Donia's picture standing in the weed-choked ruins of the Royal Theater, aka The Last Picture Show. Then we browsed the bookstore(s) for a while and Donia chatted a bit more with McMurtry, although that day he was not much of a conversationalist. This most prolific of modern novelist/screenwriters, surely a millionaire many times over, was working all alone in one of his cavernous storefronts, doggedly unloading and shelving some of the truckloads of books he buys up from secondhand bookstores around the country that are going out of business. In person he is exceedingly polite, soft-spoken, and utterly fixated on his goal of establishing the largest used-book collection in the world.

We also stopped at Wichita Falls, another city with a boarded-up downtown. Even the falls were turned off. Really. Apparently the real Wichita Falls washed out in a flood ninety years ago. In 1987 the city built a new Wichita Falls from scratch in the city park downtown, next to the Wichita River. The new falls are made of a terraced stack of red rocks about twenty feet tall. The water flow is supplied from the river, via a 3,500 gallon-per-minute pump. Unfortunately, recent rains have washed lots of mud and debris into the river upstream, so the pump had to be shut down for a few days to prevent damage at its intakes.

We celebrated our fifteenth anniversary at McBride's Steak-house. There may not be many people left in Wichita Falls, but one still remembers how to make a good Beefeater martini, and another can simmer ranch beans and grill a Kansas City sirloin to perfection. Donia and I toasted our happy years together, our dream retirement life, and the successful conclusion of our own private Tailgate Scandal a couple of days earlier.

This story involves the tailgate on our big Ford diesel pickup truck, which must be carefully raised and lowered at the right times during the hitching and unhitching process so it is not accidentally rammed against the trailer hitch-pin, which is made of a much harder metal than the tailgate. You would think we would know when to close the tailgate and when to leave it open, after nearly a whole year on the road. But you would be wrong. First I, and then Donia, just three days later, goofed up and bashed the hitch-pin against the tailgate. (I am convinced that Donia rammed the tailgate on purpose, just so I'd stop feeling stupid.)

So we had to go to an RV store near Dallas and buy one of those tailgates for dummies that are impossible to screw up because they have a cutout place in back for the hitch-pin to pass through. Installing the new tailgate was the easy part. Getting rid of a forty-five-pound, fire-engine red, bashed-in tailgate was the challenge. We considered three basic options: (1) leaving it by the curb in a fancy neighborhood with a "free to a good home" sign on it; (2) propping it up on the lawn of the county courthouse like avant-garde metal sculpture; (3) dumping it off a bridge into the Brazos River.

In the end we did the responsible thing: Snuck around until we found one of those huge railroad-car-type construction dumpsters with no one around, and pitched the tailgate in. Donia stood guard behind the truck covering up the license plate from view, so that, if there were federal agents sitting at the IHOP three hundred yards away eating pancakes and watching us through binoculars, they couldn't trace us through our license plate and make us take the tailgate back.

Speaking of cover-ups, while we were in the Dallas area we decided to take a cigar walk downtown around Dealey Plaza, the place where President John F. Kennedy was shot back in 1963. Donia, though she boasts of being a native Texan, had never seen the place. The famous grassy knoll where the alleged second gunman stood has become a veritable shrine now, with framed pictures of JFK and Jackie hanging on the fence, and hucksters selling books and audiotapes about what "really" happened.

Our favorite was a shady-looking guy peddling tours in his big convertible limo, just like the one Kennedy rode in that fateful day. Once the guy realized that Donia, Cleo, and I were not going to pay money to ride in his car, he went ahead and gave us his spiel for free anyway, about all the different conspirators involved, and where they all stood to fire their shots, and how then-Vice President Lyndon B. Johnson secretly engineered the assassination, because blah, blah, blah ad infinitum. Yeah, sure, pal. Whatever you say. We moved on down the street and left the guy giving the same pitch to new people who had walked up.

We will be here at our lakeside golf villa for another day; then we plan to continue north through Kansas and Nebraska, and spend some time in the Dakotas exploring the Badlands and Mount Rushmore. In mid-June or so, a left turn will take us to Montana, to visit our North Carolina friends Pete and Robin (the house deconstruction-meisters, remember?) at the summer cabin they built out of recycled lumber in the mountains near Kalispell. Their place has no plumbing or electricity, so most of their houseguests have to use a flashlight to see their way to the outhouse. But *we* travel with our own plumbing and electricity— ha ha ha! Is this RV the greatest, or what?

After Montana, a long, slow arc through Wyoming, Colorado, and New Mexico will land us back in Texas next fall for the wedding. So if you know any interesting folks or yummy restaurants in those parts of the country, let us know.

Love,
Mark

44 Why Do You Like Full-Timing?

It's a chilly October night at a Kentucky state park in the Appalachians. A young park ranger in a khaki uniform sets up her tape deck in an open-air pavilion and teaches folk-dancing steps to a sparse but spirited crowd. Mark and I sit on bleachers— another retired couple on one side of us, a homeless tent-camping family on the other. Three of the homeless children now dance exuberantly to their own beat on the wooden dance floor. My foot starts tapping to the music. A five-foot-three truck driver named Shorty and an earnest third-grader both want me for a partner, so I have a delicate decision to make. Five months ago I was dressed in a business suit, sitting in meetings to decide the agenda items for visiting consultants. Now I am dancing the Virginia Reel with an eight-year-old Appalachian boy under a cold, starry sky. Pinch me, I must be dreaming. Oh, wait a minute—this is our real life!

Total Freedom

The question is, how could we *not* like this fantasy life we are leading? To be "off the clock" for the first time since college is like being reborn with a whole new identity. It's a recreational witness-protection program, minus the evil hit men. Nobody knows where we are, and we're free to do anything we want.

As retired full-timers, we are liberated not only from the meetings, memos, and office politics of the workplace, but also from yard work, house chores, traffic jams, and the millstone of too much furniture and other possessions. We are freed from a daily routine. We can sleep as late as we please. No more exercising around the same old track; now we are walking or biking or hiking in a beautiful place we have never seen before.

Of course, the flip side is, we have also left behind our "comfort zone," the easy world of knowing where everything is and what's going to happen when. On the road, it's anything goes: You get lost, things break, places don't turn out the way you thought they would be. The pay phone is out of order, the laundromat is closed. You're always having to scrap your plans and do something else.

Coping with these conditions tests your flexibility and resourcefulness. You didn't realize you could change that tire until you had to. Surrounded by strangers, you learn to tolerate and even appreciate people's quirks and differences. You get used to doing without things you took for granted before. You learn to loosen up and go with the flow. For control-type personalities, this can take a while. But it's a worthy goal—really, it's the most profound freedom of all. Mark and I are still working on it.

Living in Nature
In our old life back in the East Coast megalopolis, nature was something you enjoyed on a weekend every now and then. Now nature is the medium we live in every day. Sometimes we are so surrounded by woods and water and wildlife we feel like part of the ecosystem.

I always wanted to retire to a place of natural beauty, but I never dreamed of such variety. We camp beside a Wisconsin lake glimpsed through tall pines. We listen from our Myrtle Beach campsite to the roaring Atlantic surf just over the dunes. Along the Big Bend of the Rio Grande, we share our campground with javelinas, shaggy little wild pigs gliding out of the brush at dusk to snoop for crumbs. I love watching the trees of America change with climate and terrain—from the tall, graceful palms of the subtropics, to scrubby desert mesquite, to the arching live oaks beside rushing creeks that let you know you have reached the Hill Country.

Mark and I like the West for the enveloping quality of the natural world out there, even if it's just miles of empty sky and desert. We hear a lot about the disappearing wilderness, and on an absolute scale I am sure it's true. But as we loop around the United States, our overriding impression is of vast, uninhabited stretches of pure nature that overwhelm the small signs of human civilization.

Out here in America's wide-open spaces we revel in the big-dome skies that are a stage for weather pageants of every description. Sun, shade, heat, humidity, wind, cold, clouds, rain—all carry more interest and impact than they used to in our climate-controlled world back home. The wind blows so hard in south Texas that it fights you for the trailer door. A strong thunderstorm rocks our little house, the rain a cozy drumming sound on the thin, strong roof. One summer we played cat and mouse with tornadoes chasing us across the Midwest. You have never seen greens, purples, blacks, and browns like those of a Minnesota sky on a tornado day. Our NOAA weather radio is a great companion when the weather rumors start.

In the dry West, we love the instant-cool effect of stepping from hot sun into shade. We seek the perfect weather balance—seventy-five degrees, with 40 percent humidity and a light breeze. "Air like velvet," we call it. It's amazing how often we find it. Yet try as we might to avoid freezing temperatures, they have caught us time and again—in the early frosts of the Grand Tetons in August, in the blue northers that sweep through central Texas, dropping the "mild" winter temperatures from seventy-five to twenty-five in a few hours' time. Snowbirds or not, we have awakened to a dusting of snow on numerous spring and fall mornings.

Endless Variety

Most people like having a place to call home, being a part of a fixed community, with familiar friends and activities around them. They enjoy getting away on vacations, maybe even spending whole seasons away from it all. But in the end, they need a place to come home to. This is the feeling of "roots" that so many non-full-timers say is more important to them than the fun of roaming the land.

Mark and I feel just the opposite. We're happy as birds, trading an anchored lifestyle for the adventure and variety of nonstop travel. We never tire of the changing scenery, following maps through unfamiliar terrain, getting off the highway to explore new places. The concept of "home" is an abstraction to us, at least for now. Each of us was born in one place, lived and worked in several others, and spent the majority of our career years in various suburbs of Washington, D.C. None of these places did we ever think of as home. We have adopted the Escapees slogan, "Home Is Where You Park It." When we are in travel mode, which is most of the year, we love the novelty of having a whole new place to live every few days. Last week we were on the prairie, then in the mountains. Now we're in the desert. Tomorrow we'll camp beside the Pacific Ocean.

Campgrounds across America are surprisingly quirky and different from one another. In my mind's eye, I can still picture nearly every place we stayed, even after two or three years' time. The slightly rundown RV park on Lake Nelson in Wisconsin, where I sat on the dock surrounded by the lovely North Woods landscape, happily doing needlework in a twenty-mile-per-hour wind. Our campground in Enid, Oklahoma, where all the sites radiated out from a center green like spokes on a wheel. *Circle the wagons, boys!* A place called the Landing Zone in Arco, Idaho, just purchased and renovated by an ex-helicopter pilot who named the individual campsites after his Vietnam buddies, some of whom never made it home. And the many parks across the land where our windows framed fantastic views—like the stark, knife-edged wall of the South Dakota Badlands, or the majestic Organ Mountains outside Las Cruces, New Mexico, so named because they resemble a giant pipe organ jutting up against the eastern sky.

Nonstop Learning

During our working days, the emphasis was not so much on learning new things as on getting more efficient at the old ones. That abruptly changed when we took to the road. Now, no matter where we go, we always discover something we never knew before. About cactus plants, about RV weight ratings, about nineteenth-century architectural details, about geology, or animals, or regional barbecue customs. Mark and I are natural-born students, I guess. We read all the brochures and plaques, listen to the ranger talks, study the exhibits, and say Wow! We take notes, even though there will never be a quiz.

Sometimes our exploring takes a deeply personal turn. We look up relatives we have not seen in years, and some we've never met before. A distant cousin directed Mark to a historic storefront in Helena, Montana, where a plaque described how part of his family had been merchants on the frontier. One of my distant cousins showed us an area of rural Texas hundreds of miles from where my relatives live now. Here were places I had heard about but never thought I would see: my grandmother's girlhood home, a white frame farmhouse now listed in the local historic register; a crumbling one-room schoolhouse on Double Horn Creek, where the family camped on deer-hunting trips; a cemetery tucked away in a stranger's back pasture, filled with the faded tombstones of my pioneer ancestors. The grave of a girl who would have been my great aunt had she not died at the age of two.

We also learn fascinating things from strangers we meet along the way. We talk with truck drivers and waitresses, rock-shop owners and welders, ranchers and rodeo guys, American Indians and Basque people and Canadians and Mexican-Americans and others so different in outlook and culture from those we lived among in suburbia. People are amazingly open, we have found, when they're chatting with travelers they are never going to see again. We love the stories they tell us, sometimes funny, sometimes sad or angry, mostly just straightforward, describing things important to them. The retired couple we met in Forks, Washington, who had wrested custody of their granddaughter away from their own drug-addicted daughter and were struggling to raise the girl themselves. The harp builder in Pigeon Forge, Tennessee, who told us how he had lost an entire kennel of German Shepherd puppies in three days to tropical distemper, and after that could never bear to work with dogs again.

On one memorable evening in Copper Harbor, Michigan, we shared a campfire and roasted marshmallows with a young neighboring couple. James drove a truck; Laurie was a pharmacy technician. With our faithful dogs curled up at our sides, we reminisced far into the night about the past dogs in our lives that we had loved and, finally, lost. I thought about all the nights, going back maybe 20,000 years, that small nomadic groups must have spent camping beside great bodies of water with their domesticated wolves, huddled around fires just like this one, gazing up at the same stars overhead. Could it be, we RV full-timers just inherited an extra measure of the wandering spirit from our early *Homo sapiens* ancestors?

45 Cheney Lake State Park, Kansas

May 29

Dear Friends and Fans:

Mom and Dad tell me it's Memorial Day Weekend, a holiday that officially marks the end of any campground tranquillity for the next ten weeks.

Here at Cheney Lake State Park, I guarantee you, tranquillity is already gone. We're awash in beer. Pickups have been pouring in since Thursday night towing all manner of trailers, pop-up campers, boats, and those roaring little "jet-skis" that sound like chainsaws. Overnight, a tent city has sprung up.

By 7 a.m. the campground is filled with kids zooming around on bikes and rollerblades. The picnic tables are covered with the food and cooking gear of campers making breakfast outside. The bathhouses are jammed with teenaged girls washing their hair and chattering like prairie dogs. And certain undisciplined real dogs are running loose all over the place, including one insanely friendly blue-heeler that looks like a little spotted pig. As dusk falls, folks fire up their grills and put their TV sets outside on the picnic tables, turning up the volume so they can hear over the sound of motorboats taking their last spins around the lake. Makes you proud to be an American!

Dearly Beloved

Well, I realize it's been a long time between letters. But I've been busy—mainly helping to plan Trav and Amy's wedding. It's quite amazing, the way these Humans get hitched up. Now you take dogs—we meet, we sniff, we "just do it," and that's that. But with people, it takes months of planning. Like, where the wedding is going to happen, what kind of food they're going

221

222 Steeles on Wheels

to eat, who's going to say what, which kind of car they're going to leave in after it's all over, et cetera.

And before the wedding the "bride" and "groom," as they are called, actually get to go to certain fancy stores and pick out all the presents they want to get! Then their wish list is put on this big computer and people can call up on the phone or even the Internet and send them a present, just like that! Plus, the guys and girls in the wedding have to wear certain kinds of clothes that all match, and they pick somebody to carry the ring, and somebody else to carry flowers in a basket, and to get it all right they have to practice the whole thing the day before the real wedding. Then after they practice it, everyone has to go out and EAT together, and this dinner is another thing that takes weeks of planning. I get tired, just thinking about it!

Actually, I was kind of hoping I would be given a role in the ceremonies. There is a legendary precedent for this in our family: When Mom and Dad got married back in 1984, Dad's so-called "best man" was his dog Mike (who I gather was a SAINT, unlike myself). Mike wore a white silk scarf and stood right beside Dad during the whole thing, so the story goes. And now I hear my golden retriever friend Holly, in Myrtle Beach, might be "ring-bearer" in her big sister's wedding later this year. They would tie the ring to a pillow, then tie the pillow onto Holly's back, and she would walk in a dignified way down the aisle to stand by the bride and groom. So I've been practicing walking around in a saintly manner, hoping my Humans will get the hint.

The Wolf Lady, and Other Tales of Texas

I know Dad has written a few e-mails about Texas, but you haven't gotten the full story. For example, I don't believe he mentioned the people at the neighborhood rodeo who brought their wolf to sit in the bleachers with them. The wolf was gentle as a kitten, but the lady was a wild woman. When Mom found out this person, Joan, was a hairdresser in her former life in Colorado, she makes the mistake of inviting her to our trailer after dinner to give her a "trim."

So, here comes Joan, and after scarfing down a plate of Mom's pineapple upside-down cake, the Wolf Lady whips out these tiny little scissors and starts chopping. Hair is flying everywhere and Mom's face is like, UH-OH. She looked like Mary Martin in *Peter Pan* when Joan got finished. Then the next day, the folks got ME sheared; I looked like Bo Peep's sheep when the groomer got done. Misery enjoys company, I guess.

Also, there was the day I stole the show at an outdoor bar in Luckenbach, Texas, the one made famous in the song by Jerry Jeff Walker. Actually, this bar is all there is in Luckenbach, Texas. People in cars or riding on huge motorcycles come to sit at picnic tables or on logs under the big old live oak trees and drink Lone Star beer. Some of them also get up on stage and try to play Willie Nelson songs on their guitars. But the crowd that day liked ME better than the musicians—a beautiful, well-behaved, fluffy white dog (this was right before my haircut). I was much in demand, cruising up and down the picnic tables, getting little munchies when Mom and Dad weren't looking.

Swimming with the Sharks

As a rule, sheepdogs like myself aren't big on swimming. But at a state park up near Frio, Texas, Mom and Dad looked so cool in that little Frio River, I decided to give it a try. I invented a technique called "dog paddling"—you work your front and back paws back and forth madly, just keeping your nose up out of the water. Mom and Dad were laughing and clapping like crazy, egging me on. A major Cleo triumph! Then I tried it again at a state park in Oklahoma, and just yesterday I swam again in this lake in Kansas where we are now. So I guess it works in all the different states.

Except yesterday I had no sooner started swimming than I was surrounded by a herd of screaming kids splashing around with their inflatable swimming toys and trying to pet me, and catch me, and hug me, et cetera. That kind of stuff doesn't mix well with dog paddling, so we had to give it up for the moment.

I have nothing against kids in general, but it drives me nuts when they run around wild. I can't help it. My mother was a border collie. My father was a Great Pyrenees. That's sheepdog, folks, any way you cut it. I see something running—or riding, or even walking fast—I HAVE to go after it. There could be wolves out there waiting to eat it! So I dash after it, butt it in the rear with my nose, try to herd it back where it belongs. Like that kid on a bike that zoomed right through our campsite just about dusk.

Too bad Gene Autry isn't still alive. He could write a ballad about me, "Back in the Doghouse Again."

Love 'n' Licks,

Cleo

46 Is It Difficult to Travel with Pets?

There are no statistics available on four-legged RVers, but from our observations, about one rig in four has a pet on board. Most of the ones we see (and hear) are dogs; there are some RVing cats, but they tend to stay indoors. We have seen a few birds, too, but they're generally confined to cages. Since Donia and I have never traveled with a cat or bird, we can't really comment on that experience. No offense to all you terrific tabbies and tweeties out there, but this will be a dog-centered discussion.

In the wild, canines are natural pack animals that roam the territory with their pack-mates, rustling up food wherever they can find it. I'm no animal psychology expert, but it seems to me that traveling full-time with retired humans is right up a dog's alley. I would bet they are actually *happier* living in the tight quarters of an RV than in a roomy suburban house. We met one couple who had previously full-timed in a large motorhome but now divided their time between a condo and a compact class-C rig. They told us their mixed shepherd was much calmer and better behaved since they had traded down to the smaller rig. From the dog's point of view, the smallness of an RV must make it cozy and secure, comfortingly denlike. Sentinel-type dogs like Cleo can keep an eye on the entire pack at once, by lying in a single strategic spot.

The critical factor in RVing with a dog is the animal's temperament. Say your Fido has an easygoing disposition, curls up and goes to sleep while you're driving, loves other adults, lets children crawl all over him, greets other dogs with a tail wag, faithfully obeys you even though he would dearly love to chase that squirrel, and happily takes his exercise in a weed-choked vacant lot if that's the best spot available. No question, Fido is going to be a joy to take along, wherever you may go.

But then there are those who go RVing with Fifi, who is restless and attention-seeking, yappy around people and snappy toward other dogs. She barks incessantly or eats furniture whenever she's left alone, slips her collar and runs away every chance she gets, and is highly choosy about what she will eat and where she will poop. This dog is bound to bring her owners—not to mention their campground neighbors—more aggravation than pleasure on the road. But we sure have met a lot of Fifis out there. Love is obviously blind where house pets are concerned.

Size alone has little bearing on a dog's travel personality: Friendly Fido may be a 15-pounder and Fearsome Fifi, a 120-pound giant. Breed seems to have a lot more to do with it. Some canine types are just not cut out for a life of constant change, daily encounters with strangers, and long periods of travel in a truck cab or RV. Hounds, for example, do not strike me as your ideal road dog. They tend to bark and bay hysterically when excited, and they love nothing better than running free with their noses to the ground.

Dogs bred to be watchdogs or herders may be overwhelmed by the "workload" of always being on guard in new surroundings. This often translates as aggressiveness when someone approaches the pack or RV—and a barking, snarling, lunging pet can put its owners in a very uncomfortable position, if not outright legal peril. We thought Cleo would get used to our new lifestyle in time, but during our first year on the road, she became even more jittery and erratic in behavior, not less. It may have been a comical sight to us when she butted someone from behind like a sheep that had strayed out of line, but I'm sure it was anything but funny to the stranger on the other end of that cold nose.

Later on in our full-timing life we did get a very different kind of dog, but as part of our book deal with Cleo, we are not allowed to talk about #2. Let's just say that if you were looking for the perfect road dog—gentle, obedient, relaxed, and unequivocally friendly to dogs and other people—you could not do better than a female golden retriever. Preferably one on the short-haired side. Donia and I have always been big-dog fans, but I can definitely see advantages in traveling with smaller dogs. In the confined interior of a motorhome or trailer, they don't take up as much floor space or shed as much hair as larger breeds. They eat less, so it's easier finding space to store their food. And they give the illusion, at least, of being cute, nonthreatening little playthings. This means small breeds are easier to get into campgrounds, especially resort-type parks where people spend several months at a time. Because of the prevailing attitude that large dogs are rougher and more dangerous, some campgrounds impose a twenty- or a forty-pound limit on pets, hoping to screen out the more aggressive breeds. I guess they figure there is only so much damage a toy poodle can do.

Some campgrounds will accept pets but charge a dollar or two extra, apparently on the principle that pets require additional maintenance. Many places post stern signs about keeping dogs on six-foot leashes at all times and disposing of their droppings. Some campgrounds ban dogs from all sections of the park except for small pet exercise areas that really offer no chance for exercise at all. We saw the extreme example of this in a Las Vegas campground connected to a big casino-hotel. The RV section was basically an asphalt parking lot marked off into sites and dotted with utility hookups. When Fido needed to do his bathroom business, he had to walk for several hundred yards across the hot asphalt to a group of fenced-off dog runs paved with "pee-gravel."

In these situations, the best thing to do is put Fido in the truck and drive to a local park or other open area for at least one daily romp. In our travels, nothing has delighted us as much as the few off-leash public parks we found where local dog owners can let their pets run and play together freely. The ultimate off-leash dog paradise is Marymoor Park in Redmond, Washington, not far from the sprawling wooded campus of Microsoft's headquarters. Among Marymoor's acres and acres of sports and enter-tainment facilities is its riverfront pet park complete with open fields, mulch-covered paths, poop-scoop bag dispensers, trash cans, and "beaches" along the river where dogs from all over mingle, wade and swim, and race each other to retrieve sticks and tennis balls.

Off-leash parks are rare, however, so most of the time we are looking for dog-friendly campgrounds to stay in. We feel most at home in relaxed, slightly rundown places that border on big open fields and cheerfully accept dogs. With Cleo on board, how could we be comfortable in a fully fenced park where every square foot is beautifully landscaped and monitored?

We remember fondly one park in Cheboygan, Michigan, where the registration clerk welcomed us with a plastic baggie

---

 Other Lessons Learned

- Ask any veterinarian you visit to make copies of reports or notes on pet treatments so you can take them with you.

- Most veterinarians habitually prescribe their preferred brands of pills and powders. If possible, tactfully tell a new vet about what has worked well in the past and see if he'll let you stick with that. Carry a supply of your pet's old brand with you whenever you can.

- For everyone's peace of mind, make sure your pet's shots are always up to date. Carry with you the original and at least one copy of any documentation you might need to show as proof of inoculations.

- Double-check your pet records before crossing any inter-national border, and have them ready for officials to in-spect. You definitely do not want to be crossing into Mex-ico or Canada, or returning to the United States, if your pet's rabies shot is out of date.

continued

- Full-timers need to replace their pet's old ID tag with a new one containing only the animal's name, owners' names, and phone number to call in case of emergency. It's pointless to put a mail-forwarding address on the tag; that would just confuse matters if someone found your dog and was trying to contact you.
- For economical poop-scooping, buy a whole roll of plastic bags from a supermarket produce department. (Sandwich baggies are plenty big enough for the twenty-pounders.)
- Keep a mini flashlight near the front door to use for dog walks after dark. You can hold the flashlight end in your mouth, leaving both hands free for poop-scooping. (Cleaning up after a dog while holding onto a leash is one of those tasks that really requires three hands—like putting away your change after buying an ice cream cone.)
- Keep a pair of no-nonsense, rubberized shoes near the front door for dog walking on rainy days—and in dew-soaked grass that can leave your feet sopping wet even on the sunniest mornings.

containing a big dog biscuit and a short printed reminder of pet regulations. As pet owners, we don't need a lot of signposts with dire warnings. We *know* that our dog is not supposed to run wild around the campground and that it's our responsibility to pick up after her. Most RVing pet owners are extremely conscientious about following these two cardinal rules. Do all the signs and posted threats really help keep the bozo minority in line? We wonder.

Another important consideration: Dog-friendly or not, how crowded is the campground? Cleo's nervous nature made life a lot more relaxing for us when we stayed in relatively empty places than when we were in a campground teeming with campers, bikes, and other dogs. The more jam-packed a place is, the harder it is to keep a dog from barking excitedly, tangling with other leashed pets, getting in the way of traffic, or squatting on someone else's campsite.

Full-timing with a pet requires some advance planning in the veterinary department. First of all, you would probably not be happy traveling with an unspayed female dog, who would attract a horde of suitors from the campground and surrounding vicinity whenever she came into heat. Male dogs, too, are going to be easier to handle on the road if they're neutered. Before we left Virginia we had Cleo's shots all brought up to date, and we made a "Cleo" file folder containing documentation of all her past medical problems, inoculation records, and current medications. It's especially important to have copies of a current rabies certificate with these records.

Since there's no health insurance involved in veterinary visits, it's pretty uncomplicated getting medical treatment for a dog on the road. Campground managers can usually recommend a local animal hospital. Once we walked into a small-town post office to pick up our mail and asked the postal clerk if there was a good veterinarian in town. Several people waiting in line overheard us and piped up with the name of their favorite. Luckily they all mentioned the same one.

Dogs, like humans, also need grooming from time to time. It turned out that Cleo's skin was sensitive to many plants we never encountered while living in Virginia, so allergic rashes became an ongoing issue on the road. Eventually we had her long, fluffy coat trimmed down to about half an inch during warm weather. At least, now we could see where we needed to apply the cortisone ointment.

I am sure that if you lined up all the hassles associated with taking a dog on the road, they would outweigh the benefits on a strictly practical level. A dog has to be fed, watered, walked, brushed, cleaned up after, and disciplined in close quarters—all without disturbing other campers. Campgrounds are filled with a staggering variety of distractions that can send obedience training right out the window—wild birds to chase, kids on bikes, other pets to sniff, old campfires and picnic tables surrounded by savory bones and bits of trash. In rainy weather, a pet forces you to go outside several times a day and get soaking wet when you would otherwise be staying warm and dry inside. Moreover, you can't just take off sightseeing for the entire day and stay through dinner if you have a dog locked up back in the trailer. But who can measure all of that against love?

Dog people, of course, gladly put up with all these inconveniences and more, for the primal pleasure they get from their loyal furry companions. On the plus side, many people feel more secure having a dog that will woof protectively whenever strangers approach the RV. People also get more sunshine and fresh air when they must exercise a pet outdoors—whether it's serious trail hiking or just walking in circles around the campground.

And a dog on the end of a leash is a conversation starter—a great way to meet your neighbors in a new place. At one of our winter Texan parks, the non-pet owners envied those of us who lived down in the "pet ghetto" at the far end and knew all the other pet owners and their dogs by name. "You guys are more friendly than the rest of us are," one woman said wistfully. "You've got a built-in excuse to get outside and socialize—you have all the fun!"

I suggested that she get herself a golden retriever puppy and come join us.

47 Front Royal, Virginia
June 16

Guess you never expected to see us back east so soon? Well, neither did we. But right after Cleo sent out her Memorial Day letter, we got a voicemail message from the real estate agent in Front Royal informing us we had a contract on our cabin. Somehow, Mark and I didn't figure that listing the Best Revenge would mean we'd actually *sell* it. Not for months and months, anyway. Maybe even years. But the real estate gods work in mysterious ways, as we should all know by now.

Finalizing a contract by phone tag from a state park in Kansas was a bit of an adventure. We did the usual backing and forthing on terms, all via the campground's single pay phone and a fax machine at the marina's convenience store. The store clerk was a real saint about our fax needs; in the end we felt like *he* should get a commission. During this phase, the agent would leave us messages on our 800 voicemail number. We would promptly call him back, only to be told that he was tied up and would have to call us back. We finally convinced the receptionist that there was no way to call us back, so she started dragging our busy-bee agent to the phone whenever we called.

Eventually the final papers were faxed, and the closing date was set for the last week of June. Feeling elated and remorseful at the same time, we got out our maps and drastically modified our summer travel plans, still hoping to get to Montana somehow by the end of July, after winding up our cabin sale. But first we had to get back to Front Royal, clean out the place, put our keeper stuff in storage, and say our good-byes to old friends who had always believed we would give up this RV nonsense and move back to the cabin some day.

There were a couple of states we wanted to visit on the way, so we could fill them in on our RV travel map. You may laugh, but we take our sticker-map very seriously! And we definitely don't want to leave awkward white gaps in places we won't be getting to for a long time. (It always drives us crazy to see RVers whose maps are all filled in except for one state, like Nebraska, for example. They went to Iowa, Missouri, Kansas, Colorado, Wyoming, South Dakota, every surrounding state—*what happened to Nebraska???*)

We needed Missouri and Arkansas for our map, and even though we already had Tennessee, we wanted to drop by Memphis, too. There were several famous barbecue places Mark was determined to try—and he also wanted to see Elvis Presley's museum-home at Graceland. So off we went. From Kansas to Montana, by way of Virginia.

The rest of Kansas was a blur, and before we knew it we were in Branson, Missouri. There is a nice Escapees park nearby, and we did the standard Branson thing, going to a couple of big-name shows and eating more dreadful all-you-can-eat buffet food than we ever thought possible. Just before we left, one of our friendly fellow Escapees told us we just had to go to Mountain View, Arkansas—not Mountain Home, the well-known retirement spot, but a tiny burg south of there. *Oh, great,* was our first reaction. Just what we need when we're trying to hurry eastward. But his description of this Ozark music mecca was so appealing that we added it to our itinerary.

And were we ever glad we did. Our three-day stay in Mountain View turned out to be one of the high points of our whole year. We camped at an RV park adjacent to the Ozark Folk Center, a fabulous living history museum. Visitors could listen to all-day mountain music performances, or stroll around the pioneer village watching traditional craft demonstrations such as broom making and wood carving.

But Mountain View's real drawing card was the jam sessions that took place around the town square every evening. Area musicians just sort of showed up one by one, toting their instruments, and joined one group or another playing on the courthouse lawn. This bunch would be doing gospel music, that one over there jazzy blues, and yet another pure mountain ballads. Spectators wandered from group to group, sitting on folding chairs and benches that dotted the grass and sidewalks. No money ever changed hands. These men and women—some of whom were hired by the state to play days at the Ozark Center over the summer—played on their own time at night too, just for the fun of it.

The next morning we stopped by the campground office and found it rocking with another jam session that blended the sounds of guitar, banjo, mandolin, fiddle, autoharp, dulcimer, squeeze box (concertina), harmonica, and a dozen singing voices. RV guests crowded together on window sills and desktops, listening to old-time favorites like "Wildwood Flower," "Will the Circle Be Unbroken?" and of course, "Amazing Grace." It was as if we had experienced a glorious transformation, had actually shed our tourist skins and been welcomed into the heart of a real community's real life.

And then, onward to Memphis! Mark loved touring Grace-land—seeing how Elvis, this suddenly rich country kid, built his dream playhouse and filled it with toys, circa 1960. For me, the top Memphis attraction was Mud Island, a long, skinny city park with a scale model of the Mississippi River molded right into the pavement. The "river" was four inches deep and six blocks long, complete with running water and tiny maps of major cities engraved on its banks. I had great fun hopping from state to state along this miniature Mississippi, like some kind of map-crazed Gulliver in the Land of Lilliputians.

On the final leg of our journey back to what used to be home, all was going well—except, at the campground where we stayed the final night before Front Royal, Cleo pulled one of her sudden pranks that scared the heck out of us. During our twilight dog walk we stopped to chat with two friendly kids, a girl about ten and her little brother, maybe eight years old. The boy was standing there bouncing a basketball on the pavement as we talked. Cleo was being perfectly friendly, but then out of the blue she leaped forward and, with no growling or biting, knocked him right over.

We rushed to pick up the kid—who was startled and crying, though not otherwise hurt. As for Cleo, she was being perfectly friendly again.

Anybody out there want a loony white sheepdog? No kidding, I think it's about time to set that one out by the curb with a sign on her collar: *Free to a Good Home.*

Cheers to all from the Almost-Hobos,

Donia

48 When Do You Plan To Settle Down?

The concept of having no home base is hard for many people to grasp. Folks we meet along the way invariably ask us how long we intend to keep living this way, assuming the ultimate goal is to find a house somewhere and hang up the keys to our rig. "As long as we're still having fun" is the short answer we give them. Friends and family members are even more perplexed that we are voluntarily living in a succession of campgrounds, some of them crowded and downright seedy, when we could be living in our own nice house somewhere. "So, how long do you think you'll keep doing this before you settle down?" loved ones would ask casually, during every phone chat in our first year.

As long as we still owned the Virginia mountain cabin, everyone figured we would eventually tire of our lengthy vacation and return to a pleasant life of retirement in Front Royal. Even after we sold the cabin and became official full-timers, we received many helpful suggestions about other places we might consider living. My daughter Curry extolled the virtues of Cape Cod. My son Travis urged us to build a wood and stone ranch house in the Texas Hill Country (cattle optional). Mark's mother reminded us how lovely the mountains of North Georgia were, and his Colorado cousins pointed out a spread that was for sale right down the road from their place in Durango. It took a very long time for them all to realize that our full-timing lifestyle was a goal in itself.

Two main factors keep us on the road right now. First of all, we *like* our hobo lifestyle, going where we please and not owning a house on a foundation. Second, it seems Mark and I have very different ideas about "a place to settle down." We realized this in a restaurant one night when we each jotted down our top five dream-house priorities on a napkin, just for fun. When we exchanged napkins, I was flabbergasted (see box). Here I am, married to this man for over fifteen years, and I'm just now learning that he pictures us living in a nice in-town neighborhood ten minutes from the bridge club, while I want a custom-built ranch in the boondocks? Fortunately, as long as Factor #1 remains the case, we don't have to deal with the issue of Factor #2.

RV full-timing is actually the perfect way to explore home-base options. It gives us a chance to stay for an extended period

 Mark and Donia's Dream House Priorities

Mark's List
1. Is located west of the Mississippi River.
2. Is in a mid-sized town or suburb, large enough to have several duplicate bridge games each week.
3. Is low-maintenance or no-maintenance.
4. Has a few decent golf courses within a thirty-minute drive.
5. Is close to an airport with good service to major cities.

Donia's List
1. Is a really cool custom-designed home, one of a kind. Not large, but distinctive and different. Layout is tailored to our personal tastes, lifestyles, and hobbies.
2. Is situated in a western state, on at least ten acres, with some trees. Is set apart from other houses.
3. Has a beautiful view of natural surroundings, including mountains and water—the property borders on a river, stream, or lake.
4. Has a big front porch or deck with comfortable rocking chairs overlooking the view.
5. Has an underground sprinkler system for vegetable and flower gardens, powered by an old-fashioned prairie windmill.

in any area we are interested in, to see what the climate and shopping and local bridge club are really like. Mark loves the Rocky Mountains, but we learned firsthand that even summer temperatures can dip below freezing at high altitudes, and the first snows of winter often arrive in September. I always dreamed of having a place with both water and mountain views, but that combination is hard to find—especially in the West, where water is scarce and mountain property is pricey if it's within forty miles of a supermarket. So, we keep moving on and looking more. The way we figure it, we only have enough savings for one dream house in our lifetime, so we better pick the right place to put it.

Everybody seems to agree that the only place in America with perfect year-round weather is San Diego, California. Maybe so, but that is not a place we want to be. So we think about becoming "Persephone campers"—RVers who spend half the year in two different climate zones, or sit still half the year and travel the remainder. This offers the advantages of living in a familiar setting complete with a bridge club, telephone, friends, and fast Internet connection for at least part of the year, balanced by the freedom to hit the road again when hitch itch strikes. But is it better to have a permanent home in the Sun Belt and travel north all summer? Or vice versa—join the snowbirds who live up north and go south for the winter? Or perhaps a third option—have our house in the temperate zone where the springs and falls are perfect, and take two long RV trips, three months in summer and three months in winter? These are ideas we happily kick around while driving, without feeling the slightest pressure to make a decision any time soon.

At our winter Texan campgrounds, we have had a chance to see what winter life is like for the many retirees who stay home in the northern latitudes for late spring, summer, and early fall, then migrate to a snowbird park for the late fall through early spring. We listen with great interest to the back-home reports of friends from Michigan and Missouri, New Hampshire and Canada. From a thousand miles away they are dealing with house-sitters who turned out to be unreliable, frozen pipes, lawn and

garden problems, real estate hassles, and late-season snows that
keep them from getting back home to take care of these things.
Mark and I have deeply mixed feelings about living in a house
again, for any part of the year, wherever it may be located. All
our dream-house dreaming aside, we both fear getting sucked
into furnishing and decorating a house, maintenance chores, lawn
upkeep, and all the other homeowner responsibilities that would
weigh on us during travel times. If I had a garden, would I really
want to leave it for half the year to go roaming? If we had a real
home town, would we really want to be absent for half its special
events every year? It seems that the Persephone lifestyle would
position us uneasily between two worlds, each one tugging at us
while we were living in the other.

Still, it doesn't hurt to look, and think about someday settling
down. Everywhere we go, people are living in beautiful, creative
homes that lend us ideas. Mark loves plantation-style houses with
tall windows and wide verandas, and the Spanish mission-style
homes built around a central courtyard. In Texas I was enchanted
by the LBJ dogtrot cabin. The drive from Austin to Fredericksburg is like a museum tour of magnificent ranch fences and
arched entry gates topped with wrought-iron cowboy art. Outside
Billings, Montana, we saw a handsome wooden barn with tall
double doors that would make a perfect storage garage for an RV.

Sometimes we see historic commercial buildings that we fantasize about renovating into houses—like a 1940s-vintage Sinclair
station in mint condition, with double service bays that could be
converted into a high-ceilinged bedroom wing. Of course, these
places are always smack in the middle of downtown, surrounded
by concrete and asphalt. But no problem—it's just a fantasy! We
realize that the real problem is, the minute we settle down and
put all our architecture eggs into one basket, we will lose the
bountiful variety we enjoy on the road. We'd rather *ooo* and *ahh*
over all these different lovely places than own just one of them.

At the moment, we're solidly in the More We Do It, More
We Love It phase of full-timing. Our list of places to go and
things to do keeps growing longer. We want to attend more of

the large RVer rallies like Escapees "Escapades" and Good Sam Club "Samborees," which are a blend of convention, campout, and outdoor university. Guided caravans of RVers leave every month on communal jaunts to Mexico, Canada, and Alaska. You can even put your RV on a barge for a floating caravan down the Mississippi River. We are curious to see the hordes that boondock all winter on vast public lands outside Quartzsite, Arizona, creating a gypsy city of one million in the desert. And as I write this, we still have to go camping in six more states, including nearly all of New England, to fill in all the gaps on our U.S.A. sticker map.

Working for pay or in exchange for campsites is something else that a great many full-timers do, either full- or part-time.We have seen ads for everything from managing a campground full-time, to seasonal gigs selling fireworks, to caring for puppies in a breeding kennel—all of them including a full-hookup site plus salary. Having worked at a desk for the same company for more than fifteen years, I'm dying to answer every ad and work at a wildly eclectic line of jobs in different parts of the country, one after another, sort of like a career sampler. As time goes on, I envision us moving even less frequently than we do now, choosing maybe three or four places a year where we would stay for several months and work.

Each month the RV magazines arrive filled with yet more articles about fun things to do and see. Among these are inspiring stories about volunteer work done by people like us who live on the road. We subscribe to the newsletter of the Care-A-Vanners, a Habitat for Humanity group that coordinates RVing volunteers on home-building projects. We were also intrigued by an Escapade class about RVers who receive Red Cross training as mobile disaster-relief volunteers in the aftermath of floods, earthquakes, hurricanes, and other wide-scale calamities. I want to do it *all* before we hang up the keys.

The flexibility of full-timing can be a great advantage for people who need to travel to different parts of the country to take care of family business, or be present for happy family events like graduations, weddings, or the arrival of a grandchild. Or for unhappy events. We learned this firsthand when Mark's father was diagnosed with a sudden illness requiring surgery and possibly a long convalescence.

At the time we heard the news, we were heading north toward Canada for the summer. Instead of boarding the dog and storing the RV so we could fly back to Atlanta, we decided to bite the bullet and just drive the distance. This way we could keep the family together, and we would have our own home and belongings with us. We left New England on a Thursday at noon and drove straight through, pausing only briefly at truck stops and highway rest areas. How convenient, to be able to lie down in our own bedroom for a two-hour nap at 6 a.m.! By 8 p.m. Friday night we were all hooked up in our Atlanta campground, ready to go to the hospital the next morning and remain on the scene as long as we were needed.

In our travels Mark and I have run across many variations of full-timing. People seem to move in and out of it with ease. Several couples at our winter Texan campground had full-timed for years but found the physical demands more difficult as they grew older, so they moved into mobile homes right there in the RV park. Others have fun living on the road for a while, then have to call a temporary halt to deal with medical problems. They may park the rig and rent an apartment, or live with relatives, until they recuperate enough to travel once more. We met one couple who had full-timed for five years, given it up for a condo in Florida, decided that they hated their stationary existence after a few months, and sold the condo the following year to take off again in a brand-new rig.

It's so encouraging for us to see these examples of the full-timing life as an evolving process. When you realize that even the biggest decisions aren't necessarily forever, it makes them a whole lot easier to deal with.

49 Rockville, Maryland
June 24

My Dear, Dear Friends and Fans:
Job burnout. It happens to the best of us: Corporate CEOs, rocket scientists, book editors, even fluffy white sheepdogs.

So, this is my announcement that I'm taking a sabbatical, staying with Aunt JJ and Dr. Ken, some excellent friends of ours who have a big new house in a place called Rockville, Maryland. A place where houses actually SIT ON THE GROUND and do not move around on wheels. By the time you get this e-mail, I'll be communing with the squirrels in Ken and JJ's tree-shaded backyard, or taking it easy on their cool kitchen floor, chilling out in the peace and quiet. If all goes well, I may just roll it over into early retirement.

You may be wondering: How did all this happen?

Well, as the one-dog security force for the Steele family, truck, and trailer, I did okay for a year. One year and twenty-four days, to be exact. But the stress was wearing me down big-time— all that constant moving around to different campgrounds, and strange new people always getting in my face, and chained-up dogs barking at me when I was only trying to have a peaceful walk. As Mom's compassionate friend Teresa observed, "Poor Cleo—for her, every day is like the first day on a new job."

My performance reviews were getting worse, not better. The beginning of the end was a couple of weeks ago in a campground where I kind of lost it for a moment—like, I jumped forward and sort of knocked down a little kid who was bouncing a ball right in front of me in a very annoying way. ("You wanna play ball, Kid? OKAY LET'S PLAY BALL! WHAMMO!") He wasn't hurt, and I apologized and everything, but these things go in your permanent record, you know.

The final straw happened during our farewell bridge party at the Best Revenge in Front Royal. I got aggravated at a guest who was trying to pet me while I was lying upside down on the couch just trying to take a nap. So I nipped at his hand a little. Well, okay, it was more like I BIT him. They didn't have to call 911 or anything, but there was much caterwauling and running for peroxide and bandages. And of course the worst part of it all was, IT INTERRUPTED A BRIDGE GAME.

Ironically, the victim was none other than Dr. Ken, the alpha-male of my new household! One day he's nursing a bleeding finger, and the next day his wife's begging to have me come live with them. This is definitely one for Ripley's Believe It Or Not.

I guess this is a good time to say a few words about my new folks. JJ (whose real name is Debra, go figure that out) is a bigwig who teaches people how to catch money cheaters in this stock market thing. "Securities fraud," they call it. And she is one tough cookie. So if you've got some of those stocks, don't go pulling any scams, or she'll nail you and put you away where the sun don't shine.

Dr. Ken is a computer expert who works at a university, a really smart guy, just got his Pee-H-Dee in something called Artificial Intelligence. Except I'm hoping he will soon move on to Real Intelligence and get e-mail on his HOME computer, too—because otherwise my e-writing career is going to be seriously hampered. (In the meantime, if you want to e-mail me, send it to my old Mom and Dad, and they'll see that I get it.)

There is one other new family member I haven't mentioned yet, and that's my old pen pal, Daisy the Cat. Daisy and I have had our differences in the past, but now by this strange twist of fate, she's my SISTER. I'm OK with this, however. Mainly because Dr. Ken and JJ are always setting bowls of cat food up on the kitchen counters where they think I can't reach it, and then they go off to work. Heh, heh, heh. Love ya, Daisy! Whatta great kitty!

Of course, I'm going to miss my full-timing Mom and Dad a lot. We had some great times at all those campgrounds and

244 Steeles on Wheels

lakes and woods, and especially the crumb buffets under picnic tables and barbecue grills. But life is full of changes, and everyone agrees this is for the best. A workaholic sheepdog like myself will never be a happy-go-lucky Lab or golden retriever.

Anyway, I've lucked into a really cushy deal here, and I just hope I don't blow it. Aunt JJ and Dr. Ken are building me a beautiful new deck to lie on. And a fenced-in play yard complete with one of those little doggy-doors into the basement, so I can come in and out whenever I please.

I overheard JJ telling Mom and Dad that the way you train dogs to use the doggy-door is, you line up little pieces of hot dog leading through the door to the other side, so they go through the flap to get the hot dog, and then they see how it works. Awesome curriculum! You better believe I'm going to be a slow learner on this one. Heh, heh, heh. Next time you see me I'll probably have my Pee-H-Dee in Doggy-Door Navigation.

Love 'n' Licks Forever,
Cleo

50 Do You Ever Have Regrets?

New people often ask us, delicately, if we have any regrets about full-timing. I guess they find it hard to fathom that two people who never spent a single night in an RV could suddenly sell their house, buy a truck and trailer, hit the road, and find happiness. Really, Donia and I are amazed, too, but so far we can honestly say we have had not a single second thought about our full-timing choice.

Of course, there are a couple of things that we wish had turned out better. And, as in every lifestyle, there are a few downsides that come with the territory. But the bottom line is, if we divided everything into good and bad, and all the good things were put in a bushel basket, the downers would barely fill a teacup.

Our biggest regret so far is still the first-year Cleo Crisis. In hindsight, we dragged it out far longer than we should have, putting all three of us through months of discomfort before finally admitting that a life of constant travel was just not working for our uptight sheepdog. Donia bawled like a baby the day we left her behind with our friends in Maryland, Cleo flashing us a baffled look from their front door as we drove away without her. The only consolation was in learning within a couple of weeks that she was completely at home in her cushy new digs. Now, whenever we visit, Cleo greets us with licks and hugs—but then curls up snug beside her new Humans. I doubt she'd choose to rejoin us today, even if invited.

While we have never regretted leaving our fixed address in Virginia, we do miss our old friends. A steady diet of strangers begins to feel lonely after a while. We meet lots of nice people in our travels, and even stay in contact with some of them via e-mail. We value the friendly hugs we always get from fellow

Escapees. But these "hello, good-bye" acquaintances can never match long-term friendships from the past.

Well, never say *never*. We do run across lots of full-timers who rendezvous with other RVers around the country for group campouts or caravans. Their happy hours and cookouts look like so much fun, and some day we hope to be part of such a traveling troupe. For now, Donia and I plan our rendezvous around bridge events, meeting our old D.C. pals at tournaments once or twice a year, in various cities determined by the schedule of the American Contract Bridge League. These happy reunions, which consume so many of our working friends' hard-earned vacation days, mean more to us than they will ever know.

As for our family members, they are scattered up and down the East Coast, and—while they may fret about the distances that separate us—we actually see them as often now as we did while living in Virginia. The distances are really psychological.

 Mark and Donia's Top Ten Pet Peeves

1. Super-friendly fellow campers who immediately launch into a way overly detailed account of their health problems, their dog's veterinary history, and the total incompetents who manufactured their current RV.
2. Campground owners who lament how hard it is to make a living, how much they pay for taxes and insurance, how many government hoops they have to jump through, and how obnoxious customers are.
3. Extended periods of rain that turn dirt sites to mud. Wet shoes and clothes and dog fur. Towels that never dry out between uses, but just stay damp until the next high pressure system arrives.
4. Laundromat dryers with clogged vents or other problems that prevent clothes from getting completely dry.

continued

5. Rampant development in pretty areas of the country we thought were our secret discoveries. Most galling: the subdivision of the Texas Hill Country into three-acre ranchettes, and the suburbanization of Las Cruces, New Mexico.

6. Wall-mounted pay phones with no place to sit, not even a shelf to set down a piece of paper to write on. Quirky off-brand pay phones that block 800-number calls.

7. Campgrounds with dirty, mildewed toilets and showers, trash and debris in the campfire rings, junk piled up around the weedy perimeter, and long-clogged sewer drains or broken electric hookups that the management hasn't bothered to fix.

8. Meaningless hype put forth by tourist brochures, guidebooks, and ads—making every small-town museum sound as grand as the Louvre, and every obscure historical attraction as impressive as Colonial Williamsburg.

9. Cramped, fully fenced campgrounds where there's no place to walk a dog except on somebody's campsite.

10. Dealing with business matters and health-insurance snafus by pay phone, when the right person is never at his desk and will have to "call us back."

We keep reminding our parents, siblings, and children that if we're needed in an emergency, we can get there by air within twenty-four hours, or by fifth-wheel in one to five days, as we proved in our thirty-two-hour sprint from New England to Atlanta when my father had his surgery. Our only regret is that our families tend to live in mega-cities like Atlanta and Manhattan, instead of RV-friendly places like the Texas Hill Country and southern New Mexico.

Try as we might to avoid guilt trips, I worry a little about resentment on the part of our friends and younger relatives, most of them still slaving away at their jobs while Donia and I enjoy our freewheeling, self-indulgent lifestyle. When we visit people who are still saddled with a nine-to-five workday, I wonder how they *really* feel about the two happy hobos turning up, like the idle lord and lady of the manor, expecting to be entertained. I feel like we're imposing—even though we always stay in our rig. Anticipating early retirement, we never realized how lonely it would feel, being the first among our peers to quit working. Here we are living this storybook life, and everyone is too busy to enjoy it with us!

Another psychological downside of this lifestyle is the abundance of worriers, alarmists, and fearmongers that haunt the RVing universe. These people are quick to recount disastrous experiences with lemon rigs, or the grave dangers of failing to check every electrical outlet for proper polarity. They repeat certain horror tales of people they heard about who ventured into Mexico and ran afoul of the *federales*. They imply that you are a complete reckless fool if you don't retorque your lug nuts every morning and repack your wheel bearings every six thousand miles. The RV magazines do their part, as well. I estimate there are six cautionary "What-If" articles published, for every one genuinely dangerous RV experience reported. Perhaps it's just a reflection of the insecurity some people feel, living in a state of constant change.

I don't mean to be cavalier on the subject of safety, but in all our travels, staying in a wide variety of eyebrow-raising places, we never had a single sinister thing happen to us. Our most dangerous mechanical failures have been tire blowouts (but only one while cruising at highway speed). And the closest thing to crime we encountered was an overnight break-in of an unoccupied trailer at a seasonal campground in Minocqua, Wisconsin. The sheriff was called to investigate, but it turned out the only damage was a couple of broken flower pots on the patio—the suspected perps a couple of local preteens known for this sort of prank.

I suppose I should add Noise and Lack of Privacy to the downside teacup. These are definitely two conditions that full-timers have to get used to. In the noise department, an RV engine makes a throaty roar that can totally drown out your hearing while you try to talk on an outdoor pay phone or sleep through a neighbor's early departure. Many campgrounds, for the convenience of travelers, border on interstate highways, which means we often live with the racket of huge trucks grinding past around the clock. We have also stayed at campgrounds located near small airports or railroad tracks, or surrounded by noisy, dusty construction projects. These details—never revealed by maps and guidebooks—make sense when you consider that the "trailer park" is seldom welcomed in a locale's best neighborhoods.

But the monotonous noise of vehicles and construction equipment tends to fade into the background after a while. The closer sounds of specific campground neighbors can be much more annoying—although, in truth, noisy campers are rare. When RV-ing families and groups of tenting teenagers spend the whole day outdoors, they are so pooped that they usually turn off the music and hit the pillow long before the standard "quiet time" of 10 p.m. rolls around.

Our most notable noise challenge took place in an Austin, Texas, park that was populated by many working people. The clock radio in the adjacent trailer, positioned just four feet from our bedroom window, clicked on at 5:20 every morning and screamed country music for two hours straight. Unfortunately, the owner was not there to turn it off; for days on end his trailer was locked and his pickup truck gone. I finally solved the problem by flipping off the outside circuit breaker for two hours one day. This fooled the clock radio into starting two hours later, about the time we'd normally be getting up anyway. The power was not off long enough to seriously disrupt the neighbor's refrigerator, and we left a note so that when he finally returned he'd know to reset his alarm.

The privacy issue is a very individual thing. I'm sure some folks wonder how anyone can stand to live in a fiberglass box on wheels, parked just a few feet away from somebody else's fiberglass box on wheels. This prospect alone is probably enough to discourage many people from full-timing. But honestly, lack of privacy is not such a big deal. Most campers go out of their way to respect the privacy of neighbors in tight quarters, keeping their eyes averted and their TV volume low in open-windows weather. You can always pull your shades down if you're feeling crowded or don't like the view.

Donia and I have come to appreciate a campground's spaciousness more than any other factor. There's a big difference between campsites that are spread out and buffered by trees, and sites lined up as close together as possible to save costs for the owner. The campground's occupancy rate is another major quality-of-life issue. A no-vacancy campground on a holiday weekend will make you feel claustrophobic no matter how widely spaced the sites are. Our favorite scenario, of course, is the park that has huge sites surrounded by greenery and is only 25 percent full.

The subject of full-timing negatives would not be complete without a description of Donia's Worst Day Ever, a collection of petty fiascoes that all occurred one Monday in May in Grapevine, Texas. To begin: Donia drops Mark off at local golf course, returns to do laundry in outdoor washers on bathhouse porch. While laundry washes, Donia walks to pay phone at park entrance to call health plan's mail-order pharmacy. Computer mysteriously canceled coverage, then reinstated it. Rep claims unfilled prescription mailed back to Mark two months ago (it wasn't) when coverage canceled. Rep doesn't understand the problem—why not just ask doctor for another prescription? (Because doctor is two states behind us now!) Rep will speak to supervisor and call Donia back. Rep doesn't understand—nobody can call Donia back!

Meanwhile, huge thunderstorm boils up. Donia gets soaked, waiting on hold for rep. Donia returns to trailer to find Cleo totally freaked out, digging hole in carpet to escape thunder and lightning. Donia shuts Cleo in stall shower with security blanket. Speeds off to see if Mark has been rained out. Now sun comes out. Mark nowhere in sight, still on the back nine. Donia remembers clothes in washer and Cleo in shower, speeds back to campground. Walks Cleo. New thunderstorm strikes just as clothes are being removed from outdoor dryer. Damp clothes spread on furniture, Cleo back in shower, Donia back to golf course. Mark finally appears. Nothing in freezer for dinner. Donia drives around Grapevine thirty minutes in downpour, looking for supermarket. Ritzy new Dallas suburb, many malls and boutiques and freeways, but no groceries? Mark and Donia go home to trailer, eat rice and canned beans. Laugh a lot. Decide in the end, full-timing still worth it. We'll dry.

51 Council Bluffs, Iowa
July 8

✉ I'm happy to report that Donia and I are finally back on track again, heading west toward Montana. Our "brief" detour to Virginia lasted a lot longer than we expected, due to the usual screwing around on the part of all the bankers, real estate people, settlement attorneys, and clerks who acted as though they had never shuffled papers for a house sale before. But we all have been through this Last-Minute-Lou drill, right?

In fact, we still haven't closed on the house. We finally gave up in disgust, presigned some papers, and hit the road. Here we are at the western edge of Iowa already, half a continent away. Settlement is now supposed to take place tomorrow. But not to worry—they have fax machines in Iowa. And we don't expect any further hassles. In our hearts, it's already a done deal. Our only home is now a thirty-four-foot trailer.

It was sad to say goodbye to a place that has been such a big part of our lives for almost two decades. But the emotion was offset by the tons of work we had to do—quite literally, tons—getting the house and our gear squared away. We hauled truckloads of junk out of the basement to the county dump—or "transfer station," as it is called today. We spent several days packing up things we just can't part with—like family photos, favorite pieces of furniture, and treasured knickknacks. *No, I am not going to throw away the cute little ceramic zebra, okay?* (That was me, not Donia.)

Over the past year we have met many RVers who are total full-timers—they went cold turkey and got rid of every single thing they owned, except what they could pack into their RV. But we are not quite ready to do that, yet. Out back behind the old-fashioned general store in Front Royal, we rented a ten-by-fourteen-foot storage locker—a bargain at $60 a month. And the rental manager is even willing to arrange for a moving van to pick up our things and haul them to us some day in the future, so we don't have to come back to Front Royal from wherever we are.

All this time we were having daily visits from the lady who is buying the cabin—a jolly German grandmother who currently lives just down the road in her daughter's "mother-in-law suite." Meeting her was comforting, in a way. She was genuinely excited about having the place for her own, and is even keeping the Best Revenge name, which comes from the saying, "Living well is the best revenge." Her glee over owning a house with this name has something to do with her ex-husband, the details of which we didn't much want to delve into.

Because of the real estate delays, we had a chance to invite our old friends out for a farewell weekend of bridge playing on the deck overlooking the Blue Ridge Mountains. This particular session was immortalized by Cleo's taking a bite out of Ken, one of our dearest friends—an incident you've already heard about. Then Ken and his wife JJ astounded us all a couple days later by adopting our impossible mutt and rescuing her from a life of canine campground crime.

After the guests had gone and we were down to the final cleanup, I noticed Donia slipping out onto the deck at odd times, just looking out over the valley below. The shimmering line of the Shenandoah River, almost invisible now through the screen of leafy trees along the bank. The now-dilapidated treehouse partway down the hill, which we had built for little Travis the year we were married. And the line of purple mountain peaks you can see on a clear day, way off to the southwest. One party weekend, we had dubbed them the Thirteen Sacred Hills, though there actually could be twelve, thirteen, or fifteen of them, depending on how you defined "hill." I knew Donia must be standing there saying good-bye to these sights, which we would probably never lay eyes on again.

But you know Donia. There were rugs to vacuum, and closets to sweep! In the famous words of somebody-or-other, "The die is cast—we have crossed the Rubicon!"

We are both relieved to be on the move once more, but we really, *really* miss Cleo. She was such an integral part of our travel routine—everything seems to remind us of her. The campground in eastern Iowa where we stayed last night was full of dogs of all varieties. I took a long walk to smoke a cigar, but it really was an excuse to chat with all the dog owners and play with their pooches. Two nights ago we ended up at the same rural park near Champaign, Illinois, where we stayed last fall. We walked around the grassy field in back where we had romped with Cleo, recalling what a treat it was when we found campgrounds with space where she could run free. Of course, we know she is in a better place now with JJ and Ken, who can give her a stable lifestyle. We know, we know. But we miss her nevertheless.

We're eager to get to Montana and the Great West after our long detour. So we drove hard the past week, looking for long, pull-through sites where we could just leave the truck attached to the trailer overnight and take off quickly the next morning. We haven't been to the grocery store in ages, so each night we have what the kids used to call Wacky Dinner—anything we can put together out of canned goods, leftovers, and whatever else we can find in the fridge. Last night it was pasta puttanesca—olive oil, garlic, peppers, pimientos, olives and red pepper, accompanied by (canned) wax bean vinaigrette. For lunch we have eaten cheese and crackers for three days straight. It gets to be a fun game, after a while. *How many more states can we get through before we give up and go to the grocery store?* You should try it some time.

The record East Coast heat has made itself felt in the campgrounds, for sure. Our first night on the road we couldn't stay at the first place we stopped because their electricity had failed with the heavy air conditioner use. We had to keep driving from Pennsylvania into Ohio before we found a place to camp. And in Illinois all the campsites were taken except ones with only fifteen-amp service, which meant no A/C. Luckily we had passed through the eastering cool front as we circled the Indianapolis beltway (wow, what a thunderstorm!), and the night cooled comfortably.

At the moment we are in an RV park attached to a casino in Council Bluffs, Iowa, right across the river from Omaha, Nebraska. We were forewarned that all RVs had to vacate the campground from Friday night till Saturday night, to make room for a state championship barbecue cookoff taking place here over the weekend. But they let us boondock in the casino parking lot for free during that time, and we still got the complimentary breakfast coupons and the use of the bathhouse. Then we could move back into the campground and hook back up Saturday evening. Let's see, championship barbecue, casino blackjack, free breakfasts . . . yeah, okay, I'll take it.

Best of all, I now have a new career to pursue—Itinerant Barbecue Festival Judge. I learned about this while Donia and I were walking around sampling delicious ribs and chicken and sausage that were not deemed cosmetically attractive enough for competition. Each team of contestants would grill eight slabs of ribs, pick the three most perfectly beautiful ribs to submit as their entry, and then give the rest to all us lucky spectators drooling on the sidelines. Believe it or not, there's a *shortage of qualified judges* for all these festivals across the country, and a couple of the big national barbecue associations hold one-day judge-training sessions. I just *know* I could do this.

So all you folks out there who predicted that we would eventually tire of being bums and yearn to get back to work again— okay, you were right. You get the last laugh!

Love 'n' Licks,
Mark

P.S. Every now and then we wonder if some of you are getting our e-mail at work, or someplace else you don't welcome long, rambly letters. So if your systems administrator is objecting, or if you've forgotten who Mark and Donia are, let us know. We can easily "unsubscribe" you from our e-list. And we won't be offended, honest.

52 "You're Living Our Dream!"

In my mind's eye I carry a snapshot album of unforgettable moments from our life on the road. The most memorable one of all occurred on the back lot of a tire shop in Memphis, Tennessee. A young repairman lay on his back under our axle, working on our latest tire problem. "Where y'all from?" he asked by way of friendly conversation as I stood by watching him work.

"We don't have a house anywhere, we just live in the RV and travel around," I explained.

For a moment he paused, wrench in hand, and rested his head back on the pavement with his eyes closed. "Man, I am *happy* for you," he said softly. His words hit me like a blow. There was no resentment, no sarcasm—just a gentle tone of wonder and yearning. Not a day passes that I don't think about the young tire guy in Memphis.

Along the way we have met legions who fantasize about freedom on wheels—from retired bridge players we meet in small-town clubs to mini-mart clerks along the interstates. As one ready-to-chuck-it-all motel owner in Montana told Mark and me with undisguised envy: "You're living our dream!" Saddest of all are those who lament, "We always wanted to go full-timing, but then my husband/wife got sick and passed away before we could get on the road."

If the lifestyle appeals to so many, what is it that keeps so many from taking the plunge? It is a relatively economical way to live—though the opposite is often assumed. "Wow, you must be rich!" is a reaction we've gotten over and over. The fact is, our freewheeling life costs much less than the total amount many retirees spend on their homes, boats, weekend cottages, landscaping services, recreation, and vacation trips.

People who think they could not afford our lifestyle will no doubt be surprised at the results of a survey conducted by Stephanie Bernhagen and Jaimie Hall, authors of a newsletter and Web site focusing on full-time travel. Here are the results, based on responses from 324 full-timers who reported how much it costs them per month to live on the road:

Monthly Living Expenses for RV Full-Timers

Amount	
Under $700	11%
$700–$1,499	21%
$1,500–$1,999	27%
$2,000–$2,499	17%
$2,500–$2,999	6%
Over $3,000	18%

Data provided by *RV Lifestyle Newsletter* and http://www.rvhometown.com.

It is a true cross-section of America we meet, living on the road. Our fellow full-timers are plumbers and writers, highway construction workers and clergymen, salesmen and nurses—along with retired people from every possible walk of life. And RVing is a great equalizer. If the CEO of a Fortune 500 company were parked next to us in a $1.5 million luxury bus conversion, we could no doubt get him to reveal the most intimate details about his holding tanks simply by asking. Your bank balance and social status count for nothing in the average campground. Adaptability, common sense, how pleasant and considerate you are—these are the currency of the RVer's realm.

Combining work with travel to make ends meet is highly feasible and can be loads of fun, according to those who have done it. At one end of the spectrum is the traveler, young or old, who needs to work full-time to make a living, and thus seeks a position that offers good wages, benefits, and advancement opportunities in addition to mobility. At the other end are retirees looking for part-time or less intense work, possibly in exchange for free campground hookups, propane, and laundry privileges. In between are a host of jobs you probably never dreamed of, advertised every month in RV periodicals and Web sites. You can wear a fuzzy bear costume and work at a theme park. Travel around selling ads for campground brochures. Join the carnival and run the Dunk-a-Clown game. Ride the county fair or home show circuit demonstrating nonstick cookware. Or sell Christmas trees and pumpkins in season.

Escapees CEO Cathie Carr, an enthusiastic booster of the full-timing lifestyle, began RVing as a teenager in the early 1970s, traveling with her younger brother and their parents Joe and Kay Peterson, cofounders of Escapees. "I remember waking up some mornings and Dad would say, 'Do you know what state we're in?' Or, 'Well, here we are in Wyoming!' " Cathie recalls. "Our family loved traveling so much. We were all together, we had everything we needed right there in the RV, every day was an adventure—at the end of a trip we would ask ourselves, why are we going back?"

Cathie began full-timing herself at the age of twenty-one, back in the mid-1970s. As a union millwright, she traveled to power plants around the country, following union work. She observes how different life was for the pioneering full-timers, back then: "When the club started up in 1978, there were eighty-seven members. Hardly anybody had ever heard of full-timers—RVers were considered 'trailer trash.' Joe and Kay worked hard to overcome that cheapskate image, to convince the world that full-time RVing was a respectable alternative for people who wanted to escape the usual rat race and bring something different and adventurous into their lives."

Escapees has enjoyed a steady upward climb since those days, to a current membership level of about 65,000. The club adds about 6,000 new member families a year. "At the beginning we served a less affluent, work-while-you-travel group," Cathie Carr says. "We still cater to the budget-minded, but we expect some changes as the baby boomer crowd discovers this alternative lifestyle. RVers are definitely getting younger. At an Escapade a couple of years ago we asked everyone seventy and older to stand up. Then, people in their sixties. When it came time for the fifties and forties groups to stand up, they were out there in unexpected numbers."

Along with the new demographics have come new conveniences that make full-timing a lot easier than it was for the RVers of thirty years ago—or even ten years ago. "In the old days it was hard to keep in touch from the road, but now we have cell phones," Cathie points out. "Just to get cash with an out-of-state check was a huge struggle. Now ATMs are everywhere." Campgrounds are also scrambling to accommodate the needs of today's RVs with amenities like wide and level concrete sites, 50-amp electrical service, instant-phone hookups, and sixty-foot pull-throughs for the monster rigs that are hitting the road in ever-growing numbers. "The infrastructures of older campgrounds just can't handle the newer rigs," Cathie says. "Escapees is buying a park in California, and the existing sites are so narrow we are putting two together to make each new site."

Despite these changes, the things that propel people into full-timing are still the same: independence, self-reliance, and above all, freedom from stress. After decades of being lost in the pursuit of money, status, promotions, big houses, and expensive toys—"Like a greyhound chasing the fake rabbit he will never catch," in the words of Kay Peterson—many full-timers are quietly elated to rediscover a simpler and happier version of themselves through full-time RVing.

In "normal" society full-timers often feel like lone rangers, but when Mark and I attended our first RV Escapade—parked along with some two thousand fellow Escapees at the Elkhart County Fairgrounds in Goshen, Indiana—we had the pleasure of becoming part of the gleeful majority. Full-timers were there in such concentrated numbers that the people who still owned houses seemed to be the weirdos, for a change.

We camped in the middle of the harness-racing track, a vast mudhole after a week of thunderstorms and heavy rain. "Woodstock for Geezers," Mark dubbed it. But everyone took it cheerfully in stride, tying plastic bags around their feet to wade through ankle-deep puddles en route to line-dancing lessons, Bingo games, or scheduled seminars on RV weight limits, caravanning in Mexico, and getting the most out of your radial tires. These folks were obviously living their own dream, and doing it with gusto.

In my mind's eye I see another sublime snapshot from our first year on the road—this one set at an Ozarks campground. Mark and I had stopped there on our way back to Virginia to sell our cabin and become full-timers for real. We listened, teary-eyed, as a circle of local musicians played "Will the Circle Be Unbroken?" in the campground office. Hand-lettered on the back of one guy's mandolin, I glimpsed poignant words of wisdom from the Oglala Sioux Chief Black Elk: The Journey Is All There Is.

Those six simple words said it all.

Epilogue
Austin, Texas
October 19

✉ Dearly Beloved,
We are gathered here at the computer to tell you about the joining of Amy and Travis in matrimony, an event so momentous that it took us a whole week to get up the nerve to describe it over the Internet. There was a bit of a skirmish over who would do the actual writing. "You do it, you're better at this." "No, you do it, I couldn't possibly." "No, you have to do it, you're the mother!" Such is the quality of debate when you live with one person in a thirty-four-foot space.

For warm-ups, the wedding-week preliminaries included everything Travis had dreamed of—which we mature, plan-ahead grown-ups had told him he couldn't possibly combine with something as regimented as a wedding. Silly us! A nonstop "house party" (complete with guitar playing and midnight high jinks in the pool) reigned at the hotel where Travis, his groomsmen, and most of the guests were staying. And in place of a bachelor party, there was an all-day, coed barbecue and beerfest in a friend's backyard, where Trav himself got to do the cooking.

And at long last, the wedding—what can I say about the wedding itself, without sounding like, well, Maria von Trapp in *The Sound of Music*? The Miley family threw a fabulous bash! Early on, Amy and her mother and older sister had chosen a dramatic hilltop estate with a panoramic view as the ceremony and reception site. The wedding was planned for 6 o'clock to take advantage of the golden twilight glow for picture taking. It all came off like a dream, including the weather—clear and warm, with a gentle breeze.

Here are a few of my favorite things:

- The bride, radiant in a simple white taffeta gown, her hair done up in a halo of curls. And the groom, beaming in his knee-length black Armani frock coat, looking like a nineteenth-century riverboat gambler who has just been dealt a royal flush.
- Zillions of twinkle lights in the trees that came on after dusk, casting a magical glow over the dinner tables on the lawn.
- Beribboned champagne glasses in all different shapes and sizes, which the guests got to take home as souvenirs.
- The sprightly dinner music, jazz classics by the likes of Louis Armstrong and Ella Fitzgerald, handpicked by the bride and groom. (Hmm, *wherever* did Travis get such good taste?)
- And when the 11 o'clock hour rolled around—much too soon—the vintage '58 Rolls Royce sedan that pulled up under the twinkle lights and whisked the bride and groom away, as the guests blew sparkling soap bubbles to see them off.

Alas! It all sped by faster than I could take it in, and like a live theater performance, it only happens once. But I bask in the afterglow still. And with any luck my pictures will turn out.

As mother of the groom, I had little to do but arrange the rehearsal dinner, groomsmen's accommodations, and getaway limo. But you know *me*—I managed to wring a full measure of fretting and dithering out of these simple tasks.

Long in advance we had made reservations at the nicest RV resort in Austin—tree-shaded sites, picnic tables with no rotting boards, uniformed staffers buzzing around in golf carts, and a phone hookup right at our site. And the clincher: Way back in the spring, as soon as Amy and Travis had announced their engagement, I had purchased a set of little plastic weights in the shape of fruits to keep the tablecloth from blowing away. We would be entertaining wedding guests on the picnic table that weekend, I reasoned. It would never do to have the tablecloth flapping in the wind!

For weeks—from such locales as Great Falls, Montana, and

Wyoming's Grand Tetons—I had been in voicemail contact with the catering director of the Mexican restaurant where the rehearsal dinner would be held. The planning was based on sixty guests, but by the time we rolled into Austin the count had reached ninety. The catering director remained calm about this number. The only hitch was her failure to obtain the mini-piñatas I had requested for table centerpieces. She was adamant: The ones she saw in Austin were cheap and ugly. I would have to go to San Antonio to find anything decent.

Yeah, right, I'm really going to San Antonio this week! So, I immediately embark on a mad scramble all over Austin to find suitable Mexican doodads to decorate the tables. Mark and I started our search at the Piñata Palace, right in the middle of Austin's largely Hispanic east side. (Mark: Seemed to me a logical place to start, anyway.)

We saw some adorable little tabletop piñatas at Piñata Palace, *exactly* what I had in mind. But now I wasn't so sure. They looked a little flimsy. (Maybe even cheap and ugly?) In any case, it would never do to just snap up the first thing we saw! So we moved on. Right through the entire "Party Supplies" and "Mexican Doodads" sections of the phone book.

Mark bailed out after the first day. My daughter, Curry, just off the plane from Massachusetts, naively volunteered to help me look the second day. She, too, was ready to kill me after six hours of driving from one end of Austin to the other. All the Mexican doodad shops seemed to be featuring figurines related to Dios de los Muertos (Day of the Dead, aka Halloween), and it would never do to have death skeletons decorating a wedding rehearsal dinner.

Finally, Commonsense Curry (firmly vetoing a last-minute dash to San Antonio) dragged me back to the Piñata Palace, where we stocked up on cute little piñatas, Mexican toys and noisemakers, and brightly wrapped candies. I privately agonized that the guests might think these items tacky—but it was a done deal. The decor was decided. Time to stop worrying. (Mark: Ha!)

Ha! Mark and I arrived at the restaurant an hour early on

Sunday to find our banquet room in a state of chaos. *Had these people never catered a dinner before??* There were too many tables, pushed too close together, and not enough of the teal blue tablecloths from the rental place. The silverware was neatly wrapped in the wrong napkins. The catering director was nowhere in sight. It was looking like freak-out time for the mother of the groom.

But the energetic young waitstaff scrambled around to set things right, and when they hauled out some colorful *serapes* to substitute for the missing tablecloths, I realized it was All Going to Work Out. In the end, the fajitas and margaritas were great, *and* the table decorations turned out to be the hit of the party. The children played with them, the wedding party posed for pictures with them, and the guests grabbed them all up to take home at the end of the evening.

The next morning family members dropped by our RV open house, all of them no doubt mightily impressed by the cheese tray, the grapes, and the fact that the picnic-table tablecloth didn't blow away. Then suddenly it was afternoon—time to get dressed and head for the main event.

Oh, yes. I left out one small detail about the wedding: The Austin judge who was scheduled to perform the ceremony never showed up. The guests were seated, 5:45 came and went, and no judge. Cell phones were nervously pulled out, the judge was called, but she did not answer. Then 6 o'clock came and went, and still no judge. "Is there a judge in the house?" one of the groomsmen joked.

Well, yes, in fact, there *was* a judge among the guests. Mark's sister Kathy, who is a magistrate in Georgia and regularly performs wedding ceremonies, calmly agreed to do the honors, pausing just a few moments to read over Trav and Amy's handwritten vows. At 6:20 p.m., Judge Kathy stepped to the front, and the wedding proceeded in its full glory—another adventure for the It-All-Works-Out column. Most of the wedding guests never even realized what had happened.

The next morning the Austin judge met with the newlyweds

and officially signed their license. She apologized profusely for her secretary's schedule screwup and gave Trav and Amy back their prepaid $100 fee. So they ended up with some extra spending money for their honeymoon—in addition to a great story to tell the grandchildren someday.

As all you parents out there well know, seeing your children happy is the greatest feeling in the world. And now I have the added joy of a new daughter-in-law who is smart, creative, devoted to my son, and blessed with a special knack for bringing beauty into the world of everyone around her. What a fabulous catch!

Here's hoping that all of your offspring are happy, your trees festooned with twinkle-lights, and your snafus destined to All Work Out.

Love,
Donia

Mark's Glossary of RV Terms

Amperage: The amount of electricity available for use in an RV, or in any single RV circuit. Campground hookups commonly supply a total of 30 or 50 amps.

Back-in: A campsite that is closed off at the rear and must be backed into to enter. (Opposite of **Pull-through**.)

Big rig: One of the larger, heavier RVs, generally in the thirty- to forty-five-foot range, that are hitting the road in ever-greater numbers. May be a fifth-wheel trailer, motorhome, or bus conversion. Also refers to an eighteen-wheeler.

Black water: Sewage from the toilet, containing human wastes.

Blue boy: Small, portable wastewater tank for transporting waste from an RV holding tank to a nearby dump station, without having to move the RV. Typically, blue-boy capacity ranges from five to thirty-two gallons.

Boondocking: Relying solely on internal utility systems while camping without electric, water, or sewer hookups. Often refers to staying in noncampground settings such as parking lots or undeveloped wilderness sites.

Brake safety cable: Steel lanyard that connects a trailer break-away switch to the tow vehicle. Pulls the switch if the trailer and tow vehicle separate unexpectedly, applying the trailer's emergency brakes.

Bus conversion: Large and generally luxurious motorhome built on the chassis of an inter-city-type bus.

Caravan: A group of RVers traveling together for security and sociability, often to a faraway or challenging destination such as Alaska or Mexico.

Catalytic heater: Special furnace—generally wall-mounted or freestanding—that converts propane gas to heat without open combustion. More fuel-efficient than a typical furnace, and consumes no electricity.

Class A motorhome: Motorized RV built on a chassis specifically manufactured for the purpose. Most range from twenty to forty-five feet in length.

Class B van conversion: Motorized RV created from a modified van. Generally includes a raised roof for additional headroom.

Class C camper: Motorized RV built on a truck or van chassis. Distinguished by the bunk over the truck cab. Commonly sixteen to thirty feet long.

Domicile: The state in which a full-timer claims legal residence. (See **Legal residence**.) For a traveler, the one true and fixed place to which you plan to return any time you are away.

Dry camping: Parking in a campground or undeveloped area with no utility hookups. Same as **Boondocking**.

Dual-fuel appliance: An appliance that operates on either of two sources of power, such as a water heater that has both a propane burner and an electrical heating element.

Eighteen-wheelers: Slang term for large highway freight trucks.

Enclosed underbelly: Refers to the underbody space of an RV in which the chassis, holding tanks, wiring, and pipes are shielded by a layer of heavy fabric, plastic, or sheet metal.

Escapees RV Club: A large and active RVer support group based in Livingston, Texas. Members sometimes known as "SKPs." Offers services, publications, campgrounds, social activities, and resources aimed primarily at people who live on the road full-time, or at least a large part of the year. Motto: "Sharing the Lifestyle."

Extended cab: A pickup truck driving compartment that is expanded to include storage space or fold-up seating behind the driver and passenger seats.

Fifth-wheel trailer: Bilevel, towable RV that overlaps the bed of a pickup truck, or other specially modified truck, and connects to a special hitch located over the truck's rear axle. The overlap results in a shorter, easier-to-handle package than a traditional, tow-behind trailer. (See **Travel trailer.**)

Ford Power Stroke: Small, powerful, popular diesel engine introduced by the Ford Motor Company in 1995.

Freestanding dinette: Traditional table and chairs for meals in an RV dining area. More flexible than the fixed table and benches, similar to a small restaurant booth, found in many RVs, particularly older ones.

Full-timer: A person who lives all the time in a motorhome, fifth-wheel trailer, or travel trailer. Purists insist that a full-timer cannot own a permanent home, vacation cabin, or any other fixed dwelling.

Generator: Device that uses propane, gasoline, or diesel fuel to generate electricity for RV use when hookups are not available, such as when boondocking. Motorhomes need built-in generators to run the house air conditioner while being driven.

Good Sam RV Club: A commercial membership organization that offers a host of publications, directories, products, and services. Inspects campgrounds and offers membership to those that meet its standards. Individual Good Sam members receive discounts at member campgrounds. Local chapters of Good Sam are noncommercial, oriented toward camaraderie and community service.

Gray water: Wastewater from the kitchen and bathroom sinks and from the shower, containing soap, soil, and food bits.

Has his "ears on":   Is equipped with, and paying attention to, a CB radio.

Hitch itch: Restlessness that full-timers feel after being stationary in one location for an extended period. Ready to fasten together the RV and the tow vehicle, stow the hoses and cords, and get back on the road!

Hitching: The process of coupling a trailer and tow vehicle, or a motorhome and towed vehicle, to make ready for travel.

Holding tanks: Sealed sanitary receptacles, normally ranging in size from twenty to eighty gallons, mounted beneath an RV to contain black water and gray water until it can be emptied at a dump station or into a campsite sewer hookup.

Holding-tank gauge: A set of monitor lights inside the RV living compartment designed to reveal how full each holding tank is. Monitor sensors inside the holding tanks often become fouled by debris and give inaccurate readings, thus causing much RVer aggravation.

Homeowners liability insurance: Financial protection should someone be injured in or around your RV, or by you or your pets or dependents, wherever you are. Included as a matter of course in traditional homeowners policies, it must be purchased separately, or specially included in RV insurance, by those who own no fixed dwelling.

Honey wagon: Tank truck equipped to visit a stationary RV and evacuate the contents of its holding tanks for sanitary disposal. Honey wagon service is offered in many areas that are popular with long-term boondockers.

Hookup, full: RV park utility setup that makes fresh water, electricity, and a sewer drain conveniently available at each site.

Hookup, partial: Normally, a utility setup where electricity or water, but not sewer, is available at each site. In many public campgrounds, a partial hookup includes only electricity at the site, with water available at shared water faucets around the campground.

Hookup, shared: Electrical boxes, water spigots, or sewer drains that are centrally located between two sites, for use by RVs parked on either side. Often means one RV will be on the wrong side for convenient hookup and will need to stretch cords or hoses under or around the unit to connect.

Hugs: Customary embrace shared by members of the Escapees RV Club upon meeting.

Instant phone: A telephone jack, with dial tone, immediately available for use at a campsite.

Legal residence: The state where a full-timer chooses to pay taxes, register vehicles, vote, serve jury duty, and otherwise call home. (See **Domicile**.)

Leveling boards: Short pieces of lumber, in a range of thicknesses, placed under the trailer tires as needed to raise the low side of the rig when parking on unlevel campsites.

Mail-forwarding service: Private company or club service that receives and stores mail for people living on the road, then packs it up and sends it to them upon request.

Mobile home: Oversized trailer designed for residence rather than travel. Generally is towed only once, when new, from its manufacturer to a prepared site, where it is permanently installed.

Modem hookup: Telephone jack in a campground office, laundry room, or other common area available for plugging in a laptop computer to retrieve e-mail or otherwise access the Internet.

Monthly site: Campsite in an RV park reserved for long-term rental at a rate significantly below standard daily fees. Often occupied by permanent residents. Many parks offer a monthly rate on their regular sites for travelers staying only a month or two.

Motor coach: Term frequently used interchangeably with **Motorhome**. More recently, it refers to a luxurious bus conversion.

Motorhome: Any RV in which the engine and living areas are combined in one vehicle. (See **Class A, Class B**, and **Class C motorhomes**.) In larger units, the driver and passenger seats rotate to become living room seating when the RV is parked.

NOAA weather radio: Special radio for receiving weather reports and warnings broadcast in the United States by the National Oceanic and Atmospheric Administration.

Overhead clearance: What neophyte RVers must watch out for when learning to drive their rig—i.e., tree branches, protruding awnings, carport-type roofs, and other obstacles too low for a twelve-foot-high vehicle to pass under safely.

Pass-through bath: RV bathroom located between the bedroom and living area, in which toilet, sink, and shower all share one large, open space closed off by doors at either end.

Persephone campers: RVers who spend half the year in two different climate zones, or who sit stationary half the year and travel the remainder; named for the Greek goddess Persephone. According to an ancient myth explaining the seasons, Persephone was abducted by Pluto to reign with him in the underworld. She pined so for her parents, Zeus and Demeter, that Pluto allowed her to live half of each year in the sunlit world.

Pet restrictions: Rules requiring owners to keep their dogs leashed in camp, and to pick up and dispose of their droppings. In long-term or resort-type campgrounds, restrictions may also include a size limit on pets or strict regulations on where they may be walked.

Pocket Mail: Proprietary handheld device that conveniently clamps to any telephone handset to receive and transmit e-mail without a computer, modem, or phone jack.

Pop-up camper: Compact trailer that folds out into a small, three-compartment living unit. Sometimes called a pop-up tent because of its canvas-and-screen walls. Too lightweight for full-timing, pop-ups are popular with family weekend campers.

Propane: Liquefied petroleum gas used to fuel RV furnaces, cooktops, water heaters, and other appliances.

Pull-through: An RV site that is open on both ends and can be entered and exited without backing up. (Opposite of **Back-in**.)

Quartzsite: Arizona desert town to which some one million snowbirds flock every year for a large mineral and gem show, flea market, and swap meet. Many RVers boondock in the surrounding desert for the entire winter season at little or no cost.

Rig: The combination of a truck and a trailer, or a motorhome and a towed vehicle. More broadly, any RV.

Rio Grande Valley: Area at the very southern tip of Texas popular with year-round retirees and snowbirds, who are welcomed as winter Texans.

RV: Recreational vehicle. Self-contained living unit that can be readily moved from place to place, either under its own power or when hitched to a pickup truck or other tow vehicle.

Satellite TV: Television reception system based on a dish antenna receiving digital signals beamed from one of many communications satellites orbiting the earth. Provides good reception virtually anywhere in the United States.

Seasonal site: Campsite in an RV park reserved for long-term rental at a rate significantly below standard daily fees, even below monthly fees if reserved in advance and prepaid for an entire season or more.

Slide-out: Section of an RV's structure that pushes out, by means of an electric motor or hydraulics, to provide added living space when the unit is stationary.

Snowbird: Seasonal traveler who spends the winter in a warm climate.

Solar panel: Roof-mounted array of silicon wafers, and associated wiring, that converts sunlight into electricity to power RV lights and appliances and recharge batteries. Used primarily when hookups are unavailable, and particularly valued by long-term boondockers for its silent operation, as compared with that of a generator.

Three-quarter-ton truck (half-ton, one-ton):   Rating system for pickup trucks based on engine power, braking ability, suspension system, and transmission. Complex formula does not directly correlate to weight of truck or weight the truck can carry or tow. However, *for safety, it is crucial to strictly heed vehicle manufacturer's data on towing capacities and weight limits when matching a truck and trailer.*

Toad: Slang for an automobile or small truck towed behind an RV to provide local transportation when the larger unit is stationary.

Trailer brakes: Electrically operated auxiliary brakes on a trailer's wheels that help bring the entire rig to a stop when the tow vehicle brakes are applied. Trailer brakes are also designed to stop a runaway trailer automatically if it separates from its tow vehicle because of hitch failure.

Travel trailer: Towable RV that hitches to the rear of a tow vehicle. Somewhat more awkward to handle than a fifth-wheel trailer (see **Fifth-wheel trailer**), travel trailers are preferred by RVers who want to leave their pickup truck bed free to carry motorcycles, ATVs, personal watercraft, or other bulky gear.

Truck camper: Small, self-contained living unit that slides into the bed of a large pickup truck. When stationary, the camper can be raised on telescoping legs, and the truck driven out from under it for separate use.

Twelve-volt system: Electric wiring, lights, and appliances that operate off a rig's twelve-volt house batteries. Generally includes all RV equipment on board except for microwave ovens, air conditioners, and large television sets, which require 120-volt current from a campground hookup, a generator, or some other special source.

Utility hookup: See **Hookup, full; Hookup, partial; Hookup, shared.**

Washer-dryer hookup: Water spigots, a drainpipe, and a heavy-duty electrical outlet located in an RV's large closet to accommodate on-board laundry equipment.

Winter Texans: Seasonal campers who spend the cold months of the year in (where else?) Texas.

Information Resources

This list is a highly selective and subjective one, including only resources that Mark and I personally find helpful or interesting. Most offer references or links to a vast and ever-expanding network of additional RV information. Some Web sites include sections on RV books, complete with links to online bookstores for instant purchase.

Please realize that phone numbers and addresses—particularly Web addresses—are perishable. If you should find any of the following material out of date, we apologize.

ORGANIZATIONS

Escapees RV Club
(membership includes *Escapees* magazine)
100 Rainbow Drive
Livingston, TX 77351
888-757-2582
www.escapees.com
The Web site is an excellent guide to Escapees services and campgrounds, local chapters, political issues affecting full-timers, and Escapees social functions, including their many special-interest "Birds of a Feather" groups and their annual spring and fall Escapades.

Family Motor Coach Association
(membership includes *Family Motor Coaching* magazine)
8291 Clough Pike
Cincinnati, OH 45244
800-543-3622
www.fmca.com
We have heard many good things about this organization and its services from motorhoming members across the country. The group's mail service and publications are top-notch.

Good Sam Club
(membership includes *Highways* magazine)
P.O. Box 8530
Ventura, CA 93001
800-234-3450
www.goodsamclub.com
Check the Web site or magazine for information on this group's wide array of membership benefits and services, including numerous regional Samboree rallies, plus an extensive online directory of campgrounds.

Life on Wheels Enrichment Program
University of Idaho
P.O. Box 443224
Moscow, ID 83844
866-569-4646
www.lifeonwheels.com
Gaylord Maxwell's educational organization sponsors rallies at college campuses around the country each year, with seminars aimed at enriching the RV lifestyle for seasoned campers and newbies alike.

Loners on Wheels
P.O. Box 1060—WB
Cape Girardeau, MO 63702
888-569-4478
www.lonersonwheels.com
We hear repeatedly how much the LoW organization has helped single, divorced, and widowed RVers find camaraderie, social activities, and support services within the larger, couples-oriented RV community.

BOOKS AND PERIODICALS

Complete Guide to Full-time RVing: Life on the Open Road,
   by Bill and Jan Moeller
Trailer Life Publications
800-234-3450
A straightforward reference guide to RVing by a veteran full-timing couple, with special emphasis on selecting, equipping, maintaining, and customizing your rig.

Home Is Where You Park It, by Kay Peterson
Survival of the RV Snowbirds, by Joe and Kay Peterson
Travel While You Work, by Joe and Kay Peterson
RoVer's Publications
100 Rainbow Drive
Livingston, TX 77351
888-757-2582
Escapees founders Joe and Kay Peterson, the "Mother and Father of Full-Timing," write with warmth, humor, in-depth knowledge, and a great deal of perspective on the full-time lifestyle.

Movin' On: Living and Traveling Full-Time in a Recreational Vehicle, by Ron and Barb Hofmeister
Bookmasters
800-247-6553
R&B Publications
121 Rainbow Drive #2179
Livingston, TX 77399
www.movinon.net
This is the third revised version of the popular RV book that helped lure us into full-timing. Warmly personal and highly informative, it combines astute technical advice with travel tips, memoirs, and photos to create an authentic portrait of RV life. The Hofmeisters' Web site is chatty and engaging, focusing on their travel adventures and philosophical reflections based on twelve

years of full-timing. It also features guest articles, a reader exchange, and a fun mystery-photo game titled, "Where Were We?"

On the Back Roads: Discovering Small Towns of America,
   by Bill Graves
Addicus Books
Box 45327
Omaha, NE 68145
800-352-2873
www.addicusbooks.com
Collected travel essays by *Trailer Life* magazine's whimsical back-
page columnist, who writes about out-of-the-way places and their
colorful residents with insight and charm.

Selecting an RV Home Base
Trailer Life Books
800-234-3450
A succinct forty-page booklet listing residency data for all fifty
states, including taxes, vehicle licensing and registration, voting,
fishing licenses, and where to find additional information.

Take Back Your Life: Travel Full Time in an RV,
   by Stephanie Bernhagen
Bookmasters
800-247-6553
www.rvhometown.com
"Anyone can do it" is the key message here—people too young
to retire, families with children, even the physically disabled.
The author and her husband began full-timing in their thirties,
working as they traveled. The book includes input from fifty-
six younger full-timers, plus detailed sections on finances, home
schooling, and jobs. The Web site has a similar upbeat, encouraging tone, along with many practical tips and resource listings. With
Jaimie Hall, Bernhagen also coedits the *RV Lifestyle Newsletter*
(available through the Web site).

Trailer Life Directory: Campgrounds, RV Parks & Services
800-765-4167

Woodall's Campground Directories
800-323-9076

Workamper News
201 Hiram Road
Heber Springs, AR 72543
800-446-5627 or 501-362-2637
www.workamper.com
Web site has feature stories about working on the road, sample job listings, and subscription information for the printed periodical, which offers extensive employment ads.

MotorHome magazine
P.O. Box 54461
Boulder, CO 80322
800-678-1201

RV Companion magazine
P.O. Box 174
Loveland, CO 80539
888-763-3295

Trailer Life magazine
2575 Vista Del Mar Drive
Ventura, CA 93001
800-825-6861

RV WEB SITES

www.newrver.com
An abundance of practical information on everything from free campgrounds to tax issues, with links to technical RV-info sites and an excellent Q&A section for newbies.

www.rvclub.com
Has an "RVing 101" section with a quiz for wannabees, tips for easing into the lifestyle, and articles written by experienced RVers. Also features a Frequently Asked Questions department and some RV classifieds.

www.rversonline.org
"RVers Helping RVers" is the slogan of this noncommercial Web site, which has articles, editorials, travelogues, and an "Ask Our Advisors" department where volunteer experts answer reader questions on such subjects as propane appliances and trailer towing.

www.trailerlife.com
Includes campground listings, state tourism information sources, vehicle tow ratings, links to new and used RVs for sale, and many in-depth technical articles and resources.

www.woodalls.com
Focuses on how to get started, places to rent an RV for a trial run, travel and tourism information, and an online version of Woodall's campground directory.

www.workersonwheels.com
Offers work-wanted and help-wanted classifieds geared to traveling workers, plus a Q&A section, tips on how to get started, and other support features. Coleen and Bob Sykora also publish a Workers on Wheels e-zine and *Life As We Live It,* an e-newsletter about full-timing (available through the Web site).

OTHER RESOURCES

American Contract Bridge League
2990 Airways Blvd.
Memphis, TN 38116
800-467-1623 or 901-332-5586
www.acbl.org
Okay, we admit this isn't really an RV resource. But we wanted to make sure all the RVing bridge players out there knew how to access the ACBL's online directory of local bridge clubs all around the country. Newbies are welcome.

Index

checklists, 4, 12, 60–61, 68–69, 166, 198–99
Cheney Lake State Park, KS, 221–24
Cherokee, NC, 4–8
Christmas, 128–29, 149–50, 152
cities, 74, 90
Clark, George Rogers, 104
Class A motorhome, 9, 268
Class B van conversion, 9, 268
Class C campers, 9
Cleo, 1, 4, 6–7, 19–20, 65, 105–6, 226–27, 234–35, 253–54. *See also* pets
  horses and, 105–6, 113–14
  letters from, 8, 26–28, 51–55, 84–87, 111–15, 131–35, 151–54, 170–72, 221–24, 242–44
  veterinary treatments, 37–38
clothing, 56–61
Complete Guide to Full-Time RVing: Life on the Open Road (Moeller and Moeller), 279
Compuserve, 108
computers, 7, 23, 34
Copper Harbor, MI, 51–55, 72
Cordele, GA, 151–54
Cotton Eyed Joe, 114, 121
Council Bluffs, IA, 252–55
credit cards, 31, 43
Curry (daughter), 21–22, 36, 263
cyber-cafés, 108

Dallas, TX, 213–14
Degeneres, Ellen, 143
directories, 82, 281
dishwashing, 100, 112, 116
dogtrot cabins, 201–2

domicile, 268
downtown areas, 128, 211–12
Doyle, Bob, 144
driver's license, 195, 196
driving. *See* maneuvering
dry camping, 268. *See also* boondocking
dual-fuel appliance, 268
dump stations, 6, 101
Dutchmen factory, 73, 75

Eat Your Way Across the U.S.A. (Stern and Stern), 136–37
Eddyville, KY, 92–95
eighteen-wheelers, 268
elder-care facility, 196
electricity, 96, 98–100, 267, 275–76
Elkhart, IN, 73–76
El Norteno, 137
e-mail, 2, 7, 43, 50, 65, 107–10, 121–22, 255. *See also* telephones
emergencies, 241, 247
emergency rooms, 165–66
enclosed underbelly, 269
entertainment center, 57–58
Escapees, 276
Escapees RV Club, 258–59, 269, 277
  campgrounds, 114, 121–22, 189, 233, 259
  mail service, 40–41, 43, 189
  RV Escapade, 259–60
  volunteerism, 190–91
exercise, 139
express mail, 42
extended cab, 269

Family Motor Coach Association, 277
Family Motor Coaching, 276